BABYLON

Joan Oates

BABYLON

WITH 137 ILLUSTRATIONS

THAMES AND HUDSON

THIS IS VOLUME NINETY-FOUR IN THE SERIES
Ancient Peoples and Places
GENERAL EDITOR: GLYN DANIEL

Frontispiece
Pieter Bruegel the Elder, *The Tower of Babel, c.* 1568, the second of two
fanciful paintings of the fabled tower by this artist. For a more likely,
though still largely conjectural, reconstruction see ill. 111. Museum
Boymans-van Beuningen, Rotterdam.

Filmset and printed in Great Britain by BAS Printers Limited,
Over Wallop, Hampshire

Contents

Acknowledgments

The textual and archaeological evidence now available for ancient Babylonia is far more extensive and complex than may be apparent from this book. In trying to provide an informative yet readable narrative I have ignored much that is of interest and glossed over many controversies. Thus the footnotes, although necessarily selective, are intended to lead the general reader to further knowledge and the serious student to more analytical sources. To compress 2000 years of Babylonian history and culture into a single volume has proved a daunting task. Such value as there is in this synthesis owes much over many years to the generous sharing of views and information by colleagues far too numerous to mention. To them I am deeply grateful. My debt is especially heavy to Miss J. M. Munn-Rankin, Mr J. V. Kinnier Wilson and Mr Nicholas Postgate, who read portions of the manuscript and made many helpful suggestions. The errors that remain are entirely my own.

I must also thank those who generously supplied information and illustrations: Bay Ercüment Atabay, Prof. Taha Baqir, Prof. R. J. Braidwood, Dr Muayad Damerji, Prof. R. H. Dyson, Jr, Sayid Antran Evan, Dr T. Holland, Prof. Dr B. Hrouda, the late Prof. H. Lenzen, Mr Larry Majewski, Dr G. R. Meyer, Mr T. A. Oates, M. André Parrot, Prof. E. Porada, the late Prof. Fuad Safar, Dr Isa Salman, Dr E. Sollberger, Mr C. K. Wilkinson, Prof. D. J. Wiseman and Dr Charlotte Ziegler. I am also grateful to the late Prof. Dr E. Kühnel for permission on behalf of the Deutsche Orient-Gesellschaft to publish material from the Babylon excavations.

Finally I must thank most warmly Prof. Glyn Daniel for his patience and encouragement throughout the very long gestation of this volume, and most deeply of all, my husband, without whose practical help it would never have been finished and many of whose ideas appear inevitably without acknowledgment.

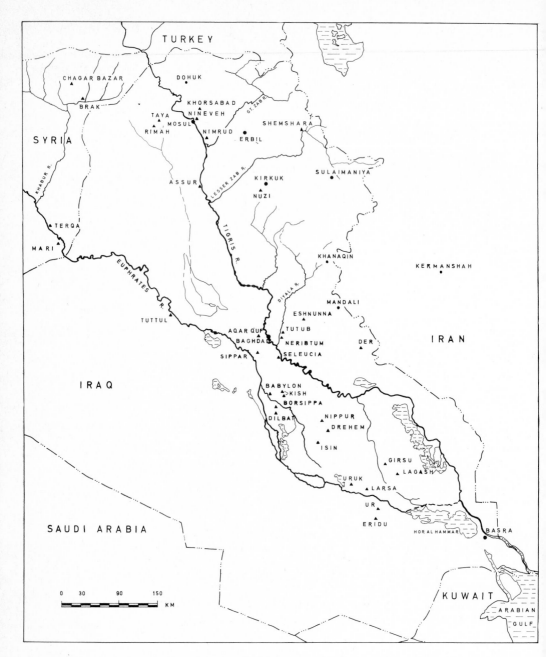

1 Map of Mesopotamia showing ancient sites mentioned in the text.

1
Introduction

What city is like unto this great city ... that great
city that was clothed in fine linen and purple and
scarlet and decked with gold and precious stones and
pearls! ... Babylon, the Great, the Mother of
Harlots and of the Abominations of the Earth.
(Book of Revelation)

So wrote a New Testament prophet, and, although the allusion was to
Rome, the sentiment accurately expressed the ancient world's view of
Babylon. Today, 2000 years after the city was 'cast down and found no
more', the name still conjures up in our minds a vision of opulence and
splendour stained with the smear of pagan decadence so enthusiasti-
cally applied by writers of the Hebrew world. There can be no doubt
that Babylon was the most impressive city of its time, yet it was not a
settlement of great antiquity nor indeed of any importance until well
after the time when Mesopotamian civilization had acquired its very
characteristic and persistent form. It was not to Babylon that 'kingship
first descended' before the time of the legendary Flood, nor is the name
to be found among those cities recorded from their distant past by
diligent Babylonian scribes. While the city-states of Sumer (the   2
southernmost part of Mesopotamia) vied with one another for power
and prestige, Babylon was at best an unimportant village. Indeed its
name remains unknown until the end of the 3rd millennium BC,* 1000
years after the invention of writing and several millennia after the
founding of the earliest farming villages in what was later Babylonia.

By contrast, Nineveh, Babylon's greatest rival in the ancient world,
could trace its past far back into the shadows of prehistory: here the
earliest occupation so far discovered can be dated to the beginning of
the 6th millennium. And in the south, Ur of the Chaldees and nearby
Eridu were farming communities, already with their local shrines, by   8
the close of the 6th millennium and the seats of dynasties some 2000
years later when history begins. Babylon's pre-eminence in the ancient
world lay not in historical claims to primacy but in a happy coincidence
of history and geography. As we shall see later in more detail, at a time
when the ancient centres of civilization in Sumer were suffering both
from the loss of agricultural land through salinization of the soil (an
unfortunate side-effect of over-irrigation) and the loss of vital and
highly profitable maritime trade routes, a local dynasty at Babylon
produced a series of able rulers, most notably Hammurapi, who were
quick to capitalize on a political situation in which there was no one

*All dates given in this book are BC unless otherwise indicated.

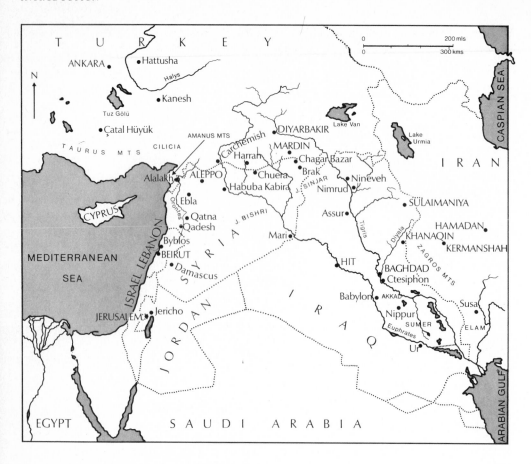

2 Map of Western Asia showing ancient sites and modern towns and political boundaries.

dominant power and on the geographical position of their capital, a factor that was to remain of major importance in Babylon's later history. Not only did Babylon lie within that small area of Mesopotamia where its two great rivers, the Tigris and the Euphrates, approach most closely to each other, but its situation at the northern end of the alluvial plain gave it potential control of two of the most famous roads in the ancient world. The main overland route from western Anatolia through Assyria to southwestern Iran – the later Achaemenid Royal Road from Sardis to Susa, which was probably in use as early as the 7th millennium – skirted the rim of the plain to the east of the Tigris. At the same time Babylonia was the natural terminus of the Khorasan Road, later the main artery of the Parthian and Sassanian Empires from their winter capital at Ctesiphon up the Diyala Valley to Hamadan (Ecbatana) and beyond. The advantages of this situation, both commercial and military, were fully appreciated and exploited by a succession of Mesopotamian dynasties and undoubtedly dictated the establishment, within 80 km of one another, of 'the most remarkable sequence of historic capitals in the world'.[1] The first of these was Kish, one of the earliest 'seats of kingship'. Then followed Agade, the city of Sargon and his successors, Babylon itself, and later

Seleucia-on-the-Tigris, Ctesiphon and finally Baghdad. Thus it is to the geographical background of Babylonian history that we turn first in telling the story of its greatest city.

Geography and economy

As a geographical term Babylonia refers to the southern portion of the modern country of Iraq, ancient Mesopotamia, encompassing the land roughly between Baghdad at its northern limit and the head of the Arabian Gulf. Historically, the term Babylonia reflects a relatively late unification of the country under Babylon's First Dynasty early in the 2nd millennium, though the word itself is of even later origin. From very early times the northern part of this land was referred to as Akkad (in Sumerian, *Ki-uri* or simply *Uri*) and the southern as Sumer (*Ki-en-gi/Kengir*). To the north, and in particular in the Upper Tigris Valley in the region of Mosul (ancient Nineveh), lay that part of Mesopotamia known later as Assyria, to the Babylonians, as Subartu.

The land of Babylonia is a flat alluvial plain laid down by the Tigris and the Euphrates whose floods, unlike the annual inundation of the Nile in Egypt, are both violent and unpredictable. In ancient times rain was scarce and the country depended almost exclusively, as it does today, on artificial irrigation for its crops. Vast areas are, and were, desert, with low scrub growing only along river banks or in seasonal water-courses and shallow depressions where subsoil water is retained close to the surface. This vegetation, together with the drought-resisting xerophytic plants that burgeon after winter rain, provides valuable grazing for camels and sheep. Once irrigated, the very fertile alluvial soil made Babylonia one of the richest granaries in the ancient world. Its principal crops, then as now, were barley and dates, both native to the country.

Babylonia, though potentially rich in agricultural products, lacked such essential commodities as stone, timber and metal ores. Indeed, with the exception of the ubiquitous mud of the alluvial plain, which served as the medium for building and provided clay for pottery and other containers, the country was virtually devoid of natural resources. For this reason trade was of crucial importance, and at an early period an extensive network of routes grew up linking Babylonia with the rest of the Near East. The rivers, in particular the Euphrates, and their tributaries served throughout Mesopotamian history as the major trade routes to and from all parts of the country; they were used also for the movement of people, supplies and in later times military contingents.

Within the immense stretches of desert, and especially in the southernmost part of the country, there existed large areas of marsh and lagoons abundant with wildlife. It is thought that expanses of permanent swamp along rivers once formed a more prominent feature of the landscape than at present; such swamps are now virtually absent from the northern Akkadian part of the plain. The earliest people for whom we have evidence in Sumer, late in the 6th millennium, were farmers who occupied what is now desert land but may then have lain along the fringes of marshes or lagoons that would have supplied additional resources. Indeed, recent archaeological work, particularly

3

in neighbouring Saudi Arabia, confirms the likelihood of even earlier prehistoric populations, with economies based on the hunting and collecting of wild foods, for whom the marsh environment would have seemed a virtual paradise.[2] These vast waterlogged areas were, and are, a changing feature dependent on flooding and periodic subsidence related to tectonic movements in the nearby Zagros Mountains and the Arabian Plateau to the south and west.[3] New areas are occasionally created as a result of severe flooding; one of the best-attested examples is the formation of the Hor al Hammar in Sassanian times, early in the 7th century AD. Such shifting conditions have so served to conceal archaeological remains, however, that within the present marshes there are no *visible* traces of occupation before the 2nd millennium BC.

In Babylonia settled occupation outside the marshes occurred, of necessity, along the water-courses, tending to concentrate in areas favourable for irrigation, separated by long stretches where the river ran through desert or swamp. This pattern produced in ancient Sumer two groups of cities separated by an area of open desert known in Sumerian as the *Edin*. It will be seen in later chapters that this geographically imposed isolation seriously hampered attempts to unify the country, and that the tendency to separatism of the city-states which it encouraged was a constant background force in Babylonian political history. The sluggish Euphrates, with its relatively high bed, provided a more easily exploited source of irrigation water than the faster-flowing Tigris; thus the earliest villages yet known in Sumer – Ur, Eridu and Uruk (Warka) – are found along its course. We know little of the pattern of settlement in prehistoric Akkad, which was later

3 The marshes of southern Babylonia are depicted in a series of stone reliefs from Nineveh now in the British Museum. These once lined the walls of the palace of the 7th-century Assyrian king Sennacherib. Detail showing Assyrian troops attacking the local Chaldaeans in their reed boats. After King.

4 Map of southern Iraq showing the probable 3rd-millennium courses of the Euphrates. The modern river channels are drawn in solid line. After Adams; and Gibson.

to see the rise of the Semitic-speaking dynasties of Sargon at Agade and Hammurapi at Babylon.[4] This is in part an accident of archaeological discovery, but is largely the result of shifting river channels, heavy silting and the existence of large numbers of later towns whose ruined mounds, like the alluvial silt itself, tend to obscure surface traces of earlier occupation. Indirect evidence strongly suggests, however, the presence here of prehistoric farming communities contemporary with those known in Sumer and on the eastern rim of the alluvial plain, sometime in the 6th millennium.

4

Archaeological surveys and historical sources both confirm this pattern of shifting water-courses and associated concentrations of population. They also indicate the later maintenance of some originally natural water channels as 'canals'. It is clear too that at no time did the Euphrates occupy one single channel. In the earliest period for which we have evidence there seem to have been three major branches, running respectively through Kish, Cutha and Jamdat Nasr, settlement apparently having been heaviest along the easternmost branch.[5] By the 3rd millennium the Kish channel was undoubtedly the most important, just as Kish was the major city. The earliest documentation for the then apparently minor Babylon branch comes later in the 3rd millennium; it was not until the end of the 2nd millennium that this channel became the most important of the Euphrates courses. It remains today an impressive river, although the main Euphrates channel now flows even further to the west.

With this short summary we may perhaps attempt to assess the possible formative role played by these various environmental factors in the development of Mesopotamian society, although to do so briefly must lead to gross over-simplification. Indeed any such comments must be highly speculative since the diversity of processes that can be observed begin well before the advent of writing. Nonetheless it seems incontrovertible that the peculiar physical environment of southern Mesopotamia, with its exceptional agricultural potential but its lack of natural resources, was a positive stimulus, although certainly not the only one, towards the growth of the world's first cities. It is well known that some of the world's oldest farming communities lie to the north of Babylonia, within the mountainous regions of Iran, Iraq, the Levant and Turkey and on the adjacent rain-fed grasslands, where those plants and animals that were to lend themselves to early and successful domestication – sheep, goat, cattle, pig, barley, emmer and einkorn wheat – were readily available in the wild state. Although it is axiomatic that the development of farming and herding preceded the growth of cities, it is significant that the first cities not only in the Tigris and Euphrates valleys but also along the Nile and Indus arose outside those 'nuclear' areas where agriculture was first practised. Clearly, more intensive agricultural techniques were required in areas marginal to those endowed with adequate wild resources, and most of all in those regions, such as Sumer, that were climatically unsuited to simple rain-fed farming. Not only did technical innovations such as irrigation and the plough, both attested before the dawn of history, make possible the intensive occupation of these otherwise unproductive areas, but the employment of such techniques helped increase agricultural efficiency and even the proportionate yield of the land. These developments served to free some members of the community for part, if not whole-time, specialization, and led ultimately to a definite polarization of society into those who controlled resources, such as land, manufacturing or trading enterprises, and those dependent on them. The viable size of settlements was directly related to these technological advances. Increased production resulted also in surpluses whose redistribution ultimately required special social and political institutions.

Although recent surveys undoubtedly demonstrate that *large-scale* integrated irrigation schemes did not appear in Babylonia until after the development of the political phenomenon known as the city-state was well advanced, there can be little doubt that the necessity to control scarce water supplies amicably and distribute them equitably must have been a strong cohesive force within early village communities in Babylonia.[6] Even the most modest irrigation schemes demand a level of local co-operation that would have been unnecessary under conditions of rain-fed agriculture, although co-operation is perhaps too strong a word in view of later textual evidence for the Babylonians' love of litigation, especially over water rights!

Thus in Sumer the growth of specialization, the internal differentiation of society and especially the development of community agencies to collect and distribute agricultural and manufactured surpluses, can be seen as clearly related to, though of course not an *inevitable* result of, the deficient environment. Such technological and economic developments were essential to local growth and prosperity; they also led to more effective methods for the acquisition of raw materials, not only for everyday necessities but also for a growing market in luxury items and the manufacture of products with which yet more imported goods could be acquired. At the same time, the open nature of the Babylonian terrain served both to discourage social isolation and to facilitate the rapid spread of new ideas, whether technical or political, while the lack of raw materials engendered an outward-looking attitude that was to influence political thinking and encourage expansion. This can be seen in the archaeological evidence already by 5000 BC and more specifically in the extensive trading networks of the late 4th and early 3rd millennia. In such ways the physical environment of Babylonia influenced and almost certainly served to accelerate the growth there of urban society, though we must remember that it was the people themselves who created their institutions within the limitations imposed on them by external forces.

Sources

Writing was invented in Mesopotamia as a method of book-keeping. The earliest texts known are lists of livestock and agricultural equipment. These come from the city of Uruk (biblical Erech), from an archaeological stratum designated by the excavators as Uruk IV (*c.* 3100 BC). Like most later Babylonian documents, these were made of clay, the writing having been inscribed on the damp tablet with a reed or wood stylus. The Uruk IV script consisted of pictographs which were later to develop into the more stylized cuneiform (wedge-shaped) writing. A system of numbers was also in use at this time, a stroke indicating units and a circular impression, tens. Stone inscriptions are found too, but stone is rare and clay plentiful in Mesopotamia; for this reason clay remained the most common writing material for over 3000 years, until the disappearance of cuneiform writing about the time of Christ.

Babylonian documents survive in enormous numbers because of the virtually indestructible nature of clay when dried and especially when baked, either deliberately or in an accidental fire. By far the greatest number of these documents are economic in content, dealing with such mundane transactions as sales of land and loans. There exist also royal inscriptions, usually records of a king's military campaigns or building activities; letters, myths, proverbs and other literary texts; school practice tablets; mathematical, astronomical and other 'scientific' texts; and many other varieties. The actual tablets vary considerably in size and shape, although the most common form was rectangular and of a size to be held conveniently in the hand. One of the largest tablets known, a vassal-treaty of the time of the Assyrian king Esarhaddon, is some 46 × 30 cm, while many economic dockets measure as little as 2.5 cm across.

Although the meaning of the pictographs is generally clear, the earliest tablets cannot be 'read' because each pictograph is a logogram or 'word-sign' which tells us only its meaning and not its spoken sound. In later cuneiform, a single symbol or 'sign' could stand for a whole

5, 6 The earliest written documents known (*above*) are clay tablets (ht of largest 3.4 cm) from Uruk inscribed in a pictographic script in which each sign stands for the pictured object or some closely related word. (*Right*) Sometime after the invention of writing the scribes found it convenient to turn the tablet in such a way that the pictographs lay on their backs. In time the pictographs assumed phonetic as well as ideographic values and the later cuneiform or 'wedge-shaped' writing became conventionalized and simplified.

word as in the earliest texts, but had as well one or more syllabic readings, deriving sometimes, though not always, from the word for which the original pictograph stood. In time a single cuneiform sign came to have many different 'pronunciations' or readings. Thus the interpretation of groups of such signs is not always clear. The wide range of cuneiform documents available to modern scholars is potentially enormously revealing, but their comprehension is made difficult both by such problems in the transliteration of the various ancient languages and by the often damaged or fragmentary nature of the tablets themselves. Moreover, accident of archaeological discovery gives an often distorted view of ancient history. There may have been recovered, purely by chance, large numbers of documents from one particular king's reign, whereas equally by chance we may know nothing of contemporary or succeeding figures who were historically of greater importance. This point is strikingly illustrated in the recent discovery of a large archive of late-3rd-millennium cuneiform tablets at Tell Mardikh (ancient Ebla) in northern Syria, revealing not only a hitherto unknown dialect of early Semitic but also the presence of a previously unsuspected state with the power and prestige to treat on equal terms with the kings of Assur and perhaps even Agade. Thus so-called 'Dark Ages' in Babylonian history are as likely to reflect a paucity of written documentation as a political or economic decline. Our view of ancient society is further distorted by the fact that many archaeologists have chosen, often for quite commendable reasons, to excavate the public rather than the private quarters of ancient cities. Such policies have led to the recovery of large numbers of temple and palace archives, revealing much of the everyday activities and business affairs of such large corporate institutions, while the life of the ordinary citizen remains remote and often little understood.

Perhaps more serious interpretative difficulties arise simply from the enormous gap that separates 20th-century AD ideology from the concepts of Babylonian thought and society. The necessity to translate in terms of a modern language ideas and institutions that almost certainly have no modern counterparts is a serious barrier to real understanding. Moreover, it is often the case that what was widely known and implicitly understood is not expressed in the written documents. One can imagine, for example, the difficulty of reconstructing modern banking operations from the evidence of a few ledgers or the form and significance of the Church of England from a hymnal and a book of prayer.

Attempts by modern scholars to reconstruct the history of the ancient world are further hindered by the fact that the Babylonians never wrote history in the modern sense. Nor are there Babylonian social or economic studies or political commentaries. This is not to say that the Babylonians were unaware of or unconcerned with their past or with social problems. On the contrary, much of their literature was written to explain the development both of the physical and the spiritual world. We read in numerous documents of the concern of various rulers for social justice and of the measures taken by them to ensure its propagation, while certain aspects of 'history' are meticulously recorded. Scribal explanations of cause and effect often

Uruk IV c. 3100	Sumerian c. 2500	Old Babylonian c. 1800	Neo-Babylonian c. 600 BC	SUMERIAN Babylonian
				APIN epinnu plough
				ŠE še'u grain
				ŠAR kirû orchard
				KUR šadû mountain
				GUD alpu ox
				KU(A) nunu fish
				DUG karpatu jar

appear to us naïve, but in the context of their comprehension of the universe and their place in it are perfectly consistent. In Mesopotamia the understanding of self, so essential to western philosophy, was clearly of secondary importance to the understanding of the external world.

The prime precept of Western consciousness 'know thyself' would have been incomprehensible to the Mesopotamian, and its corollary injunction that 'the proper study of mankind is man' would have struck him as frivolous and even dangerous nonsense. To the Mesopotamian the crucial and urgent study was the entire objective universe, without any interposition of the self between the observer and the observed. There probably has never been another civilization so single-mindedly bent on the accumulation of information, and on eschewing any generalization or enunciation of principles.[7]

The Babylonian scribe was the ultimate cataloguer, compiling and copying painstakingly detailed lists of all the facts he knew about every imaginable subject. Often these lists consisted simply of related words or phrases; sometimes they contained all names within a specific classification, such as trees, countries, animals or minerals. Such texts provide a wealth of information and tell us much of the accomplishments and the limitations of Babylonian scholarship. But with the exception of a small number of 'chronicles' and the historical allusions to be found in texts recording omens, there was no deliberate writing down of historical events. Indeed, virtually all the genres of Mesopotamian literature that purport to deal with the past appear to have been motivated by purposes other than the desire to know what actually happened – an attitude of mind not entirely unknown among more modern authorities! This is certainly true of several well-known 'historical' documents, including the so-called 'King-Lists' and the 'Weidner Chronicle', whose point was not so much the authenticity of their contents as the serving of a particular political purpose. The Sumerian King-List, which originated in the 3rd millennium, was a political tract in which the primary aim was to give an account of the various dynasties that ruled in Babylonia in accordance with the theory that legitimate kingship could reside in one city only at one time, an ideal that was seldom realized. Thus it arranges successively dynasties that we now know ruled simultaneously. The later Assyrian King-List is biassed by an attempt to legitimize the line of King Shamshi-Adad I, which was of non-Assyrian origin, while the 'Weidner Chronicle' establishes a scheme of dynastic history whereby the rise to power and overthrow of each dynasty is alleged to depend on the piety or impiety shown in turn by each king to the main temple of Babylon, at a time when we have little evidence even for Babylon's existence![8] Such texts are not without historical value. Indeed they provide the very foundations upon which Babylonian history is based, and give a revealing insight into contemporary political thought. Nevertheless it is essential to understand the motivation behind such documents and to appreciate that they were not intended as literal records of events.

People

The earliest ruling dynasty at Babylon was founded in the 2nd millennium BC by a Semitic-speaking people, that is, people speaking a language of the same family as later Arabic and Hebrew, whose origins would appear to lie in the desert country to the west of Mesopotamia. These people adopted almost in its entirety, however, the native Mesopotamian culture – education, religion, art, mythology, literature – which can be attributed largely though not entirely to an earlier Sumerian-speaking population. Who these Sumerians were and whence they came remains an unanswered and much-argued question. The ancient Semitic languages of Mesopotamia – Akkadian, Babylonian and Assyrian – were distinguished and deciphered only little more than a century ago, although the people who spoke them were well known from biblical sources. All traces of the earlier Sumerians had completely vanished, however, and the survival in cuneiform of an older non-Semitic language was but slowly recognized. Indeed for a time the view that 'Sumerian' was merely an ingenious system of cryptographic writing, devised by Babylonian priests in order to lend an air of greater mystery to their sacred writings and render them incomprehensible to the vulgar and profane, received much scholarly support. But we now know that the Sumerians formed the predominant strain among the population in Sumer at the time of the earliest cuneiform records. Their language is agglutinative, not inflected like Semitic or Indo-European. In structure it resembles Turkish, Finno-Ugrian and some of the Caucasian languages. In vocabulary, grammar and syntax, however, Sumerian stands alone and seems not to be related to any other known language, living or dead. It is yet to be conclusively established whether the Sumerians represent an element native to southern Iraq or whether they came from elsewhere. The question, 'Who were the Sumerians?', is one of the most challenging and persistent in ancient Mesopotamian history and its many aspects have been confounded in what is now referred to as the 'Sumerian Problem'.

The Sumerians are usually credited with the invention of writing, though even this cannot be established with certainty. In the pictographic Uruk IV script each sign was a picture of one or more concrete objects and represented a word whose meaning was identical with, or closely related to, the object portrayed. It is impossible to determine the actual language in which these tablets were written, since no attempt was made to indicate morphological or grammatical elements and the simple pictographic sign could stand for any one of a group of related words in any grammatical form or language. Scribes in the succeeding period (Uruk III) also used pictographic signs; these texts are thought to have been written in Sumerian because of the occurrence of the Sumerian personal name En-líl-ti. By the time writing had developed to the point of representing grammatical elements, the language written was clearly Sumerian. On this basis it has seemed reasonable to assume that the Uruk III texts were also written in this language, and probably the earliest pictographic tablets as well. It should be noted, however, that the Uruk III pictographic

7 A short inscription on the back of this Early Dynastic seated stone figure reveals that it was dedicated to the god Ningirsu for the life of the Sumerian scribe Dudu. Ht 39 cm. Iraq Museum.

writing was not confined to southern Babylonia, the area later most strongly associated with Sumerian influence, but was widely used also in the northern part where we first find evidence of the Semitic Akkadians.

The problem of Sumerian origins and the composition of the prehistoric population of Mesopotamia is further complicated by other linguistic evidence. Some scholars believe that the Sumerian vocabulary is composed of two distinct layers: Sumerian itself, together with a number of loan words borrowed from another as yet ill-defined language, assumed to have been that of a native 'pre-Sumerian' population.[9] A number of arguments are put forward in favour of this view. Firstly, certain geographical names are thought not to be Sumerian. These include the names of some of the earliest cities as well as the two rivers, Tigris and Euphrates. Secondly, certain words referring to such basic activities as farming, gardening, brewing, pottery, leatherwork and building are thought to belong to this 'substrate' language, while the Sumerians are credited with the vocabulary for shipping, cattle feeding, sculpture, writing, education and law. And thirdly, a number of cuneiform writings with purely phonetic values seem to reproduce what are interpreted as non-Sumerian words apparently perpetuated in Sumerian writing but not speech. If this view proves valid, the certain conclusion must be that the Sumerians borrowed their system of writing from some other linguistic group and there must remain the possibility that the Uruk IV tablets are written in this unknown language. But here one must hastily emphasize that there is much disagreement among Sumerologists as to the presence of this earlier 'substrate' language. Unfortunately our knowledge of the structure and syntax of Sumerian comes almost

8 A sequence of temples excavated at Eridu strikingly demonstrates the continuity of culture in Sumer from the prehistoric Al 'Ubaid period until Sumerian times. Temple plans and cult fittings persist, and the foundations of the later shrines actually enclose the remains of their predecessors. This photograph shows the walls of the latest 'Ubaid temples in this long sequence, under the corner of the heavily eroded Ur III ziggurat.

exclusively from a period when the language had virtually ceased to be spoken, and there remains no evidence from which to reconstruct the shifting of dialects and pronunciation that must have taken place from the time these supposedly non-Sumerian words were first in use, at the most conservative estimate some 3000 years before. Not only is there uncertainty about how the unwritten language changed throughout this long period – a span of time perhaps even greater than that separating us from the sack of Troy – but scholars have recently demonstrated that some at least of the alleged 'substrate' vocabulary is undoubtedly Sumerian.[10] A cautious assessment would be that although we may reasonably suppose that the prehistoric population of Mesopotamia was heterogeneous, there is at present no unequivocal evidence by which to establish the presence of this theoretically pre-Sumerian linguistic stratum.

Neither the acceptance nor the rejection of this thesis finally solves the 'Sumerian Problem'. Equally, it is clear that for the historical periods 'Sumerian' is used in a cultural sense to describe a population of mixed linguistic elements. The impossibility of identifying with certainty the linguistic affiliation of any prehistoric group is axiomatic but there is growing reason to believe that the Sumerians formed at least part of the indigenous population. Archaeological data indicate a striking degree of continuity from the time of the earliest agricultural settlements in Sumer to the period when the written language can be identified as Sumerian and the presence of a significant Sumerian-speaking population is thus firmly established.[11] At no point is there convincing evidence for an 'invasion' of new people, nor – and perhaps this is a more telling argument – can we identify any hypothetical homeland from which the Sumerians, with their unique language and culture, may have come. This failure becomes the more obvious as our archaeological knowledge of the lands bordering on Mesopotamia increases.

Mesopotamian archaeologists, for want of a better method, describe prehistoric cultures in terms of their characteristic pottery. Not only does pottery survive in greater quantity than any other type of artefact, but it is susceptible to rapid changes in fashion or technique and is thus a useful general chronological indicator. The archaeologist identifies a pottery style, and by extension the associated archaeological assemblage, by the name of the site at which the particular type was first discovered. Thus the earliest farmers in Sumer were the creators and bearers of what is called the Al 'Ubaid culture, named after a small site near Ur where its distinctive painted ware was first discovered. This characteristic and easily recognized pottery has been found over a very wide area in Western Asia, far beyond the boundaries of Babylonia. This fact, together with the knowledge that use of the Sumerian language appears to have been confined largely to Babylonia and even there predominantly to its southern reaches, has been used by philologists to 'prove' that the 'Ubaid people could not have been Sumerian. Such an argument has no validity since the spread of cultural traits need not imply the migration of people. Moreover, archaeological data now demonstrate beyond any reasonable doubt that the homeland of the 'Ubaid people was in Sumer, indeed precisely in

9 The earliest Al 'Ubaid pottery is found only in Sumer but by the latter part of the 5th millennium this style occurs throughout Mesopotamia, northern Syria and even in Saudi Arabia. These examples come from Ur and the small site of Arpachiyah near Nineveh. After Woolley; Mallowan and Rose.

that area later most closely associated with the Sumerians, while excavations in northern Syria have recently shown that Sumerian 'culture', like that of the 'Ubaid people, spread northwards over much of the same 'foreign' territory. Evidence for contact between the 'Ubaid and contemporary peoples to the north, south and east suggests that already by 5000 BC the population of Sumer may have been linguistically mixed, though there remains the strong presumption that Sumerian was dominant. In the conditions of growing prosperity and cultural advancement for which there is clear evidence in Sumer during the 5th millennium, one would expect an increase in the indigenous population, whoever they may have been, and a gradual rapprochement between neighbouring communities whose habits and ways of life may originally have differed.

Yet another people, speaking a language known to us as 'Akkadian', are well documented in early Sumerian texts; their predecessors may well have composed part of the ' 'Ubaid' population. The Akkadians are first recognized from personal names in Sumerian documents, certainly by the middle of the 3rd millennium in tablets from Fara (ancient Shuruppak, home of the Babylonian Noah) and possibly earlier still in the archaic texts from Ur; at the same time 'Sumerian' scribes at Abu Salabikh, not far from the holy Sumerian city of Nippur, whose documents are closely comparable with those from Fara, bore largely Akkadian names.[12] There is also evidence for the borrowing of Akkadian words into Sumerian from a very early period, while Semitic names appear in the Sumerian King-List for kings of city-states, especially in Akkad.

The Akkadians borrowed the Sumerian system of writing, but it is not until the latter part of the Early Dynastic period – sometime around 2500 BC – that texts can be distinguished as actually written in Akkadian. These include a number of votive inscriptions of kings and officials at Mari on the Euphrates in Syria, presumably a Semitic-speaking region. The Akkadian character of these otherwise 'Sumerian' inscriptions is betrayed only by a few Akkadian spellings, and the statues on which the inscriptions are carved appear in every other respect 'Sumerian'. Of this date also are a few Akkadian inscriptions on stone recording sales of fields; these come largely from cities in Akkad, but there are two from Adab further to the south.

The original homeland of the Semitic-speaking peoples is thought to have been Arabia, whence a number of major nomadic incursions are attested in later periods. Semitic-speaking nomads with their specialized herding economy formed an important part of the Mesopotamian pattern of life, but it would be a serious mistake to view the Semitic element in early Mesopotamian society as no more than wandering and illiterate tribesmen. The essentially settled character of the 3rd-millennium Akkadian population has become increasingly clear and, although their cultural contribution – apart from their language which became the *lingua franca* of the entire civilized Near East throughout most of the 2nd millennium – remains to be determined, it should not be underestimated. Their influence was felt in many aspects of Mesopotamian civilization, while several of the most successful Mesopotamian kings, including Hammurapi of Babylon and his contemporary Shamshi-Adad of Assyria, were of Semitic nomad extraction. History provides many examples down to the present century not only of recurrent movements of pastoral tribes into the Mesopotamian steppe, but of their progressive infiltration into the settled lands.[13] The interaction of nomad and townsman was an active catalyst in the crystallization of Mesopotamian civilization that is too often lost in the vivid biblical imagery connected with the supposed antagonism of the desert and the sown.[14]

Although we cannot isolate separate cultural strains in Sumer in the prehistoric periods, there can be no doubt that by the 3rd millennium BC both Semitic and Sumerian-speaking peoples were present as settled elements in the population. Linguistic analysis of personal names indicates the dominance of Sumerian-speakers in southern Babylonia, with Akkadians to the north, but personal names cannot be taken as unequivocal evidence of ethnic affiliation, since they are subject to whims of fashion as geographical names are not. The last of the Third Dynasty of Ur kings, who were responsible for what is often called a 'Sumerian revival', bore a Semitic name, while many of the earlier rulers of Kish, in what we assume to have been a predominantly Akkadian-speaking area, appear superficially to have been Sumerian. Indeed, a 'Sumerian' queen of Kish, Ku-Baba, who reigned sometime around 2400 BC, was succeeded by her 'Semitic' son, followed by his son, a 'Sumerian'. The latter was deposed by his vizier who took the Semitic throne-name Sharrum-ken. He is better known to us as Sargon, founder of a Semitic-speaking dynasty at Agade, with whom we begin the next chapter.

Chronology

Absolute dates for prehistoric materials are derived largely from radiocarbon determinations. Recent calibrations with dendro-chronologically dated samples suggest that before 1000 BC there is an increasing deviation from 'true' dates back to a maximum of some 800 years at radiocarbon 4500 BC. The prehistoric dates given here are uncalibrated, and therefore too young, a convention followed in Near Eastern archaeology where many dates fall well outside the limits of present calibration curves (c. 5000 BC). From about 3000 BC onwards it is possible in Mesopotamia to estimate dates on the basis of historical sources such as the King-Lists, lists of year-names (a system of dating by 'naming' each year followed from the time of Sargon of Agade to the end of Babylon's First Dynasty), lists of *limmu* (officials appointed annually after whom the Assyrians designated their years), historical chronicles, historical synchronisms, building inscriptions, etc. Unfortunately such sources may be contradictory, and often provide only isolated fragments of information. Third-millennium chronology is also affected by two historical 'gaps' of unknown length, between the fall of the Agade Dynasty and the rise of its successor at Ur, and between the first fall of Babylon and the earliest well-documented Kassite king.

Essential to any absolute chronology is some fixed point in time. Such true dates can best be established by means of recorded astronomical events. For Assyrian chronology, for example, an eclipse of the sun in the *limmu*-ship of a certain governor of Guzana provides a fixed date in 763 BC. Unfortunately for Babylonian chronology, the famous 'Venus tablets' of the end of the First Dynasty, on which were noted certain movements of the planet, provide not one fixed point but a series of possible dates, all in agreement with these particular observations. Thus, although the internal chronology of the First Dynasty can be securely established on the basis of year-names, we have no absolute point to which to tie it, and such are the inconsistencies in the sources that chronological systems currently in use give a range of some 200 years (1900–1704 BC) for the accession of Hammurapi. The system of dating followed in this book is the so-called middle chronology, proposed originally by Sidney Smith, in which the accession of Hammurapi falls in 1792 and the sack of Babylon in 1595.[15] These are by far the most commonly accepted dates – hence their use here – although many scholars, including the present author, believe them to be too late to accord well with better-preserved Assyrian sources. Those chronologies which place the fall of Babylon later than 1595 now find little support.

Government: the city-state

By the latter part of the 4th millennium BC a number of settlements in Sumer can be described as 'urban', not only in the sense of size but also of specialized function, and by the period early in the 3rd millennium which archaeologists call 'Early Dynastic', the city-state – a political institution unknown elsewhere at this early date – had come into being. Each such state consisted of a city, occasionally several cities, with its surrounding territory, including dependent towns and villages. Occasionally leaders arose who succeeded in uniting a number of such cities into larger coalitions, but these seldom survived for long. One of the most striking characteristics of the Sumerian city-state was its individualism and its strong resistance to any form of central political control. This is especially surprising in view of the lack of natural boundaries between individual city-states; indeed Eridu, Ur, Uruk and Larsa, four of the more important early cities, were actually within sight of one another. This tendency to separatism remained an important factor in Mesopotamian history, despite many able efforts to surmount it, and the city was and remained for long the basic form of political unit.

Although the focal point of these earliest known urban centres was a temple or temple complex, a pattern whose origins can be traced back as far as the first 'Ubaid settlements, it is an oversimplification to categorize them as theocratic societies or to assume, as has commonly been suggested, that religious institutions were the sole precipitating factor in their growth. It is difficult 5000 years later to disentangle an intricate relationship between temple and community whose development stemmed from an even more remote and pre-literate past, but there is no evidence that in Mesopotamia any settlement grew up around a previously existing shrine. The temple owed its existence to and was administered by the community and in its earliest stages was

8

but one element in an intricate, and in our terms essentially secular, community structure.

Later written sources tell us that all authority derived from the gods, and all individuals whom we would classify by their functions as 'religious' or 'secular' officials acted alike as the servants of their divine overlord. The temple was the god's earthly residence and in later times accommodated his household – not only his personal attendants who performed what we should term priestly or cult services, but his secretaries (scribes), stewards and many servants of lesser status who administered his estates and engaged in commercial or manufacturing activities. In modern terms the Mesopotamian temple functioned largely as an economic organ, a central authority engaged in the collection and distribution of surpluses both in the form of agricultural produce and of the products of the specialized crafts and industries it sponsored. It is important to remember that the distinction between 'religious', 'social', and 'economic' activities reflects modern attempts to analyse the structure and behaviour of societies, and that such terms would have had no meaning in ancient Mesopotamia. We cannot be certain to what extent the later economic functions of the temple were also characteristic of prehistoric shrines, but continuity of cult is clear and suggests a gradual development of the temple as an institution rather than a radical change in its character that happened to coincide with the invention of writing, which in itself represented merely a technical advance in economic administration. Certainly such a central mechanism for redistribution was vital to the well-being of a society in which foreign trade signified not simply the provision of luxury goods but the acquisition of commodities essential to prosperity and technological advance.

In theory the Sumerian city was the actual property of its main deity, to whom it was assigned on the day of creation. This total identification of god with city was an underlying tenet of Sumerian society. The temple of the city-god was the city's central feature. Often there were smaller temples or shrines dedicated to the wife or children of the chief deity, and in the larger cities in later times a number of quite independent establishments dedicated to other members of the

10 Impression of a cylinder seal now in the Ashmolean Museum, Oxford. Cylinder seals of the late Uruk period (late 4th millennium) often depict what are thought to be community or temple herds before byres which closely resemble reed houses still built in the marshes of southern Iraq. The ringed posts probably symbolize a deity.

8

pantheon. The temples were large landowners, cultivating extensive holdings by means of sharecroppers or client labour. But despite the nominal identity of god and city, the temple owned only a part of the land of the city-state; the rest belonged to the palace or to individual private citizens. The Russian scholar I. M. Diakonoff, in an important study of the early cuneiform texts from Telloh (ancient Girsu in the kingdom of Lagash), has shown that the largest proportion of the land there in *c*. 2500 BC was privately owned, much of it belonging to what he termed the 'nobility', i.e. members of the ruling family, palace administrators and priests.[16] Labour on these large private estates was performed by a special category of 'clients' or 'dependants', whose status resembled that of the temple dependants. The commoner owned a particular plot of land as a member of a family rather than as an individual; the hereditary land held by such extended families or 'clans' could be alienated and sold, but only by certain designated members of the family. One text shows that the poor owned gardens and fish ponds.

Despite the important position of the temple in the Sumerian city, it is clear that supreme political power was at an early period vested in the secular figure of the 'king'. The titles used to identify the office of kingship varied from one city to another, perhaps owing to the manner in which the office evolved. There is some evidence to suggest that communities in prehistoric Sumer were originally essentially democratic in their structure, though not in the modern sense of this much-abused term. Indeed Thorkild Jacobsen has proposed that the earliest form of government of the city-state was a bicameral assembly of free citizens, with an upper house of 'elders' and a lower house of 'men';[17] this assembly was called into session in emergencies, acting by consensus and choosing a temporary leader to carry out its wishes. As society became more complex and the crises more serious, the position of this temporary leader is thought to have become both more powerful and more permanent, and some would see in this pseudo-historical figure the origin of the *lugal*, literally 'great man' or 'king'. Certainly there is no doubt about the authenticity of the assembly itself. *Unken*, the Sumerian word for assembly (literally, 'circle of the people'), occurs in the very earliest texts (Uruk IV), while we know from later periods not only that the assembly was an effective organ of local administration but that as late as the 2nd millennium it was empowered to write letters to the king, make legal decisions, sell real estate and assume corporate responsibility for robbery or murder committed within its jurisdiction.

Also attested in these earliest texts is the title *en*, usually translated 'lord'. The *en* seems originally to have possessed both secular and ecclesiastical power, but the political side of his office was clearly secondary and at an early period *en* became a purely priestly title. The title *lugal* and the term *é-gal* ('palace', literally 'great household') are found in the archaic texts from Ur, dated early in the 3rd millennium. Ultimately the *lugal* came to be the most powerful person in the city-state, and although his position may at first have been elective, a dynastic system of royal succession soon developed. Whether or not it reflected the origin of his position, the king's role as war-leader grew increasingly important during Early Dynastic times, and by the end of this period the king regularly led his troops to war (though 'wars' were

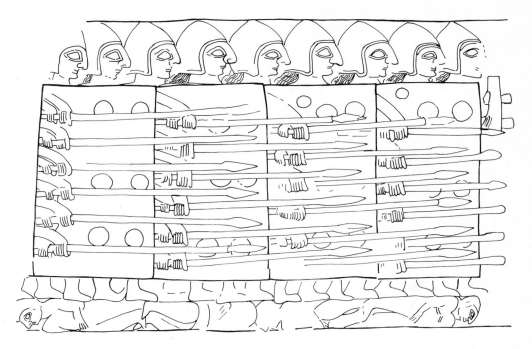

often little more than minor skirmishes and standing armies were unknown). The *lugal* also came to perform the role of 'judge' in the Old Testament sense, a 'righter of wrongs', and later he assumed the *en*'s responsibility for fertility and abundant harvests. Thus magic and ritual duties were added to his military and judicial functions to form the combination so characteristic of later Mesopotamian kingship. As kingship became hereditary, with all the prerogatives of royalty, the palace began to rival the city temple in wealth and influence.

Along with *en* and *lugal* another title, *ensi*, is known from an early period. The *ensi* or 'steward' seems originally to have been an official in charge of ploughed lands, but was in later times a city-governor. Except for a brief period under the pre-Sargonid kings of Lagash the early *ensis* were apparently not independent rulers, and none appears in the King-List. Sargon of Agade designated the Akkadian governors he placed over the cities of Sumer as *ensis*, but subsequently the term came to be used indiscriminately for either an independent ruler or a governor of a city, especially where no other title was associated with the city.[18]

According to Mesopotamian tradition, embodied in the Sumerian King-List, kingship descended from heaven after the legendary Flood and was then held by a number of cities, each taking its 'turn' (*bala*, Akkadian *palû*) as the seat of royal authority and, by implication, exercising hegemony over the whole country. The undisputed source of this supremacy was the authority of Enlil, principal deity of the pantheon, administered through the priesthood of his temple Ekur at Nippur. There is some evidence to suggest that in the early 3rd millennium there existed a league of cities which recognized Ekur as the paramount shrine of all Sumer,[19] and tradition points to Nippur as the place of assembly for the 'election' of the supreme ruler.

11 The main offensive weapon in Early Dynastic Mesopotamia was the war chariot, while heavily armed infantry attacked in phalanx formation as can be seen from this detail of the famous Stele of the Vultures of Eannatum of Lagash (*c.* 2450 BC), now in the Louvre Museum. Enemy corpses can be seen brutally trampled under foot. Ht of panel *c.* 85 cm.

12 Fragment of an alabaster Akkadian victory stele, found not far from Ur. The prisoners of war with their strange hairdos and their elbows tied behind their backs are shown in a 'neck stock'. Ht 21 cm. Iraq Museum.

The theory of kingship expressed in mythological texts is more explicit. They state that the king was nominated for office by his own city-god in an assembly of the gods meeting at Nippur. Since, to a Sumerian, city and god were synonymous, the 'council of the gods' would have been equivalent to a council of cities. The existence of such an 'amphictyonic league' can be inferred only indirectly from hints in texts whose purpose was not historical, but there can be no doubt about the extraordinary status of Nippur. Nippur was never directly involved in the petty squabbles that characterized the relationships between the other cities of Sumer, nor was it the titular capital of any dynasty, although in the late 3rd millennium the kings of the Third Dynasty of Ur may have resided there. The possession of Nippur entitled a Babylonian king to adopt certain styles and titles that implied at least theoretical hegemony over the whole of Sumer and Akkad, but the rise of Babylon to political pre-eminence led to a deliberate and successful attempt by its priests, sometime in the 2nd millennium, to replace Enlil by their own city-god, Marduk, as head of the pantheon, and thus to usurp the authority of the earlier holy city.

A history of the Sumerian city-state in the Early Dynastic period is beyond the scope of a book concerned with the later, Semitic dynasties of Babylon, though Semitic influence at this time is already clear and there remains a strong possibility that Semitic-speaking rulers at Kish once dominated the country. In the 3rd millennium Semitic influence was greatest in the north, yet the founder of a highly successful dynasty in the Sumerian south at Lagash, Ur-Nanshe, though himself the possessor of a Sumerian name, would appear to have been of Semitic origin;[20] while the earliest Akkadian (Semitic) royal inscription known from Babylonia comes from Ur, a dedication by the wife of one Meskiaga-nuna, King of Ur (2483–2448). We assume an early period of domination by the city of Kish on the basis of the later significance of the title 'King of Kish', highly prized by subsequent kings as a claim to suzerainty over the whole of the country. Indeed we know that both Mebaragesi (c. 2630–2600), the earliest Mesopotamian ruler identified by a contemporary inscription, whose titles include both *en* and 'King of Kish', and Mesilim (or Mesalim, c. 2550) ruled much of Babylonia. The latter's name is probably Semitic, but the adoption of Sumerian writing by the early Akkadians leaves us uncertain of the language they commonly spoke. Only at Mari, to the west on the Euphrates, is there unequivocal evidence for an Akkadian-speaking dynasty, and even here its cultural appurtenances are wholly Sumerian. It is not until the rise of Sargon (c. 2330) that a Semitic-speaking dynasty is genuinely attested in Babylonia.

The last of the Early Dynastic kings was an ambitious *ensi* of Umma named Lugal-zagesi (c. 2340), whose father bore an Akkadian name. Lugal-zagesi claims to have made all foreign lands subservient to him and to have ruled in peace and prosperity 'from the Lower Sea along the Tigris and Euphrates Rivers to the Upper Sea', i.e. from the Arabian Gulf to the Mediterranean. His 'empire' did not long endure and, after two decades of successful rule, he was defeated in battle and brought in a 'neck stock' to the gate of Ekur at Nippur to be reviled by all who passed by. His conqueror was Sargon of Agade.

12

2

From Sargon to Hammurapi

Lugal-zagesi's claims not only to suzerainty over Sumer but to control of the trade routes from the Mediterranean to the Arabian Gulf have often been dismissed as an exaggerated boast, but archaeological discoveries in recent years lend increasing credence to his pretensions. The possible presence of Sumerian merchants, if not more direct Sumerian influence, has long been attested both at the city of Assur, to the north on the Tigris, later to become the first Assyrian capital, and at Tell Brak in northeastern Syria, where as early as the late 4th millennium there was a large city with a lavishly furnished temple closely comparable with those known from contemporary Sumer. More recently excavations at the site of Tell Chuera, *c.* 150 km west of Brak, have revealed a 3rd-millennium shrine in which were found stone figures of worshippers virtually identical with those known from Early Dynastic sites in Mesopotamia. But most surprising of all has been the even more recent discovery of the site of Habuba Kabira South, a large walled town over half a kilometre in length, on the bend of the Euphrates east of Aleppo.[1] The pottery found in this settlement and the type of mud-brick employed in the construction of its buildings are indistinguishable from comparable materials from Uruk in the late 4th millennium. Clay sealings, found at the site, which had been used to mark some form of portable property, are identical with examples both from Uruk and from Susa further to the east in Khuzistan, seat of a non-Sumerian dynasty in the country known as Elam. Habuba Kabira

13

13 Recent excavations in northern Syria have revealed hitherto unexpected evidence of Sumerian influence in the late 4th millennium. The pottery and even the sun-dried mud-bricks found at the walled town of Habuba Kabira South, probably a Sumerian colony on the Euphrates east of Aleppo, are indistinguishable from examples from Uruk in Sumer. Aleppo Museum.

South can only be interpreted as a Sumerian merchant colony, controlling the Euphrates route northwestwards to the 'Upper Sea', a fact which puts Lugal-zagesi's claims, some 800 years later, in an entirely new light. Contemporary evidence for close commercial relations, if not indeed actual 'merchant colonies' based on Susa, comes also from recent excavations at Godin Tepe near Kermanshah in western Iran and at Tepe Yahya, some 1000 km southeast of the Elamite capital.[2] Even at this very distant site contact with Uruk Mesopotamia is clear in the presence of a very distinctive ceramic type (Jamdat Nasr) that is found over much of the then-known world and may well have served for the export of some highly prized commodity.

Lugal-zagesi's reign (2340–2316) marks the end of the Early Dynastic phase, but it is only in the final 100 years of this almost certainly very long period that historically informative inscriptions are found. The small number of surviving royal texts provide a still frustratingly limited glimpse of struggles for supremacy among the city-states and the foreign involvement that archaeological evidence proclaims and of which later mythological sources give a much more vivid, though inevitably less dependable, picture.[3] Although written documentation for what we would call political history is disappointingly inadequate, large numbers of economic texts do reveal something of more mundane affairs. Especially important are certain economic reforms instituted at Lagash. Indeed, without the royal inscriptions of the Lagash dynasty – *ensis* whom the King-List does not deign to recognize – and the records of one of their temples in Girsu, we would know very little of life in Early Dynastic Sumer. Undoubtedly one reason for the impact of the succeeding dynasty founded by Sargon lies in the vastly richer written sources available for the period, a factor relevant not only to present-day understanding of these remote times but also that of later Babylonian scribes, whose comprehension of their own past was influenced by those texts that chanced to survive.

Certainly there can be no disputing the importance of Sargon and his successors to later Mesopotamian history, but the changes in both ideology and practical politics that took place under their suzerainty appear to us accentuated by an apparently abrupt linguistic change. For the first time Akkadian becomes the language of official inscriptions, and this fact has often led to an undue emphasis on ethnic differences. We have already observed that Akkadian was almost certainly universally spoken in Akkad long before this time. There is also reason to believe that Sumerian, although retained as the proper language for legal and cultic purposes, was already dying out as a spoken language even in the Sumerian south. The imperial aspirations that are often conceived as originating with the new 'Akkadian' dynasty equally have their roots in the less notably successful but similarly aggressive ambitions of such Sumerian rulers as Eannatum of Lagash, who claimed to have defeated both Elam and Subar, the first mention of 'the North',[4] Lugal-zagesi and doubtless others for whom no contemporary inscriptions survive.

Sumerian kings are often credited with more peaceful intentions than their Akkadian successors, but a close examination of the available texts, especially those of the later rulers of Lagash from whose reigns

14 A number of victory stelae have survived as vivid evidence of Akkadian imperialism. This diorite fragment was recovered from Susa where it had been carried, probably in the 12th century, as booty from Babylonia. It shows an Akkadian soldier escorting naked prisoners. Ht 46 cm. Louvre Museum.

longer inscriptions survive, reveals pillage and slaughter to be the common-place accompaniment of their expansionist policies. Nor does the war scene from the well-known 'Standard of Ur' depict other than the callous disregard for the slain and the cruel treatment of prisoners more usually associated with the victory celebrations of Semitic kings. Sumerian mythical tradition does, however, imply some preference for outwitting as opposed to beating up one's opponent, and we should perhaps note that among the more obviously successful 'Sumerian' kings are those such as Lugal-zagesi and Eannatum whose origins may have been Semitic.

Lugal-zagesi asserts that he 'made secure the routes' from the Mediterranean to the Arabian Gulf. The archaeological evidence leaves us in no doubt that such goals were of major concern to the Sumerian cities from a very early period. With the new dynasty founded by Sargon the documentation becomes more explicit and the concern with political control as opposed to mere economic exploitation is more clearly spelled out. We are fortunate that Sargon and his successors commemorated their victories, as was already the Sumerian custom, in

11

14

the temple of Enlil at Nippur. The original statues and stelae have not been recovered, but some unknown scribe copied their inscriptions with a meticulousness worthy of a modern scholar, even noting whether the writing was on the statue itself or on its pedestal. Some of these copies survive, and it is on them that our knowledge of the history of this period is largely based.

Sargon of Agade and his successors

Sargon's real name is unknown to us – he cannot have been born 'the true (legitimate) king' – and as far as we know it could even have been Sumerian. His antecedents are a mystery and have been obscured in the haze of mythology with which later generations surrounded his name. It is possible that he was the illegitimate son of a priestess of Kish; later legend attributes to him the first of the classic stories of a baby laid in a basket and abandoned in a river. One story relates that he was brought up as the son of the water-carrier who found him and subsequently entered the service of Ur-Zababa of Kish, rising rapidly to the position of vizier. At this time Kish claimed theoretical suzerainty over Sumer, though Lugal-zagesi of Umma was clearly a powerful rival.

Sargon appears to have seized the throne in a palace revolt c. 2334. Although he assumed the coveted title 'King of Kish' it is doubtful that he resided at that city – at least, the King-List attributes to Kish five 'kings' following upon Ur-Zababa. It is not known when Sargon established his new capital, Agade, but it was this city that gave its name to his dynasty, to the language he spoke and to the country in which he lived. The site of Agade remains unidentified, though it is almost certainly to be found in the vicinity of Kish or Babylon. Indeed it is possible that the city was situated somewhere within the later city boundaries of Babylon itself.

Although we know of many of Sargon's alleged conquests and accomplishments, the exact sequence of events during his long reign of 56 years remains uncertain. Scribal records mention his defeat of Lugal-zagesi. 'Thirty-four battles' are recorded, with the victorious Sargon gaining control not only of Akkad but of all Sumer as far as the 'Lower Sea', where he 'washed his weapons' in a ritual commemoration of his victories. At some point, perhaps even early in his career, he turned to the northwest, conquering Tuttul (modern Hit), Mari, Yarmuti and Ebla (now known to be Tell Mardikh south of Aleppo) 'up to the Cedar Forest and to the Silver Mountains [the Amanus range and the Taurus]'. Mention of cedar and silver reveals clearly the motivation for this distant campaign. Later legend adds still further victories, taking him across the sea as far as Anaku, the 'Tin Country' (location uncertain) and Kaptara, Old Testament Kaphtor or Crete. A composition known as the 'King of Battle', which is preserved on a cuneiform tablet found in Egypt with the Amarna letters (chapter 4), tells the story of (?Akkadian) merchants in the Anatolian city of Purushkanda, thought to lie somewhere south of Tuz Gölü, the Great Salt Lake, who appeal to Sargon to champion their cause in some unspecified local controversy. Rich inducements are offered to the Akkadian king who is said to march with great difficulty to

15 Akkadian art is noted for its realism, perhaps best illustrated in this life-size head, cast in bronze, found at Nineveh, and often ascribed to Naram-Sin or Sargon. The head was deliberately mutilated in antiquity. Ht 36 cm. Iraq Museum.

16 Some surveyors' plans survive on clay tablets but this is the only known Babylonian map of the world. It illustrates a rather abstruse mythological treatise. Beyond the great circle of the 'Salt Sea' is an area 'where the sun is not seen'. The Euphrates flows through the middle of the map on which are marked Babylon (rectangular box), the mountains at the source of the river and to the south, at its mouth, the country of the Bit-Yakin and the marshes. British Museum. Ht 12.2 cm.

Purushkanda where his presence alone apparently brings about a settlement of the merchants' grievances. A 17th-century Hittite text also places Sargon in Asia Minor,[5] but for a number of reasons, including lack of contemporary evidence and the circulation of similar stories about his grandson, Naram-Sin, the King of Battle story has been little credited. However, a recent and as yet unpublished archive from the newly discovered kingdom at Ebla (Tell Mardikh), contemporary with the dynasty of Agade, is reported to contain references to merchant colonies at this time in Anatolia.[6] There seems little doubt that Sargon deserved his epithet 'Great'. Indeed his exploits so captured the Babylonian imagination that it is difficult now to distinguish the man from the legend: even 1700 years later echoes of his exploits are found on the only known Babylonian 'world map'.

16

The Agade kings are credited with many administrative innovations (see below), but they had considerable difficulty in controlling their vast empire. Even during Sargon's reign, and among the cities of Babylonia, there were seemingly never-ending rebellions. The 'Sargon Chronicle' tells us that 'in his old age all the countries revolted against him and they besieged him in Agade'. Sargon claims to have crushed this insurrection, but his son Rimush (2278–2270) on his accession found the empire again torn by revolts and rebellions. He was nevertheless clearly successful in regaining much of Sargon's empire. A fragment of a vase bearing his name was found at Tell Brak in northeastern Syria and like his father he claims to have held 'for Enlil' the entire country from the Upper to the Lower Sea, together with all the mountains. Rimush was killed in a palace conspiracy, assassinated by certain of his courtiers, possibly even including his 'elder' brother Manishtushu who succeeded him, and whose name, meaning 'who is with him?', perhaps indicates that they were twins.

An inscription of Manishtushu, the restoration of which is unfortunately uncertain, suggests that he 'crossed the Lower Sea in ships', where he defeated a coalition of 32 kings gathered against him and occupied their country 'up to the silver mines'. He brought back 'black stone' from the mountains beyond the sea, shipping it direct to the quays of Agade; this was almost certainly the beautifully grained diorite in which his surviving statues are carved, in a naturalistic style striking in its contrast with the stylized conventions of the Early Dynastic period. That Manishtushu held Assyria is clear from a votive inscription dedicated to him at Assur and from a later text of Shamshi-Adad who, while restoring the Ishtar temple at Nineveh, found a number of statues and stelae recording the Akkadian king's founding of the temple.

Manishtushu seems also to have been killed in a palace revolt, to be succeeded by his son, Naram-Sin (or, correctly, Naram-Suen, 2254–

17 This marvellously modelled naked figure was found recently near Dohuk in northern Iraq. It was hollow cast in copper, technically much more difficult than bronze-casting, and weighs 160 kg. It bears a dedicatory inscription of Naram-Sin, who describes himself as 'king of the 4 quarters of the world'. The nude girdled figure resembles the bearded 'hero' common on Mesopotamian seals (ill. 20). Diam. of base 67 cm. Iraq Museum.

18 A worshipper, right, led by a god brings a goat as offering to another god who stands on the back of a dragon and brandishes a mace. The Akkadian inscription reveals that the seal was dedicated for the life of the donor by his son. Impression of a mottled marble cylinder seal now in the British Museum. Ht 4·1 cm.

2218), who was to prove a more than worthy grandson of Sargon and whose empire was possibly even more extensive than his grandfather's. Naram-Sin claims to have conquered both Arman (possibly Aleppo) and Ebla, which 'since the beginning of mankind no king had ever destroyed'. Confirmation of this triumph may recently have been found at Tell Mardikh, where the Italian excavators have discovered evidence both of a major Semitic kingdom centred on Ebla in the late 3rd millennium and of its destruction about the time of Naram-Sin. The Akkadian king claims also to have journeyed to Talhatum in Anatolia where the later Cappadocian merchants did business, 'a road which no king before had ever taken'. Indeed we know that Naram-Sin was active in southern Turkey from a stele with the figure of the king found near modern Diyarbakir.

The marvellously cast life-size bronze head found at Nineveh is
15   often said to be a portrait of this king, while recently the lower portion of a large naked bronze figure inscribed with his dedication has been
17   found not far from Dohuk in the very north of Iraq. These works, together with the statues of Manishtushu and a number of undated stelae of this time, were created with a realism that is unprecedented in ancient art. Indeed, the Dohuk statue, were it not inscribed with the name of Naram-Sin, could easily have been mistaken for a piece from Classical Greece. This is in marked contrast with works attributed to the time of Sargon which, like his politics, owe much to his Early
24   Dynastic predecessors.[7] The well-known victory stele of Naram-Sin also marks an abrupt departure from Early Dynastic convention and clearly reflects a new concept of kingship which emerged in Akkadian times. This monument was set up originally in the Babylonian city of Sippar, in order to commemorate his defeat of the Lullubi, an Iranian border tribe. It was found by archaeologists excavating Susa, whither it had been carried as booty by a later Elamite king, whose own inscription can clearly be seen on the mountain peak.

Naram-Sin's control of the north is evident also from excavations at Tell Brak, which revealed a strongly fortified administrative building of the Agade period. Both here and at Elamite Susa buildings were constructed using bricks stamped with the Akkadian king's name. So complete was Akkadian ascendancy at Susa that documents relating to local law and administration were written in Akkadian rather than the native Elamite. The widespread adoption of the Akkadian language can be seen also in texts from Gasur (later Nuzi) near modern Kirkuk, and in its employment even by a Hurrian king of Urkish in upper

Mesopotamia.[8] Only at faraway Ebla in northwestern Syria is there evidence for the writing of another Semitic dialect at this time, and even here the tablets reflect an earlier Mesopotamian influence in that they are written using Sumerian signs.

Later tradition attributed the downfall of Naram-Sin, Agade and indeed all Sumer to invading hordes from the mountains to the east, the Gutians. These people are not in fact mentioned in contemporary texts until the time of Naram-Sin's son, Shar-kali-sharri (2217–2193), who ruled for 24 years and appears to have maintained a modicum of control, at least in Sumer. A number of Shar-kali-sharri's year-names survive and provide the first mention both of Babylon and of a West Semitic people, the Amurru or Amorites, who were to play an important role in the later kingdom of Babylon and whom Shar-kali-sharri defeated 'at the mountain of Basor' (Jebel Bishri in northern Syria).

Shar-kali-sharri seems to have met the same violent end as the sons of Sargon, but in conditions of even greater turmoil. His reign was followed by a period of anarchy colourfully described in the King-List as 'Who was king? Who was not king?'. Two final kings of Agade were minor figures who ruled over little more than the city itself, although the last, Shu-Durul, may have controlled territory to the east in the region of the Diyala River. At the same time a Gutian dynasty is recorded which survived perhaps a hundred years (c. 2220–2120), although the extent of its authority remains in doubt. It would appear that Gutian domination extended at least briefly as far south as Umma, and perhaps even to Ur,[9] but independent dynasties are attested both at Uruk and at Lagash during this period. Very little material evidence of Gutian rule survives; it is interesting to note, however, that like all other invaders of Mesopotamia they appear to have taken on the colour of their surroundings, even observing the local cults.

Yet another linguistic group appears at this time, the Hurrians, whose kingdom lay in the region of Mardin and perhaps to the east, who spoke an agglutinative language totally unrelated to Sumerian, and who were to play an important role in northern Mesopotamia in the 2nd millennium. Although later tradition attributes the fall of Agade solely to the widespread destruction caused by the Gutian invaders, recent research suggests that internal difficulties and dissension were equally likely, perhaps even more significant, factors in the decline of the Sargonid dynasty. Other foreign groups such as the Elamites, the Hurrians, and indeed also the Lullubi, who feature in a late and almost certainly confused legend as the cause of much distress to Naram-Sin, contributed to the general disruption of the country for which there is evidence at the time of the later Akkadian kings.

Akkadian empire and administration

Although the achievements of the Akkadians were considerable by any standards, they were unable long to control the outermost regions of their empire nor indeed even the cities of Sumer. In this they may have been no more nor less successful than their predecessors among the Early Dynastic kings; we are, however, far better informed about both the political conquests of the Akkadians and the methods by which they attempted to maintain control over their dependent territories. We have stressed the economic motivation that lay behind the establishment of this early empire, but of course far more profit is always to be gained from looting and the imposition of heavy tribute than from honest trade, which requires a quid pro quo. A monopoly of trade is also profitable and it is clear from the inscriptions of the Akkadian kings that all these paths to greater wealth were pursued. Extensive trade, with free access for the representatives of Agade to native resources, and forced tribute made the new capital a prosperous and resplendent city. Merchants came from Asia Minor, and ships from Magan and Meluhha (southeastern Arabia and the Makran coast perhaps as far as the Indus Valley) rode at anchor along its quays; '5400 men ate bread daily before the king [Sargon]', an impressive palace establishment. That Sargon's claim to trade with the Indus was not an idle boast can be seen from the discovery in Akkadian houses at Tell Asmar of an Indus-type seal together with pottery, etched carnelian beads, and bone inlay of Harappan types.[10]

21, 22 These very realistically carved small stone heads are a feature of Akkadian art. The larger (ht 9·5 cm) is from Adab and is carved in alabaster with inlaid ivory eyeballs. The small limestone head (ht 4 cm) was found in an Akkadian house at Tell Asmar. Oriental Institute, Chicago.

In order to maintain control of this economic empire 'Citizens of Agade', including members of the royal family, were appointed as governors 'from the Lower Sea to the Upper Sea', though it is clear that many conquered cities were allowed to retain their native rulers, who were kept in hand by the representatives of the king. One of Sargon's innovations was the establishment of the office of high priestess of the moon-god at Ur as a royal sinecure, apparently in a deliberate move to ally to his Akkadian administration the loyalty of the old and once-powerful Sumerian centres. His daughter Enheduanna was, so far as we know, the first holder of this celebrated post. For the next 500 years, until the end of the reign of Rim-Sin of Larsa, this appointment was a royal prerogative which was exercised through numerous dynastic

changes and provided in Sumer a unifying link even in periods of apparent disunity. As well as being the first, Enheduanna was the most distinguished in this long line of priestesses. There survive a number of hymns that she herself is said to have composed – in excellent Sumerian! – revealing her as history's first known literary figure; even her portrait has survived.[11]

Another administrative development was a reform of the method for dating cuneiform records. Previous systems involved dating by names of local officials (eponyms), known at Shuruppak, a form that was to be used subsequently in Assyria, and dating by regnal years, attested at pre-Sargonid Lagash, a system resumed in Babylonia with the advent of the Kassite dynasty in the 2nd millennium and which remained in use until the adoption of the Seleucid calendar. Under Sargon a system of 'year-names' was adopted, each year being 'named' after some significant event of the previous year. The origins of this method of

23 Sargon's daughter, Enheduanna, is depicted on this limestone plaque, performing a ceremony of libation before a stepped altar. The plaque, now restored, was found by Sir Leonard Woolley at Ur where Enheduanna held the office of high-priestess of the moon-god. Diam. 26 cm. University Museum, Philadelphia.

dating remain uncertain. Two year-names survive from the earlier time of En-shakush-ana (2432–2403) and one from Lugal-zagesi's reign,[12] but the system was first widely employed under the Sargonid kings. Scribal lists of year-names survive from later periods and provide not only dating ready-reckoners but also records of actual events that are often otherwise unattested. The lack of any such compendia for the Agade dynasty leaves uncertain the order of events known from their largely votive texts. Indeed, relatively few year-names of the Akkadian period have yet been recovered, and only those of Shar-kali-sharri are at all revealing of historical events of the time.

Perhaps the most significant innovation under the Agade kings, however, was in their conception of kingship, and for the first time we see intimations of the stereotype Oriental monarch. Sargon's titles were comparatively modest and reflected little more than the titulary used by the later Early Dynastic kings, but under Naram-Sin a change took place so startling that it proved in the long run unacceptable. At some point during his reign Naram-Sin adopted a style previously the exclusive prerogative of the gods. On his own inscriptions his name appears preceded by the determinative for 'divinity', that is, the cuneiform sign 'god' normally written before the name of a god. The language in texts dedicated to him is even less reserved, and in these his 'servants' address him not merely as divine but literally as 'god of Agade'. On his famous stele he is depicted wearing a horned helmet: such 'horns of divinity' were normally the prerogative solely of gods. The divine entitlement to multi-tiered horns, however, and the fact that Naram-Sin has only one emphasizes his undoubtedly inferior position in the pantheon; indeed in later periods single pairs of horns usually identify lower ranks of divinity, for example, a god's attendants. Moreover, Naram-Sin is depicted on his stele significantly below and clearly subordinate to the rayed discs which are almost certainly the symbols of the sun-god Utu, in whose city the stele was originally erected.

The divinity of kings seems unthinkable in the context of a religious ethic whereby rulers claimed no more than the privilege of serving as stewards of their city-gods. The extraordinary change wrought by Naram-Sin is usually interpreted as a deliberate attempt to provide a central rallying point for an empire of widely diverse elements and one in which ancient traditions of city-allegiance remained strong. Indeed the divine Naram-Sin seems to have been conceived as a sort of presiding or guiding national 'genius'. The divine form of name was adopted by Shar-kali-sharri and the later kings of Ur and Isin, but, although there is evidence to suggest a widespread cult of the divine king under the succeeding dynasty at Ur, the principle of divine kingship was never wholeheartedly adopted in Mesopotamia. Certainly the deified Mesopotamian king was in no way comparable with the divine and absolute Pharaoh in Egypt. Even divine Mesopotamian kings, with their subjects, remained at all times subject to the will of the gods as expressed in the observance of omens, which were often taken by the examination of the entrails of animals; as E. A. Speiser once observed, 'a god incarnate would not normally be expected to take his cue from the liver of a sheep'![13]

25 The triple-horned crown of divinity can be seen clearly on this head of a god in baked clay, from Telloh, *c.* 2000 BC. Ht 10 cm. Louvre Museum.

24

25

24 (*Opposite*) Sandstone victory stele of Naram-Sin showing his victorious soldiers trampling on the enemy. Only traces remain of the original inscription but on the mountain top can be seen a second inscription of Shutruk-Nahhunte of Elam, who over 1000 years later carried this famous stele from Sippar to his capital Susa (*c.* 1159). Ht 2·0 m. Louvre Museum.

The fall of Agade

The literary tradition that later attached itself so strongly to Sargon and Naram-Sin saw them not only as two of the most illustrious figures in the ancient world but also as rulers whose disastrous final years implied some stigma of ill-fate. Naram-Sin especially is remembered as the hapless king who was himself responsible for the fall of Agade. A later poem known to modern scholars as 'The Curse of Agade' accuses Naram-Sin of sacking Nippur and desecrating Enlil's sanctuary, Ekur, his ships docking by the temple in order to load and carry off the loot to Agade. According to the story Enlil, enraged by the sacrilege, turned to the Gutians to effect revenge. In the later Babylonian version of this almost certainly apocryphal story (we know from contemporary inscriptions that Naram-Sin refurbished Ekur and dedicated statues there celebrating his victories) Babylon and Marduk are defiled, but both versions ascribe to the Gutians the role of divine avenger. The poem is of especial interest in being one of the earliest recorded attempts to 'explain' a known historical incident in the framework of contemporary thought. Thus the fall of Agade can only be understood in the context of some act that would have caused Enlil to desert the Akkadian cause. The poem also provides a vivid description of the ideal city, Agade, its buildings full of gold, silver, copper, tin and lapis lazuli, its citizens wise and joyful. When 'the good sense of Agade turned to folly', a chilling account of the ensuing destruction follows: communications were cut, brigands dwelt on the roads, irrigation systems were disrupted – always a disastrous consequence of unstable conditions – and dire famine came upon the land. Naram-Sin is depicted as sulking by himself, dressed in sackcloth, his chariots and boats lying unused and neglected.

With famine and desolation rampant, so the story continues, eight of the major deities decide that for the good of mankind Enlil's rage must be assuaged. They vow to him the total destruction of Agade and pronounce upon that city a lengthy curse:

> May your groves be heaped up like dust. . . .
> May your clay [bricks] return to the depths of the earth. . . .
> May your palace built with joyful heart be turned into a
> depressing ruin. . . .
> Over the place where your rites and rituals were conducted
> May the fox who haunts the ruined mounds glide his tail. . . .
> May no human being walk because of snakes, vermin and
> scorpions. . . .[14]

And, concludes the poet-historian, such indeed was the case. Thereafter Agade remained desolate and uninhabited. Little was he to know that over 4000 years later we should still be searching for its remains.

The Third Dynasty of Ur (2112–2004)

The length of overlap between the Gutian line recognized in the Sumerian King-List and the later kings of Agade remains a matter of dispute but is crucial to the dating of earlier kings. The period from the death of Shar-kali-sharri to the rise of the new political power at Ur known as the Third Dynasty (Ur III) was probably no more than a century, but whatever dating system is adopted the discrepancy is unlikely to exceed 100 years. During this time, although much of the north suffered severe disruption and depredation, several cities in the south, most notably Lagash, regained some local authority and autonomy. The leading figure among these later *ensis* of Lagash, and indeed one whose inscriptions imply considerable political prestige, was Gudea (2141–2122), well known to us from his many statues which are among the most human and endearing to have survived from ancient Mesopotamia. But it was a king of Uruk, one Utu-hegal (2123–2113) who – or so he himself claims – rid the country of the Gutian menace. At Ur he appointed a military-governor named Ur-Nammu who soon struck out for himself, overthrew his erstwhile protector and assumed the title 'King of Ur'. In this way was founded a new dynasty at that city in many ways as remarkable as that of Agade.

The reinstatement of kingship at Ur was marked also by a reversion to Sumerian as the official language, at least throughout Sumer. For this reason the period is often characterized as a Sumerian 'revival'. It should by now be evident to the reader, however, that both Sumerians and Akkadians had long been assimilated into a homogeneous population with common traditions and culture: while the Agade kings clearly recognized the authority of the supreme Sumerian god at Nippur and Sargon's daughter composed hymns in the best literary Sumerian, the last of the Ur III kings and the most powerful queens of the dynasty bore Semitic names. Indeed we have already seen that Akkadian was spoken by at least some of the population of Ur already in the Early Dynastic period. Certainly the deliberate use of Sumerian at this time must reflect to some extent a consciousness of the cultural heritage of Ur, but any suggestion of ethnic conflict has long been abandoned.

The Ur kings owed much to their Akkadian predecessors, not only in their styles and titles but in their concept of a Mesopotamian state and its administration. Although their inscriptions are far less revealing of political conquest than those of the Agade kings, it is clear that they held much the same territory. Ur-Nammu's name appears at Brak; control of Elam and Assur was maintained, and isolated mention is made of some formal relationship with cities as far away as Mari, Tuttul, Ebla and even Byblos, a prosperous seaport on the Mediterranean coast.[15]

The Ur III kings were clearly conscious of the administrative problems that had vexed the rulers of Agade and attempted to solve them. Risk of rebellion was minimized by careful management of their governors (*ensis*) in some 40 districts;[16] each *ensi* was accountable to the king for all that happened within his territory. Under Ur-Nammu's successor, Shulgi (2094–2047), the appointment of one such royal governor in Babylon is recorded. The control of garrisons was taken away from the *ensis* and some were posted from one city to another, possibly to prevent their acquisition of too much local power or perhaps merely to transfer able men to difficult posts. Military affairs were put in the hands of garrison commanders directly responsible to the king, and conflicts between the civil and military administration were adjudicated by the courts. An efficient corps of royal messengers kept the king informed of provincial affairs, and hundreds of cuneiform tablets record their points of departure, destinations and the meals to which they were entitled on the way. Diplomatic representatives were sent to other states and royal marriages arranged to ensure continuing good relations with foreign allies.

But the most extraordinary facet of Ur III life lay in its economic administration. Literally tens of thousands of clay tablets have been found, unfortunately by far the largest number in illicit excavations, detailing for us the operation of one of the most elaborate bureaucracies of ancient times. Nothing was too insignificant to be recorded; tallies were kept of every item entering or leaving every government establishment, and the names of those responsible for each transaction were carefully noted. Such 'book-keeping' tablets have been found in several Sumerian cities but by far the greatest number so far recovered come from Umma and a small site not far from Nippur known as Puzrish-Dagan (Sellush-Dagan), modern Drehem. This small administrative centre was founded during the reign of Shulgi, who was perhaps responsible for the extraordinarily bureaucratic establishment that developed here. Its purpose was to provide for the receipt and distribution of livestock, an important part of governmental income. Large numbers of animals – in one year alone over 28,000 cattle and some 350,000 sheep were 'accounted' – were received as enforced or voluntary contributions from *ensis* and foreign vassals, offerings to the temples, taxes and booty. From Drehem the animals were allocated to the temples of Nippur, and also apparently to the other major centres, Ur and Uruk, or were sent to various officials as 'salary' or gifts or were supplied to the royal household. If an animal died, this too was recorded; the scribes employed a daily balance sheet, with the total or deficit at the end of the day carefully totted up.

Texts from Umma also provide an extraordinary picture of day-to-day administration.[17] Daily numbers of men working in the fields, digging canals, harvesting, loading and towing canal boats were recorded. The amount of work completed was noted, and rates of work and pay minutely calculated. Female workers were tabulated cutting reeds, draining fields, harvesting and as weavers and in the mill house. Ration texts detail the issue of 'pay' in the form of beer, bread, oil, onions, seeds for seasoning and fish. Beer was a basic commodity and its quality was carefully controlled. Inspections were often carried out, according to one text by a royal princess, and in another, by a 'constable' of the king; 'ordinary', 'royal', 'strong' and 'weak' beer were brewed. Closely associated with the control of state herds was a profitable industry in wool and leather. Traders who operated by royal warrant imported a great variety of goods by land and sea: exotic foods, aromatic woods, fruits and herbs, raw materials for industries such as tanning and metal-working, timber for roof beams and ship-building. Such items were paid for largely with agricultural products such as wool, barley, wheat, dates, fish oil, dried fish and skins, although silver had by now become a standard of value. Silver served too as a medium of account, thus already fulfilling all the classical functions of money. Long lists of commodities valued in silver provide the earliest 'price index' for the staples of Mesopotamian life.[18] The documents that have been recovered were once thought to imply a royal monopoly of trade, but it is becoming increasingly clear that private persons also participated in such transactions. Indeed our view of life under the Ur III kings is revealed largely by official documents, and the lives of private individuals, who must even in this seemingly rigidly bureaucratic time have comprised the majority of the population, is scarcely apparent.

Among the many and varied documents of Ur III officialdom a special group, largely from Lagash, reveal the structure and operation of an elaborate judicial system.[19] Although the royal proclamation of social reforms and remission of debts was known already under two earlier *ensis* of Lagash, Entemena and Urukagina (probably more correctly read Uru-inim-gina), it is Ur-Nammu who is especially remembered as the promulgator of the world's first-known 'law code'.[20] Though poorly preserved this can be seen to begin with a documentation of the same concern for social justice and the correction of administrative abuse that characterized the earlier reforms. It is doubtful to what extent such royal promulgations, of which there must have been far more than have survived, were binding on the courts, which never record the appeal to written law as a basis for their decisions. Court procedure is clearly shown in court records known as *ditilla*, literally 'case closed', the phrase with which these tablets end. Proceedings were heard occasionally before the king himself, but more often by his *ensis* or his judges. Cases involved such subjects as breach of contract and disputed inheritance or property. From documents dealing with marriage law it is clear that the legal position of women was equal to that of men. Penalties were financial; *lex talionis* was unknown, or is at least unrecorded, at this period.

The contribution of the Ur III kings to Mesopotamian culture was considerable. The impact of their extensive public building programme can still be seen in almost every major city of the time. Ur-Nammu's architects redesigned the royal and religious quarter of Ur 26 and, although the structures themselves were remodelled many times thereafter, to this day the ruins of Ur preserve in essence the Ur III conception of the city. Our extensive knowledge of Ur III architecture contrasts markedly with the dearth of evidence from Agade levels, from which no major public building has yet been recovered in either Sumer or Akkad. What little we know of Agade monumental buildings comes from provincial sites such as Brak and Tell Taya.[21] Thus many architectural innovations that may derive, like so much else, from Akkadian times have been attributed to the period of the Ur III kings, when for the first time we can be certain of the existence of an established school of architecture, imposing to some extent its own technical expertise and aesthetic standards on its royal patrons.[22] One of the major contributions of this new school lay in the treatment of buildings in elevation as well as ground plan. The most conspicuous example of this new development, attested apparently for the first time under Ur-Nammu, was the ziggurat, a stepped tower surmounted by a

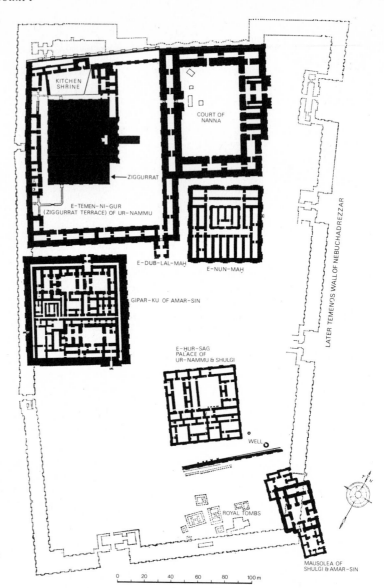

KITCHEN SHRINE

COURT OF NANNA

← ZIGGURRAT

E-TEMEN-NI-GUR
(ZIGGURRAT TERRACE) OF UR-NAMMU

E-DUB-LAL-MAH̬

E-NUN-MAH̬

GIPAR-KU OF AMAR-SIN

E-HUR-SAG
PALACE OF
UR-NAMMU & SHULGI

LATER TEMENOS WALL OF NEBUCHADREZZAR

WELL

ROYAL TOMBS

MAUSOLEA OF
SHULGI & AMAR-SIN

0   20   40   60   80   100 m

26 Plan of the sacred precinct of the moon-god Nanna (Sin) at the time of the Third Dynasty of Ur. The vaulted tombs of kings Shulgi and Amar-Sin, together with the famous Royal Tombs of the Early Dynastic period, lie just to the southeast of the outer precinct wall. After Woolley.

small shrine, best known in historical tradition from the Tower of
27 Babel but best preserved at Ur. Ur-Nammu's tower owes its excellent
state of preservation to the original casing of baked brick with which it
was enclosed and to the careful renovations carried out 1500 years later,
when the last kings of Babylon exercised their responsibility for
maintaining the ancient shrines of Sumer.

Yet another new feature was the idea of a precinct enclosing a large
open space, in the middle of which was set a monumental building.
This too served an aesthetic function in enabling the building to be seen
to advantage on all sides. The layout of religious complexes with one or
more regularly planned internal courtyards is also first known from this

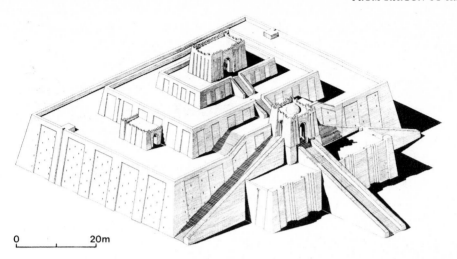

0   20m

period, although it has precedents in the 'palaces' of earlier times, such as at Brak, Kish and Eridu, and may reflect the growing demands on administration in the great shrines as well as, perhaps, some ceremonial changes. The latter would seem to have been partly responsible for the introduction of the 'Babylonian' plan, with its formal courtyard and wide (*breitraum*) cella. At Ur the ziggurrat formed the core of a sacred precinct dedicated to the moon-god. An outer wall enclosed this and three other buildings: E-nun-mah, a temple store-house; Gipar-ku ('holy *gipar*'), the official residence of the high priestesses of the moon-god; and E-hur-sag, a royal palace, probably for use on religious occasions (it is likely that the main residence of the Ur III kings was at Nippur). On the northwest side of the ziggurrat was the god's kitchen, for the preparation of his meals.

Mesopotamian building techniques create many problems for archaeologists. Although careful and frequent plastering serves to maintain mud-brick structures, their average life is short, a fact which explains in part the seemingly endless series of royal buildings. To restore a temple was a work of piety which ensured the favour of the gods; that the opportunities to earn such favour were unlimited was guaranteed by the almost exclusive use of the only readily available building material, mud. Sun-dried mud-brick is a highly versatile medium. Indeed buildings of this material can be altered or enlarged with relative ease. When more drastic rebuilding is necessary, it is a fairly simple process to level a standing structure to its foundations, at the same time providing a solid base for its successor. It was a tenet of Mesopotamian faith that a temple should be rebuilt on the same 'consecrated' site and its earlier foundations preserved. The wealthier the dynasty the more often it could afford such major reconstruction. Thus at ancient and important sites like Ur and Babylon excavation frequently reveals only long and often highly complicated sequences of stubs or walls, representing perhaps hundreds of years of occupation but telling the archaeologist little beyond the plan of the building he is investigating. Although the inscriptions of the Ur III dynasty and extant archaeological remains testify both to the wealth and piety of its

27 The ziggurrat of the moon-god at Ur, restored as it is thought to have been in the time of Ur-Nammu. This is the best-preserved ziggurrat in Mesopotamia and the recent restoration of its surviving remains enables the modern visitor actually to climb the central staircase to the first stage. After Woolley.

8

28 The earliest known 'pitched-brick' vault, Tell al Rimah, c. 2100 BC. Slanting rings of bricks were laid from each end until they met in the middle, when the gap was plugged with brick fragments. Almost certainly invented in Mesopotamia, this mud-brick technique was later reproduced in baked brick, notably in 5th-century AD Constantinople and in the Sassanian palace at Ctesiphon, still the largest unreinforced brick vault in the world. The pendentives at the corners – later a standard method of support – are not known elsewhere for 2000 years.

kings and to the increasingly professional competence of its architects and builders, we have therefore little idea of the overall aspect of their buildings, and no evidence whatsoever of the techniques of roofing employed.

At Ur vaulting was used in the Early Dynastic period, but only in *underground* structures, where lateral thrust is not a problem. We must turn to a peripheral site in northern Iraq to find evidence of the technical expertise of builders of this time. The discovery at the site of Tell al Rimah of buildings in an unusual state of preservation has revealed the structural use of radial vaulting with a skill that must imply a long previous tradition. Perhaps more surprising is the evidence for 'pitched-brick' vaulting, in which the need for centring, using less readily available wood, is virtually eliminated by the laying of successive rings of bricks with their edges across the long axis of the vault, a technique perhaps best known in the 6th-century AD Arch of Ctesiphon near Baghdad. In what is so far a unique discovery, several examples of sun-dried mud-brick vaults of this type, built on shallow pendentives and dated to the late 3rd millennium BC have been excavated at Rimah.[23] To what extent these vaulting techniques represent innovations of the new school of architecture postulated for this period remains uncertain; however, the evidence from Rimah must suggest their fairly common employment at this time. Woolley's reconstruction of domed gate chambers in the ziggurat precinct at Ur has often been criticized, yet the skill with which the provincial masons of Rimah erected what were in all essential features 'domed' structures makes Woolley's metropolitan dome wholly plausible.

At Ur the quays too were rebuilt, and a year-name early in Ur-Nammu's reign records 'the return of the ships of Magan and Meluhha into the hands of Nanna [city deity of Ur]'. Ur-Nammu's devotion to

28

27

the ancient shrines, particularly at Nippur, brought him recognition there by Enlil's priesthood and early in his reign he adopted a new title, 'King of Sumer and Akkad', which was to assume great importance in the succeeding centuries. His 'coronation' at Nippur was commemorated in a new literary genre, the so-called royal hymn, which was addressed not to the gods but to the king himself 'as a god'.[24]

The exalted position of the late-3rd-millennium kings of Ur is even more evident during the reign of Shulgi, who not only continued his father's administrative, architectural and literary interests, but went one step further in emulating the later Agade kings. Sometime early in his reign he assumed divine status. Shrines were erected for him; local manifestations of the royal god were worshipped and more royal hymns composed in his honour than are known for any other Mesopotamian king. Like Sargon and Naram-Sin Shulgi became in later times a favourite literary figure. Both the great scribal schools, at Nippur and at Ur, traced their foundation to him, and he was a devoted patron of Sumerian literature and culture, even claiming to have been trained in his youth as a scribe in the *edubba* or school. Such education was as rare for a Mesopotamian king as it was for most members of society.

The fall of Ur

We know little of the military exploits of the Ur III kings, but the monumental building programmes carried out by the early monarchs of the dynasty lend credence to their claims of prosperity throughout the land. Despite the peaceful tenor of his inscriptions, it would appear that Ur-Nammu was killed in battle, a fate rare for a Mesopotamian monarch and one which later scribes found difficult to reconcile as a just reward for his visibly pious life. The year-names of Shulgi's later years indicate increasing military activity, but tradition reveals little of the life of his son and successor, Amar-Sin (Amar-Suena, 2046–2038), beyond the fact that he continued his father's building policies and that he died from the 'bite' of a shoe, presumably a poisoned foot. He and his father were buried in the elaborate corbelled mausolea still visible at Ur. Unfortunately these were looted in antiquity, but the discovery of traces of gold leaf from the doors and sheet gold inset with inlays of agate and lapis lazuli from the walls of the associated superstructures gives some hint of their original magnificence, and of the rewards reaped by their presumably Elamite plunderers.

Like Shulgi, both Amar-Sin and his brother Shu-Sin (Shu-Suen) were deified in their own lifetimes. One of the finest examples of the new, broad cella temple plan is to be found at Tell Asmar (Eshnunna) in the shrine built by an Ur III governor and dedicated to the divine 29 Shu-Sin. Shu-Sin's inscriptions are more informative than those of his brother, and begin to foretell the disasters that were to lose the empire for Ibbi-Sin (2028–2004). In the reign of Shu-Sin we first hear of a serious incursion into Babylonia by a Semitic-speaking people from the western desert known as the Martu or Amorites. Against these marauders the king built a wall known as the *Muriq-Tidnim* ('which keeps away the Tidnum', one of the nomadic Martu tribes). A fragmentary letter, written by an 'expert' on the committee of technical

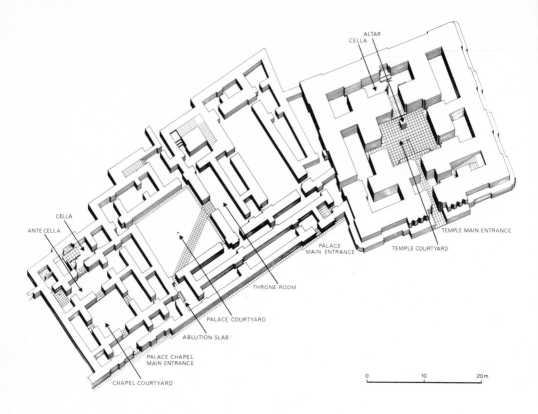

ALTAR
CELLA
CELLA
ANTE CELLA
TEMPLE MAIN ENTRANCE
PALACE
MAIN ENTRANCE
TEMPLE COURTYARD
TEMPLE COURTYARD
THRONE ROOM
PALACE COURTYARD
ABLUTION SLAB
PALACE CHAPEL
MAIN ENTRANCE
CHAPEL COURTYARD

0   10   20 m

29 Plan and reconstruction of the palace of the governors and the temple of Shu-Sin at Eshnunna. The shrine dedicated to Shu-Sin by an Ur III governor (plan, right) provides one of the finest examples of the Babylonian broad cella temple plan. It adjoins the palace, rebuilt by the governor's son, Ilshu-iliya, to include at its western end an additional chapel complex which was an almost exact copy of the temple and perhaps served as an audience chamber. After Lloyd.

advisers called in to execute this great work, gives some surprising details, including the fact that it was to extend for '26 double-hours' (some 270 km) and that the work would involve breaching the banks of both the Tigris and the Euphrates.[25]

Shu-Sin's wall proved even less effective than other great walls in history, and in the reign of his successor Amorite pressure increased. Their attacks together with raids by the Elamites compelled Ibbi-Sin to build large walls and fortifications around Ur and Nippur. One by one his various governors, encouraged by unsettled conditions throughout the country, decided to sever relations with Ur and fend for themselves. This disintegration was gradual, although in many cases it is clear that professed loyalty to Ur was in fact only formal. One such defecting governor was Ilshu-iliya, who rebuilt the small palace complex adjoining the shrine of Shu-Sin at Eshnunna, to which he added a chapel, in plan very like the temple itself, which may have served as his own audience chamber, though he himself did not claim divine honours. The plan of a later (Old Babylonian) palace reception suite at Tell al Rimah also bears a striking resemblance to the *breitraum* temple plan, although by this time the fashion for according divine honours to royalty had died out. Such evidence only serves to emphasize the significant point that the distinction between the temple cella or reception room of a god and the royal reception suite is far less rigid than our use of the terms 'religious' and 'secular' implies. Both

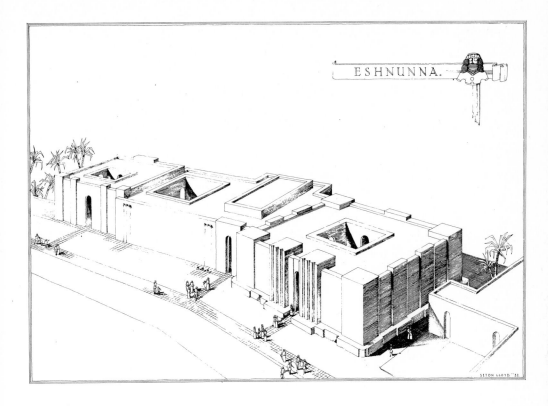

performed the same function, and the underlying similarity between the suites in which rulers, whether gods or kings, held court cannot be surprising.[26] The audience chamber of the original palace at Eshnunna, consisting of a throne room to which the paved way leads, situated between a forecourt and an inner court, and with a stair-well at one end, is a clear prototype of later Assyrian examples. Both styles of throne room can be found in the palace at Mari, clearly demonstrating the lack of any standard form for such suites at this time.

The break-up of the Ur III state, like the fall of the Agade dynasty, was remembered and repeated in later omen literature, which tells of the population over-riding the authority of the king and of numerous uprisings and rebellions. The Martu breakthrough appears to have been a very real catastrophe. It has been suggested that Sumer fell victim to a 'Maginot-Line mentality'; once the outer defences were breached there seems to have been no effective resistance. The major cities became isolated from one another, and agricultural lands were abandoned to the invaders as people sought safety within city walls. Prices reflected conditions of extreme famine and economic collapse: in the 7th and 8th years of Ibbi-Sin's reign the price of grain rose to 60 times the normal. Ibbi-Sin held out for 24, possibly 25, years. At the end his territory comprised little more than the city of Ur itself, which fell finally to an all-out attack by Elam, together with the Su or Sua, mountain people from the Zagros. Ur was ravaged and Ibbi-Sin

43

30 This magnificent necklace with its enormous beads of banded agate set in gold is one of the few surviving pieces of jewellery which can certainly be dated to the Ur III period. It belonged to the priestess Abbabashti (also read Tiamat-bashti) and was found in the temple of Eanna at Uruk. The width of the largest bead is 9 cm. Iraq Museum.

suffered an unprecedented fate, being led captive to Elam. One of the most moving of Sumerian poems records the catastrophe:

> Dead men, not potsherds,
> Covered the approaches,
> The walls were gaping,
> the high gates, the roads,
> were piled with dead.
> In the side streets, where feasting crowds would gather,
> Scattered they lay.
> In all the streets and roadways bodies lay.
> In open fields that used to fill with dancers,
> they lay in heaps.
> The country's blood now filled its holes,
> like metal in a mould;
> Bodies dissolved – like fat left in the sun.[27]

Successors to the Third Dynasty of Ur

Documents from Isin show that a certain Ishbi-Erra, a man from Mari who was in charge of Ibbi-Sin's northern troops, had established himself as a rival to Ibbi-Sin as early as the 10th or 11th year of the latter's reign. The new capital Isin (Ishan Bahriyat, some 30 km south of Nippur) was a town of no previous distinction, but the dynasty founded there by Ishbi-Erra ruled without serious opposition for the next 100 years. In outlook and in administrative policy he and his successors followed closely the precedents set at Ur. Like the kings of that city they assumed the divine style, the last Mesopotamian dynasty to do so. Although Akkadian was certainly by now the dominant spoken language, even at Ur, the Isin kings continued using Sumerian for official documents and patronized the scribal schools in which the study of Sumerian was perpetuated. Indeed Sumerian continued to be taught in Babylonian schools and survived in legal and religious usage for almost 2000 years, but after this time was never again the official language of any ruling dynasty.

Some years after the fall of Ur, Ishbi-Erra succeeded in expelling the Elamites, henceforth controlling the old Sumerian cities of the south as well as central Babylonia. His son, Shu-ilishu (1984–1975), recovered from Elam the stolen statue of Ur's moon-god, and he and his immediate successors, though they ruled from Isin, did so under the ancient and prestigious title 'King of Ur'. This was a time of peace and prosperity in Babylonia. Some of the greatest literary works of the ancient world owe their composition to the scribes of this dynasty, whose copies of older texts also provide the only extant versions of many invaluable historical and literary compositions. The latest version of the Sumerian King-List was compiled at this time with the purpose of legitimizing Isin's claim to inherit, following upon Ur, the true and proper authority of Enlil.

From the reign of Ishme-Dagan (1953–1935), and for the first time since Urukagina of Lagash, there appear references to the abolition of social and economic grievances. According to contemporary texts the city of Nippur was relieved of tax and its citizens released from certain

31 The remarkable skill of Mesopotamian goldsmiths can be seen on this Old Babylonian necklace from Dilbat. The circular rosettes and the crescent and forked lightning are decorated in the very finest granulation technique. The small figures, 3 cm high, are probably to be identified as the goddess Lama. Metropolitan Museum of Art, New York.

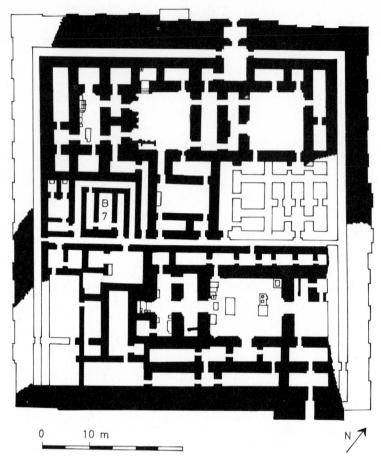

32 Plan of the Gipar-ku at Ur as rebuilt by Enanatuma (*c.* 1940 BC). The main sanctuary, dedicated to the goddess Ningal, is situated in the southeastern quarter. The residence of the *entu*-priestess would appear to have been in the northern quarter. B7 marks an enigmatic complex adjoining two small unidentified shrines. It contained three stelae dedicated to Ningal by Amar-Sin apparently re-sited here by Enanatuma. After Woolley.

0   10 m

N

obligations. Ishme-Dagan is referred to as the king who 'set justice in the land', a phrase which almost certainly implies the promulgation of social or economic reforms. The earliest collection of laws known from this dynasty – and one still largely in the Sumerian tradition – dates from the reign of his son, Lipit-Eshtar (1934–1924). Ishme-Dagan's daughter, Enanatuma, then high priestess of Nanna, rebuilt the Gipar-ku at Ur. Records of the storehouse E-nun-mah at the time of the later kings of Larsa reveal the issue of regular offerings of cheese, butter and dates for two earlier high priestesses (*entu*), one of whom was Enanatuma, made at 'the place of libation'.[28] This suggests some form of cult of the dead *entu*s, and shows clearly the high esteem in which Enanatuma was held. There was a cemetery associated with the Gipar-ku, but the vaulted tombs actually found there by Woolley are, at least to judge by their contents, of later Kassite date.

A poem composed at the time of Ishme-Dagan speaks once again of Amorites who are said to be raiding the settled lands. And early in the reign of his successor there is evidence for the establishment of the first Amorite dynasty in the south, under Gungunum (1932–1906) at Larsa.

How long his family had reigned in Larsa is uncertain. Gungunum traces his ancestry back to one Naplanum, thought to have been a contemporary of Ibbi-Sin of Ur and about whom nothing more is known than his Amorite name. Although a later version of the King-List attributes to Naplanum the founding of this Larsa dynasty, no records have been recovered for any of its 'kings' until the time of Gungunum, with the single exception of brick inscriptions of his (elder) brother Zabaya who claims only the title 'Shaikh of the Amorites'.

The Martu or Amorites

It is perhaps time to say more about these people who are alleged to have wreaked such havoc at Ur and elsewhere in the south at the time of Ibbi-Sin, and who in the subsequent two centuries were to be responsible for the founding of a number of new dynasties not only in cities in Babylonia, but also at Assur, Mari and further to the northwest at Qatna and Aleppo. The word Amorite, Akkadian *Amurrum*, comes from the Sumerian *Martu* meaning simply 'the West', a phrase used both as a geographical term and to refer to a large number of different tribes who had their origins in the western desert and whose names first appear on documents of the Ur III period. The townsmen held no high opinion of the tribal Martu; an inscription of Shu-Sin describes them as 'a ravaging people, with the instincts of a beast ... a people who know not grain' – the ultimate sign of barbarism to city-dwelling farmers – while a later poem represents them as no better than savages, living by warfare, grubbing up truffles in the desert, eating uncooked meat, houseless, careless even of burying their dead.[29] Yet already in the Fara and Agade texts we find persons designated as Martu living and working peacefully in Babylonia. Eannatum of Lagash is said to have a 'Tidnum [tribal] name', and in the Ur III and Old Babylonian periods West Semitic (Amorite) names are found in a variety of contexts which suggests their holders' complete assimilation into sedentary Mesopotamian society. Indeed it is these names that provide our only written documentation for this West Semitic dialect, since even those dynasties founded later in the 2nd millennium by men of Amorite origin adopted the Akkadian or East Semitic form of language, at least for the purpose of writing.[30]

The incursion and settlement of nomadic groups was and remains today a complex process of interaction between settled and tribal societies that has often been misunderstood. Certainly these peoples at times preyed on the settled lands: a Sumerian myth describes them as 'hovering over the walls of Uruk like flocks of birds', but in general their incursions took the form of raids or razzias, not invasions. Economic distress or poverty often persuaded nomadic peoples to seek employment as labourers on the land, or – and this is frequently attested in contemporary texts – as hired mercenaries. Others appear deliberately to have chosen the mercenary role, their pay including grants of land as well as loot from the campaigns on which they served. By such means groups of pastoralists, indeed sometimes whole tribes, came in time to acquire not only the settled ways of their protectors but

33 Most pottery of the Old Babylonian period is undecorated and dull. However this vase, found in a tomb at Larsa, is ornamented with lively incised animals and small figures in relief of the goddess Ishtar. Ht 26·3 cm. Louvre Museum.

their language and culture as well. There is certainly no direct route from the role of true bedouin to that of head of state, and those groups that became true city-dwellers had normally passed some time in the intermediate stage of dependence upon their settled agricultural neighbours.

The Old Babylonian archives from Mari, of which more will be said in the next chapter, reveal a number of West Semitic tribes pursuing their migratory role as fully fledged pastoralists or in the service of local rulers, in particular those at Mari, who were themselves of Amorite origin. A letter from a palace official to Zimri-Lim of Mari (1782–1759), a contemporary of Hammurapi, reminds him that as he is king of the Hanu, a tribal federation from whom many mercenaries were drawn, so he is 'in the second place, king of the Akkadians'.[31] Another tribal federation of this period were the Maru- or Binu-Yamina, a name meaning 'Sons of the South' which is linguistically related to the Old Testament tribal name of Benjamin. Patterns of tribal migration, and indeed tribal structure, appear to correspond closely with those that are known among modern bedouin.[32] The Amorite shaikh was called *abum*, 'father', in Akkadian, and as in modern tribal society it was he who bore full responsibility for the activities of his followers. These desert shaikhs were treated with respect and considerable diplomacy – though occasionally with some impatience – by the rulers of Mari, and a variety of letters make clear the complicated relationships between the two:

34 The inscription on this steatite vase, designed to hold some form of offering, is a dedication by a high priest of Girsu for the life of Sumu-El of Larsa (19th century BC). Ht *c.* 8 cm. Louvre Museum.

From Shamshi-Adad of Assyria to his son, viceroy of Mari:

> Tell Yasmakh-Adad, your father, Shamshi-Adad sends the following message:
>
> 'You have asked me about the waiving of all administrative and legal claims incumbent on the northern tribes. It is not appropriate to waive these claims. Should you do this, their relatives, the Rabbaya tribes, who are now on the other side of the Euphrates in the country of Yamhad, will hear about this and be so angry that they will not come back here to their home grounds. Therefore do not waive the claims against the northern tribes . . . On the contrary, reprimand them severely in the following terms: "If the king goes on a [military] expedition, everybody down to the children should immediately assemble. Any shaikh whose men are not all assembled commits a sacrilege against the king even if he leaves only one man behind!" '

A second letter is more urgent:

> Tell my lord [of Mari] your servant Bahdi-Lim sends the following message:
>
> 'I have been waiting now for five days for the Hana auxiliaries at the place agreed upon, but the soldiers are not assembling. The Hana auxiliaries did come out of the open country but they are now staying in their own encampments. I sent messages once or twice to call them up, but they did not assemble; in fact it is three days now and they still are not assembling.

35 Much of our knowledge of Mesopotamian musical instruments comes from the very life-like clay plaques of the Old Babylonian period. From the Diyala excavations of the Oriental Institute, Chicago. Ht c. 12 cm.

36 Clay plaque from Khafajah: a god armed with a dagger and bow kills a fiery cyclops. The significance of this ritual scene is obscure. Ht 11 cm. Oriental Institute Museum, Chicago.

37 Seal from Larsa and impression showing Nergal, god of the nether regions, carrying a large scimitar and a 'lion mace'. The inscription is a dedication to Nergal for the life of Abisare, perhaps the king of Larsa of that name. Ht 4·5 cm. Iraq Museum.

'Now then, if this meets with the approval of my lord, one should execute some criminal kept in the prison. Cut off his head and carry it around outside the encampments as far away as Hutnim and Appan, so the soldiers will become afraid and will assemble here quickly.'[33]

An edict of a king of Babylon late in the Old Babylonian period refers to the local population as 'Akkadians and Amurrum' but by the middle of the 2nd millennium the West Semitic peoples – whom we indeed recognize only by their names – appear to have become totally assimilated into the Babylonian population. In Syria and Palestine, however, they were to remain the dominant element in the population until a further incursion of nomadic tribes brought with them a later dialect of West Semitic, that known as Aramaean.

The Larsa kings

With the Amorite Gungunum (1932–1906) the fortunes of Larsa change. Notable among his achievements was the annexation from Isin of Ur, by which Larsa gained control of the valuable Gulf trade which had apparently languished since the fall of Ur. That there was no open conflict between the two cities, however, can be seen in the traditions of the office of high priestess of the moon-god at Ur. Daughters of both Ishme-Dagan and Lipit-Eshtar of Isin continued in office under Gungunum, and a usurper to the throne of Isin following upon Lipit-Eshtar made dedications at Ur while that city was under the hegemony of Larsa. Gungunum claimed the titles both of 'King of Sumer and Akkad' and 'King of Ur', and he and his successors did much to improve the political and economic standing of Larsa. One of the most interesting archives to have survived from this period tells of the revived sea-trade between Ur and Dilmun (the island of Bahrain).[34] The relevant documents date from the reigns of Gungunum and his two successors and reveal an active trade carried out by a group of seafaring merchants – the *alik Telmun* or 'travellers to Dilmun' – with the aid of capital invested by various private citizens who appear to have accepted none of the risk involved but received a fixed return of the profits. (Over 100 years later the Law Code of Hammurapi of Babylon attempted, unsuccessfully, to compel such investors to share not only the profits but the possible losses, §98.)

The main object of this Dilmun trade was copper, in the form of both ingots and finished products. Copper was imported in enormous quantities, on which the palace made a tidy profit in import duties. Ivory, gold, lumps of lapis lazuli, beads of precious stones, 'fish-eyes' (pearls) and other luxury items are also mentioned. In this trade Dilmun was the middle man, importing raw materials and commodities from such places as eastern Iran, Magan and Meluhha and selling to the *alik Telmun* for Babylonian products such as oil, grain and highly-prized garments. Such trade marks a noticeable change from the period of the Sargonid kings when ships of Magan and Meluhha actually tied up at the quays of Agade.

One of the major concerns of the Larsa dynasty was water. Indeed to judge by the long succession of irrigation schemes mentioned in royal inscriptions and year-names of the period, procurement of water was of major concern to all the later Old Babylonian kings. But Larsa's problems became unusually acute, apparently owing to the damming of its main canal by some unspecified enemy. In a *coup d'état* one Nur-Adad (1865–1850), 'one of the multitude', took control of the city and destroyed the offending dam. Growing conflict with Isin owed much to increasing shortages of water, and Nur-Adad's son, Sin-iddinam (1849–1843), was forced to resort to measures perhaps first taken by Entemena of Lagash (2404–2375): the channel of the Tigris was deepened and 'eternal and unceasing abundance of water' brought thence to Larsa.[35]

38 Baked-clay figure of a bearded man with an axe, perhaps a warrior, Old Babylonian, from Telloh (Girsu). Ht 19 cm. Iraq Museum.

The art forms of the kingdoms of Isin and Larsa differed little from those of the traditionally Sumerian Ur III kings. Terracotta as an artistic medium achieved a new significance, and among the smaller antiquities of the period are enormous numbers of clay plaques, poor men's dedications, mass-produced in open moulds and undoubtedly sold in the vicinity of temples.

35, 36, 38, 48, 49

Both the King-List and the royal hymns composed at this time perpetuate the fiction that Sumer and Akkad continued to be united under a single king. But it is clear that the peace enjoyed under the early kings of Isin was now interrupted by more than a century of increasing turmoil in which power see-sawed among a number of petty states. At first Isin and Larsa were the dominant protagonists, though the political pretences of their royal inscriptions were often largely fictional; but by the end of the 19th century Isin's supremacy was at an end, and Larsa, Assur and Eshnunna were the major contenders for power. At the beginning of the 19th century an Amorite dynasty emerged at Babylon, the first we hear of this city since its brief appearance in a list of imperial governors appointed by an Ur III king. The most important ruler of this new dynasty was Hammurapi, undoubtedly the best-known figure of his age and the subject of the next chapter.

3
The Old Babylonian period

39 The widespread trading connections of Old Babylonian Mesopotamia can be seen in the presence of such exotic objects as monkeys, presumably imported from either Africa or India. They are often depicted on cylinder seals of the period, sometimes mounted on poles as was this fine alabaster example, which has a hollow at the base for this purpose. From Ishchali. Ht 8 cm. Iraq Museum.

Babylon under the First Dynasty

In 1894 BC an Amorite dynasty was founded at Babylon which was to bring that city to a pre-eminence it maintained, psychologically if not politically, for nearly 2000 years. Up to this time, as we have seen, Babylon had made no mark on its country's history. Yet little over 100 years later this city ruled all Mesopotamia, albeit briefly, and subsequently it was to give its name to the whole of Sumer and Akkad, a name indeed that still remains in common use today. The language written on the cuneiform documents of this time, and presumably spoken by the majority of the population, is known to modern scholars as Babylonian, or more specifically, Old Babylonian, to distinguish it from later dialects. Archaeologists refer to the period from the fall of Ur (c. 2004) to the Hittite sack of Babylon in 1595 BC as the Old Babylonian period, though correctly speaking the changes in writing and language that signify Old Babylonian to a philologist are not generally found until the latter part of the 20th century BC, about the 4th or 5th generation of the Isin kings. Babylonian is not a new language but simply a later form of Akkadian; the earlier dialect of the time of the Agade kings and before is specifically designated Old Akkadian to differentiate it from later Babylonian forms.

Babylon's existence can be traced back to the latter part of the Early Dynastic period; at least, potsherds of this date have been reported from the surface of the site.[1] By the time of the Agade king Shar-kali-sharri the town boasted at least two temples, and under the kings of Ur was of sufficient importance to be the seat of a local governor. The name Babylon – Akkadian *Bab-ilim*, biblical *Babel*, 'gate of god' – was long thought to be merely a translation of an earlier Sumerian name *Ka-dingirra*. But the city's name is first found in the Akkadian form *Bab-ilim*, now believed to be a secondary spelling developed by popular etymology from an earlier name *Babil*, the meaning of which is unknown.[2] Much later, the plural form *Bab-ilani*, 'gate of the gods', is found. This became βαβυλων in Greek, hence the modern name Babylon.

Later and almost certainly apocryphal tradition attributes to Babylon an early importance as a religious centre. Esagila, the temple of Marduk, Babylon's chief deity, was already in existence in the Ur III period, but Marduk did not achieve his pre-eminent position in the pantheon for some centuries, indeed probably not until Kassite or even later times. Year-names of the founder of the First Dynasty, Sumu-abum (1894–1881), make no mention of Marduk and it is not until the 21st year of his successor, Sumulael, whom the rest of the dynasty regarded as their true ancestor, that any record of Old Babylonian dedications to Marduk is found. According to the year-names Sumulael made a throne for the god, finished in gold and silver, and two years later, a statue for Marduk's wife, Sarpanitum. The much later tale, that Sargon committed sacrilege by carrying holy soil from Babylon for the founding of Agade – literally for the building of a 'replica' of Babylon next to Agade – was clearly invented to give substance to Babylon's subsequent claims to sanctity.

Little is known of the antecedents of Babylon's first dynasty, though a tablet now in the British Museum lists a number of 'ancestors', presumably tribal shaikhs, reminiscent in many respects of the genealogy of another Amorite king, Shamshi-Adad, who seized the throne of Assur some generations later.[3] Nor are we well informed of events in this dynasty's early years. Sumu-abum began his reign with the construction of a 'great city wall', a project still uncompleted on the accession of his successor. Babylon's relative insignificance at this time is emphasized by the fact that Sumu-abum was unable to retain control even of nearby Kish, a city Sumulael was forced to sack. The year-names of the early kings of Babylon do record the digging of several new canals, and much of Babylon's later prosperity may be traced to the care lavished by them and their successors on the improvement of their water supply.

On the accession of Hammurapi (1792–1750) Babylon was still but one of a number of petty states. Contemporary documents reveal a highly unstable political scene in which rival kingdoms joined in ever-shifting coalitions as power fluctuated from one centre to another. They show too that a talent for political intrigue was as necessary for success as the possession of more material resources. An often-quoted letter aptly illustrates the situation:

> There is no king who by himself is strongest. Ten or fifteen kings follow Hammurapi of Babylon, as many follow Rim-Sin of Larsa, Ibal-pi-el of Eshnunna, and Amut-pi-el of Qatna, while twenty kings follow Yarim-Lim of Yamhad [Aleppo].[4]

Hammurapi's first few years cannot have been encouraging. The powerful Rim-Sin (1822–1763) dominated the south, Eshnunna controlled the region north of Babylon as far as the Euphrates, and to the far north Assur under the astute Shamshi-Adad was a growing power already in control of vast territories to the west. Rim-Sin's family is of some interest: his elder brother Warad-Sin (1834–1823) was manoeuvred to the throne of Larsa by their father, Kudur-mabuk, a clever tribal shaikh who had deposed one Silli-Adad, vassal of the state of Kazallu, who ruled Larsa only briefly (1835). Kudur-mabuk's name and that of his father are Elamite, yet Kudur-mabuk bore the titles 'Shaikh of the Amurrum and of Yamutbal' (an area east of the Tigris settled by Amorites at the time of the Ur III dynasty). It would appear that he was an Amorite whose family had at some time entered the service of the king of Elam. His sons' names, however, are pure Akkadian and his daughter was consecrated high priestess of the moon-

40 Like the Naram-Sin stele (ill. 24) this beautifully carved head of an Old Babylonian ruler was carried to Susa in the 12th century as part of the Elamite spoils of war. It is often identified as a head of Hammurapi. Diorite, ht 15 cm. Louvre Museum.

41 This small bronze statue was probably placed as a votive offering in a temple. At the front two deities, seen here from behind, hold a small bowl (cf. ill. 45); the heads and beards of the goats are covered with beaten gold foil, those of the small figures with silver foil. Ht 22·5 cm. Louvre Museum.

42 The so-called 'Investiture of Zimri-Lim' is the central portion of a large wall painting found at Mari at the entrance to the broad reception room to the south of courtyard B (ill. 43). It shows the king before the goddess Ishtar in the presence of various other deities. Ishtar is depicted in her warlike guise, with a mace between two scimitars rising from each shoulder. Painted in various shades of black, red, yellow, blue and brown. After Parrot.

god at Ur under the Sumerian name Enanedu. Indeed we see here the best-documented example of the path from nomad to Babylonian monarch. Like the Isin and Ur kings Rim-Sin was worshipped with divine honours. His rival Hammurapi never assumed the title of divinity in any form, and all subsequent kings were to follow Babylon in this respect.

Hammurapi's first few years seem to have been devoted to matters of internal administration. In his second year he 'established justice in the land', a reference to the inauguration of reforms that culminated in the promulgation of his famous code of laws. The reference is not to the laws themselves, but to the *misharum* act, a reform edict with which kings of this period began their reigns. During Hammurapi's first 30 years only 3 year-names record military campaigns, and it was not until the latter part of his reign that Babylon became a major power. Undoubtedly the dominant personality of the age was Shamshi-Adad (*c.* 1813–1781⁵), and only accident of archaeological discovery has made Hammurapi the more widely known figure.

Shamshi-Adad was a ruler of great military and administrative

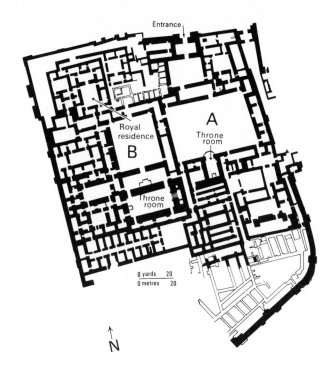

Entrance

Royal
residence
B

A
Throne
room

Throne
room

0 yards 20
0 metres 20

N

43 The great palace of Zimri-
Lim at Mari contained more
than 260 rooms and courts. A
double throne-room suite is
situated to the south of the
inner courtyard (B) which
was panelled with paintings
some 2 m in height, most of
which appear to date from the
time of Shamshi-Adad I. The
vast and complex plan owes
its final form to Zimri-Lim,
but wall paintings in the
earliest throne room, south of
courtyard A, display close
parallels with stelae of Gudea
and Ur-Nammu and date this
earliest phase of the building
to the late 3rd millennium.
After Parrot; and Hawkes.

ability. His forceful personality is intimately revealed in letters found
among some 13,000 cuneiform documents recovered from the royal
palace at Mari, an important way station for caravan and boat traffic
along the Euphrates, at that time ruled by the Assyrian king's viceroy in
the person of his younger and feckless son Yasmah-Adad. An elder and
more able brother, Ishme-Dagan, was viceroy at Ekallatum, an
administrative centre east of the Tigris above Assur, while Shamshi-
Adad himself ruled from two capitals, Assur and Shubat-Enlil in
northeastern Syria, possibly the site of Chagar Bazar, where an
administrative archive of his time has been found. The Mari archive
covers the period from *c*. 1810 to 1760 BC, and provides a day-to-day
view of contemporary events unequalled in the ancient world.[6] The
family correspondence of Shamshi-Adad and his sons is particularly
revealing of the politics of the time and includes some of the most
human documents recovered from the ancient world.

42–3

Yasmah-Adad was an indolent young man, and his father
continually takes him to task:

> Are you a child, not a man, have you no beard on your chin? Even
> now when you have reached maturity, you have not set up a home.
> . . . Who is there to look after your house? Is it not so that if an
> administrator does not carry out his functions for only two or three
> days, the administration collapses? Why then have you not
> appointed a man to this post?

Another passage recounts a great victory won by Ishme-Dagan and
continues:

> While your brother has won a great victory here, you remain there
> [in Mari], reclining amongst the women.

Other letters drive home the same message:

> As to you, how long will it be necessary for us continually to guide
> you? . . . How much longer will you be unable to administer your
> own house? Do you not see your own brother commanding far-
> flung armies?

Ishme-Dagan is not above admonishing his brother and on one
occasion writes:

> Why are you setting up a wail about this thing? That is not great
> conduct.[6]

Ishme-Dagan, though far abler than his idle brother, proved not to
be a ruler of his father's calibre. After Shamshi-Adad's death, Assyrian
power declined, and the letters suggest that Hammurapi was now in a
position to request or even order military reinforcements from the
Assyrian king. Ishme-Dagan's response on at least one occasion was
grudging, however, and Hammurapi complained of his poor support.
At Mari, Zimri-Lim, son of a former king, now recovered the throne
from the incompetent Yasmah-Adad. Zimri-Lim (1782–1759) is an
important figure in the archives, and many of the letters are reports to
him from his representatives at the court of Hammurapi. Both kings, as
was the custom of the time, maintained 'foreign advisers', who used
their position like modern ambassadors to report upon the military and
political situation. One of Zimri-Lim's ambassadors, Ibal-pi-el, is
particularly boastful of his inside knowledge of Babylonian affairs:

> When Hammurapi is disturbed by some matter, he does not hesitate
> to send for me, and I go to him wherever he is; whatever the matter
> that is troubling him, he tells me.

On one occasion when messengers were sent to Hammurapi by another
ruler, Ibal-pi-el drew them aside at the palace gate before they were
admitted to the Babylonian king, thus discovering their business. The
substance of another report to Hammurapi was acquired through the
donkey-drivers who accompanied the messengers.

Relations between heads of states were governed by a common code
of manners. The regular exchange of letters and gifts between rulers
was regarded as a demonstration of friendship and their discontinuance
tantamount to breaking off relations. Diplomatic missions were
entrusted to special envoys whose arrival and treatment were matters of
great importance. It was the responsibility of local officials to forward
messengers to the king without delay. On several occasions Yasmah-
Adad received scathing letters from his father for holding up such
messengers. Once, having written to Shamshi-Adad that an am-
bassador was unable to continue his journey, apparently because of
some damage to his chariot, Yasmah-Adad received a sharp reply: 'Is
he incapable of getting on a donkey?'[7] (A modern reader might well
ask, 'Why not a horse?', but the wild horse, *Equus caballus*, was not
native to Western Asia. The domesticated horse, in Sumerian the
'foreign ass' or 'ass of the mountains', had been introduced into

Mesopotamia only a few centuries before, and these creatures had yet to acquire the royal favour they were subsequently to enjoy. Indeed they were considered inferior animals no gentleman would ride. A letter to Zimri-Lim urges him to avoid such a barbarous and undignified custom: 'May my lord preserve his royal dignity. Let my lord not mount on horseback but ride in a chariot with mules.'[8])

The princes who ruled the petty states of the period – almost all of whom now claimed the once prestigious title 'king' – were reduced to the diplomacy and make-shift alliances that form a major theme of the Mari letters, not from positions of strength but of general weakness. Zimri-Lim requests as many as 10,000 men from Babylon, while Hammurapi receives similar aid from Mari. The tone of the letters is of interest. Whereas local administration is dispatched with concise and straightforward language, international diplomacy is carried out in the long-winded and evasive phraseology of a language in which even today, in its modern counterpart Arabic, it is impolite to say no. Rulers of equal status address each other as 'brother', overlord and vassal as 'father' and 'son', while immediate subordinates of a king call him 'lord'.

Babylon's rise to power

This scene of general weakness and defensive diplomacy changes, apparently abruptly, in Hammurapi's 29th year, when the Babylonian king seems to have adopted a more aggressive military policy; within the next few years he had established himself as supreme ruler not only in Babylonia but at least briefly in Assyria as well. A defeat (perhaps defensive) of Elam and a number of formidable allies, including Subartu (Assyria under Ishme-Dagan) and Eshnunna, was followed in the next year (1763) by the conquest of Larsa, then ruled by Rim-Sin. A letter requesting help from Mari reveals the assistance of Eshnunna in this enterprise, although the next year a great victory over Assyria and Eshnunna is again recorded. With the acquisition of southern Babylonia, previously under Larsa's suzerainty, Hammurapi succeeded to the traditional kingship of Sumer and Akkad, a title of which his later inscriptions show him to have been justly proud.

Having secured Babylonia Hammurapi turned on his old ally Zimri-Lim. Clay labels found at Mari, dated to Hammurapi's 32nd year, and originally attached to baskets in which cuneiform records were stored, show not only a military occupation of the city but the Babylon civil service already busily at work cataloguing Zimri-Lim's official archives.[9] Mari must have proved a troublesome acquisition, for two years later (1759) Hammurapi records the destruction of its walls. Assyria and Eshnunna remained stubborn pockets of resistance, but the prologue to the law code makes clear Hammurapi's control of both Assur and Nineveh. Thus at the end of his reign Hammurapi claimed suzerainty over all Mesopotamia. His inscriptions show that he regarded himself as the traditional heir not only of kingship over Sumer and Akkad, but also, although he can hardly be said to have won a comparable empire, of the Agade kings. Like Naram-Sin he styled himself 'King of the Four Quarters of the World', using this title side

43

44 Detail of the top of Hammurapi's famous Law Code Stele (ill. 50). The king is shown in an attitude of prayer before the sun-god, Shamash, the god of justice. Ht of relief 65 cm.

by side with 'King of Sumer and Akkad', a practice unknown from previous periods.

Although Hammurapi failed to establish an enduring national state, by defeating the major city-states of Babylonia and uniting the country, if only briefly, under the hegemony of Babylon he achieved a political result which was to affect the history of Mesopotamia for the next two millennia. Babylon became almost overnight the established seat of kingship, a position she was to maintain unchallenged until the Greeks built Seleucia. As a religious centre Babylon survived until the 1st century AD, while the mystique surrounding the name remains with us still. Much of Babylon's later hold over the country involved the cult of Marduk, who came to replace Enlil of Nippur as the bestower of legitimate kingship, but this religious transformation did not take place until long after the reign of Hammurapi.

Hammurapi remains the symbol of his age. However, his modern reputation as great king and legal innovator owes as much to the early discovery of cuneiform documents from his reign as to any unique attributes he may have possessed. The great stele, on which his famous law code is inscribed, was found at the beginning of this century by the French archaeological mission led by Jacques de Morgan at Susa, whither it had been carried by a later Elamite king. This monument was long thought to contain the first legal text – it remains in Mesopotamia the most lengthy – while letters published many years before the excavations at Mari reveal Hammurapi not only as an efficient administrator supervising even the most mundane matters, but also as a just and humane ruler who genuinely made the welfare of his subjects his personal care. Subsequent discoveries have shown him in truer perspective – as one among a number of able contemporaries – but one fact alone will ensure Hammurapi's lasting fame, his role as the most successful king of the dynasty that made Babylon thereafter the leading city in Western Asia. Never again did any southern city rule Babylonia, and indeed the sociological pattern imposed on the country in his time continued to be felt until the end of its history.

44

Babylonian society at the time of Hammurapi

Cuneiform texts from the reign of Hammurapi, of which the law-code stele is the most important, documents from Larsa at the time of Rim-Sin, contemporary letters from Shemshara in northeastern Iraq, and archives from Mari and Sippar provide social and economic data far greater than exist for many later periods in history, even in western Europe. Despite such unparalleled sources many aspects of Babylonian society – who people were, what they did and how their lives were regulated – remain unclear. Particular difficulties arise in the translation of terms relating to professions and social classes so far removed from our own experience, and few scholars or even institutions have had the time and money necessary to support the extensive analytical studies that will be necessary to resolve such problems, if indeed solutions are possible. Publication of the Mari texts and special studies based upon them and upon the Sippar archives have done much to increase our understanding of Babylonian society in this

45 This votive bronze statue was dedicated to the god Amurru for the life of Hammurapi by one Lu-Nanna, shown here kneeling in an attitude of supplication. On the base is a similar kneeling suppliant before an enthroned deity. A small vessel for offerings is attached to the front. Ht 19·5 cm, probably from Larsa. Louvre Museum.

46 An Old Babylonian votive figure in bronze, depicting an unusual 4-faced god, the right hand trailing a scimitar. It was found at Ishchali and is now in the Oriental Institute Museum, Chicago. Ht 17 cm.

period. Nonetheless, there remain serious uncertainties of interpretation and the following remarks must be viewed in this light.

Perhaps the most striking feature of Mesopotamian social structure at all periods is the apparent lack of other than economic stratification. Society fell basically into two groups, those who owned the means of production, especially property in land, and those dependent upon them.[10] There was never a warrior class as in some early civilizations, nor did the priesthood hold any special status. Hammurapi's legal code distinguishes three basic social classes, in Babylonian the *awilum*, the *mushkenum* and the *wardum* or 'slave', the only term readily translatable. *Awilum* means simply 'man'. Usually translated as 'freeman', there remains considerable uncertainty over the precise meaning of the word, if indeed it had one. Sometimes used to indicate a man of high class, perhaps 'noble', it is clear that *awilum* could mean also a free man of any class and occasionally any man, whether king or slave. Certainly the word bore the connotation of 'gentleman', but in its legal sense it seems to have referred to citizens in general, though how this concept was defined in Babylonia is also unclear beyond the fact that association with a city or other residential grouping was a basic aspect of Mesopotamian social structure. Citizens are indeed *maru alim*, 'sons of the city'. It is likely that *awilum* signified a landowner or head of a household, though we cannot be certain of this.

The *puhrum* (assembly) was made up of the freemen or citizens, however they were defined. Among these the 'elders' (*shibutum*) constituted a special council of advisers. In the Old Babylonian period *alum*, 'town' or 'city', and *puhrum* were used synonymously. The *shibutum* seem to have been in some way socially superior, and were perhaps the heads of the most influential families. A Babylonian proverb shows clearly that at this time membership of the assembly did not constitute the prerogative of some small favoured class:

Do not go to stand in the assembly:
Do not stray to the very place of strife.
It is precisely in strife that fate may overtake you:
Besides, you may be made a witness for them
So that they take you along to testify in a law-suit not your own.[11]

This advice is perhaps lacking in public spirit, but it undoubtedly implies that anyone who happened along could participate in the *puhrum*. The residual power of the community in the form of its assembly in an otherwise apparently autocratic social system is striking and perhaps lends further credence to the largely theoretical reconstruction of earlier Sumerian society with such an assembly conceived as the sole political force, electing even the 'king'. The positions of chairman of the assembly and town mayor (*rabianum*), even at this later time, remained rotating offices, reminiscent of the earlier *palû*.

The meaning of *mushkenum* has been the subject of many learned articles, and remains in dispute.[12] In the Old Babylonian period the term in some contexts seems to have denoted a member of a very specific group, set apart from and in some way inferior to the *awilum*.

47 Detail of ill. 45. The face, beard and hands are covered with beaten gold foil.

The essential legal position of the *mushkenum* was that he was singled out for protection as a dependant of the state or crown. Such royal dependants were supported either with rations in kind or non-alienable allotments of land in exchange for services to the palace. A possible explanation for the numerous provisions in the Old Babylonian law codes providing separately for the *mushkenum* and identifying him with the palace is that the *mushkenum*, as a non-owner of property, i.e. a 'non-citizen', was not protected by ordinary customary law. Although a *mushkenum* could speak in the assembly, he would appear to have been outside the actual jurisdiction of the *alum*.

The word *mushkenum* is the participle of a verb, possibly of Amorite origin, meaning 'to greet someone by placing the hand before the mouth [in the gesture of adoration]' – perhaps the pose of the bronze figure from Larsa. Thus *mushkenum* may have denoted someone obliged to employ this form of greeting, which was accorded to those of higher rank.[13] The basic implication of inferiority had led already in the Old Babylonian period to the connotation of pauperism, which later became the primary meaning of the word. In this sense *mushkenum* was borrowed not only by other Semitic languages but also by French (*mesquin*) and Italian (*meschino*). The basic meaning to some extent explains its confusingly ambiguous usage in the Old Babylonian period, in that each citizen would be a *mushkenum* in his relationship to the palace or temple, as indeed everyone was a *wardum* of the king.

The meaning of *wardum*, 'slave', is more straightforward, although slavery in Mesopotamia, where landowners seem to have preferred a system of tenancy to the widespread employment of slaves, differed greatly from that in the classical world. In Mesopotamia there was

45, 47

nothing comparable with the Roman *latifundia* or the mining industries where enormous numbers of slaves were employed. Most Mesopotamian slaves originated from the native population: defaulting debtors and penniless men and women often sold themselves or their children into slavery, or were seized by creditors. Babylonian merchants also dealt in foreign slaves, Subarians from the north being the most in demand, while war captives normally became the property of the king, i.e. slaves of the state. These, together with the corvée gangs attested in the Mari letters and some hired labour, constructed roads, dug canals, erected military fortifications, built temples, tilled the crown lands and worked in palace factories. State slaves were housed in special barracks, their names, ages and lands of origin recorded in special registers. Temple slaves were recruited both from prisoners of war and dedications made by private individuals.

Private slaves were relatively uncommon, and were employed largely in domestic service. Slaves born in the house seem to have enjoyed a special status, at least in this period, while the custom of adopting slaves who were to be manumitted on the death of their adoptive parents, after caring for them in their old age, suggests that the master–slave relationship was one of mutual obligation. Runaway slaves appear to have been rare, but according to one text were to be marked on their foreheads, 'A runaway – seize him!' A slave was distinguished by a characteristic lock of hair (*abbuttum*) and some apparently wore tags or fetters.[14] The average price for a slave in the Old Babylonian period was approximately 20 shekels of silver, sometimes rising to as high as 90. The average wage paid to hired labour was some 10 shekels a year. Thus it was far cheaper for a landowner to employ seasonal labour than to own a slave specifically for agricultural work. By far the most common system of working the land at this period was one of tenant farming, the tenant receiving seed, animals, and implements, for the most part in the form of non-interest bearing loans, for which the tenant returned a set percentage of the harvest.

Administration

Evidence for administrative procedures in Old Babylonian times comes from a number of sites, especially Mari and Sippar, and from the letters of Hammurapi. The degree to which royal power is exercised is perhaps the most striking feature. Final responsibility in all matters lay with the king; no matter is too insignificant to merit his attention. Under Shamshi-Adad there were efficiently organized chancellery and accounting departments, and so rapid was his courier service that he sometimes dated his letters, a practice uncommon at the time, even going so far as to specify the time of day. In the event of a military emergency fire beacons were used; these consisted of a series of signal fires by which a message could rapidly be transmitted over the entire country. Occasionally this system led to some confusion, as it was of course necessary to establish in advance what the signal was to mean. In one instance, the incompetent Yasmah-Adad was severely reprimanded by his elder brother for setting off the whole warning system for nothing more than a local raid:

Say to Yasmah-Adad, thus says Ishme-Dagan, your brother:

'Because you lit two fires during the night, it is possible that the whole land will be coming to your assistance. Have letters written to the whole land . . . and send your fastest messengers to deliver them. You should say, "A considerable body of men came on a raid into the land, and because of this two fires were lit. There is no need to come to my assistance."'[6]

Shamshi-Adad's administration was highly organized, with governors appointed over the various districts under his control. There were permanent garrisons in the towns, and additional troops were levied for each campaign, both from the settled population and the nomads. In the capture of Nurrugum, one of the most important military events of his reign, 60,000 troops were said to have been employed.[15] Before each campaign lists were drawn up enumerating the men taking part and arranging the distribution of provisions. Censuses were also instituted.

Many of Hammurapi's letters are concerned with the administration of justice and indicate the very active supervision the king exercised not only over cases tried at Babylon, but also over the decisions of courts in other Babylonian cities. Under his predecessors disputes between citizens were tried before benches of judges who sat at the gate or in the courtyard of temples. Who these judges were or how they were selected is still unknown, though they appear to have been ad hoc appointments possibly from among the 'elders' or other prominent officials. Although there is some reason to suppose that judges may have been appointed by the temple, they were not priests nor was there an ecclesiastical as opposed to secular law. Under Hammurapi there seems generally to have been a transfer of authority from the temple to the king, both with respect to responsibility for temple offices and the exercise of judicial functions. There is evidence to suggest the appointment of more permanent judges who were responsible for administrative duties as well, and officials known as 'judges of the king', first attested under an earlier monarch, Sabium (1844–1831), play a prominent role. The king himself could try cases in person, and it was possible for any private individual to appeal directly to him for justice.

In the Old Babylonian period the *puhrum* also functioned as a court of law. The town mayor and the elders seem to have settled minor local disputes; other cases were brought before the town as a whole for decision. Sometimes one of the parties and his witness were required to prove their testimony on oath. When there was a clash of evidence and neither side refused the oath, the gods could be called upon to make the decision by ordeal. In Babylonia this was the responsibility of the 'river-god', and, contrary to the rule in mediaeval times, the guilty party sank. According to the Code of Hammurapi accusations concerning witchcraft were proved by this means.

The letters of Hammurapi provide much insight into other branches of administration and the functioning of the community in general. Most striking is the time and labour devoted to public works, especially the maintenance of canals, which served both to provide water and as a major means of transport. The wealth of the king and the temples, which was considerable, included land and flocks and herds. The

48 The symbolism of this 'Maypole' with rampant lions is uncertain. The 'ribbons' end in mace-like objects or heads of strange beasts reminiscent of the 'lion club' mace carried by Nergal as portrayed on Old Babylonian seals (ill. 37). Clay plaque, ht 13·4 cm. Iraq Museum.

letters show that the governors of the larger cities were responsible for the animals pastured in their districts, and that both royal and temple herds were placed under the same chief shepherd. Accounts were rendered to Hammurapi himself, showing that at least in some instances the king controlled the collection of the temple revenues as well as his own. Tax collectors unable to exact their full dues were forced to make up the deficit themselves. The king kept a close eye on his officials, and there are letters in which the latter defend themselves to him against charges of negligence.

By the time of Hammurapi the practice of paying palace dependants by the distribution of rations had been largely replaced by the allotment of grants of land, generally held by virtue of the performance of certain military or civil duties. This system of labour service became vital to the Old Babylonian economy, providing reserves of ready labour and military personnel, ensuring the performance of services essential to the state, and as a very efficient means of farming the land. This system, known as *ilkum*, is found in both the Old Babylonian and Kassite periods. Although 'fief' is a convenient English term for rendering the Babylonian word, which signifies both service and grant, no idea of a feudal relationship between the king and his tenants should be read into the Babylonian institution. Such a grant might be made to an individual or a group; several might be held by one person. The fief was reckoned in days, and in some cases it was possible to provide a substitute to carry out some or all of the relevant duties. The length of time required in service of the crown is uncertain, but there are indications that relatively short periods may have been involved. The possession of a fief, despite the burdens attached to it, was highly valued. Many of Hammurapi's letters deal with complaints received from tenants saying they have been wrongly kept out of or evicted from their fiefs. Other letters are concerned with the granting of *ilkum*, fixing of boundaries, neglect of land, etc. They mention numerous craftsmen and professional men who are holders of *ilkum*: archers, shepherds, bakers, smiths, jewellers, cobblers, singers and soothsayers.

A number of categories of people are also mentioned in the law code as holding land in this way. Of these, the *redum* and *ba'irum* appear to have been military or police personnel. *Redum* is commonly translated 'soldier', but it would be anachronistic to think of professional soldiers in the modern sense. Warfare was largely a seasonal occupation, and the *redum* performed what one would term 'police' duties as well as taking part in military campaigns. Indeed we know from one small but revealing village archive that much of his time was spent tilling the land.[16] The owner of this archive, the *redum* Ubarrum, and his brother apparently alternated in fulfilling military service and looking after the fields at home. Ubarrum also rented and cultivated fields other than those of his *ilkum* grant, and himself owned sheep and goats which were left in the care of professional shepherds. Most of the texts deal with Ubarrum's business affairs yet they reveal a rare glimpse of the life of a small community of soldiers and farmers without soil of their own, their otherwise mundane existence interrupted by their habitual litigation, and even by a local scandal, when a girl, engaged to a village boy, runs away to Babylon.

49 The majority of Old Babylonian plaques represent deities or cult scenes. They are found in temples, and in private houses where they were probably placed on domestic altars. But the function of some, like this mastiff and puppies, is more difficult to explain. It may perhaps represent the goddess Gula whose symbol was a dog. Ht 10 cm, from Ishchali, now in the Oriental Institute Museum, Chicago.

The *redum* was forbidden to sell or mortgage his royal allotment, but those holders of *ilkum* of higher social standing, such as the *naditum* and *tamkarum*, who were not fief-holders of necessity, were free to sell provided the buyer agreed to take over the obligations. *Naditum* is often translated 'priestess', but these women, although they were attached in some way to the temple, were involved in various kinds of business transactions and played an important role in Babylonian economic life, lending silver and corn, supplying capital for trading expeditions, and so forth. The *naditum* lived and worked in the *gagum* or 'cloister', a compound associated in some way with the temple. Like the *tamkarum* (merchant) she invested her money in houses and landed property which she let out on lease. The *naditum*, although she could 'marry', seems to have been under an obligation of celibacy. Despite certain ties and duties to the cloister, the *naditum*, whose background seems always to have been wealthy, lived and functioned as a private individual. Evidence for this unique institution, which flourished in the Old Babylonian period, comes mainly from Sippar, where the *gagum* was attached to the Shamash temple.[17]

The *tamkarum* was the central figure in Old Babylonian trade, although at times he appears to have been more of a banker than a merchant. Sometimes he travelled with his merchandise, but often he dispatched *shamallu* or agents. The *tamkarum* seems essentially to have been a private capitalist; under Hammurapi however there is evidence for extensive trade in mass produce, conducted by the government, directed by official 'overseers' known as *wakil tamkari*. As an accessory task these officials collected and administered the taxes owed by the *tamkarum* and other businessmen. At times the activities of the *tamkarum* seem to have been limited by a system of permits regulating trade. One letter reads: 'We interrogated the *tamkarum* as to whether

73

he carried a royal permit and then allowed him to pass. The *tamkarum* who does not carry a royal permit, we send back to Babylon.'[18]

Another Old Babylonian profession which is treated in the laws as parallel with the *tamkarum* is the *sabitum*, traditionally translated 'ale-wife'. The *sabitum* seems to have been a tavern-keeper engaged in the preparation and sale of intoxicating beverages, but it is clear that she dealt also with basic commodities in the manner of a small broker. A tavern is not an unlikely place for the execution of such business; indeed in origin and etymology a broker denotes a retailer of wine (from to 'broach' a cask).[19] One of the most famous of Mesopotamian 'ale-wives', Ku-Baba, founded one of the early dynasties at Kish.

Babylonian law

It is time to take a closer look at the Code of Hammurapi, to which we have already had occasion to refer, and which is undoubtedly the most important single written document to have survived from this period. It is the longest coherent inscription in Old Babylonian and serves today as the standard text by which modern students learn the language. The laws are carved in 49 columns on a basalt stele, 2.25 m high. The text consists of three parts, a prologue and epilogue written in an elaborate and often archaizing style – indeed the inscription is cut vertically in the manner of the earliest cuneiform documents – and a lengthy middle section, divided by modern editors into 282 laws. The real nature and purpose of this text, and indeed the monument itself, has been the subject of much controversy. That it is not a true 'code' seems clear. It is far from comprehensive in its coverage and nowhere is there a specific adjuration of judges or other officials to abide by its provisions. Whether the text represents a recording of customary law, a series of legal innovations or even a designation of those areas in need of amendment (or a combination of all these) remains uncertain. That the provisions were not Statute Law can be seen from the fact that several abuses explicitly condemned by Hammurapi on pain of death were again 'legislated against' in a later edict of King Ammi-saduqa. The provisions of the code cover a variety of subjects, largely involving the disposition of and responsibility for property, both private and real, and deal with certain areas of commercial law. Each is presented as a conditional sentence, *if* such and such happens, *then* this penalty will follow, as the following few examples illustrate:

44, 50

> 1   If a man has accused another man and has brought a charge of murder against him, but has not proved it, his accuser shall be put to death.
>
> 22–23   If a man has committed robbery and is caught, that man shall be put to death. If the robber is not caught, the man who has been robbed shall formally declare whatever he has lost before a god, and the city and mayor in whose territory or district the robbery was committed shall make good to him his lost property.
>
> 153   If a woman has brought about the death of her husband because of another man, they shall impale that woman on stakes.
>
> 195   If a son has struck his father, they shall cut off his hand.

196   If an *awilum* has put out the eye of a *mar-awilim* [lit. 'son of an *awilum*'],[20] they shall put out his eye.

198   If an *awilum* has put out the eye of a *mushkenum* or broken his bone, he shall pay one mina of silver.

202   If an *awilum* has struck the cheek of an *awilum* who is older than himself, he shall be beaten 60 times with an oxtail whip in the assembly.

229–30   If a builder has constructed a house for an *awilum* but has not made his work strong, with the result that the house which he built collapsed and so caused the death of the owner of the house, that builder shall be put to death. If it has caused the death of the son of the owner of the house, they shall put to death the son of the builder.[21]

A striking change from Sumerian law is the appearance of *lex talionis*, 'an eye for an eye, and a tooth for a tooth', almost certainly a reflection of Amorite custom. The difference in status between the *awilum* and the *mushkenum* is evident in the examples cited.

Hammurapi's purpose in setting up this stele is stated in the epilogue, which begins:

> These are the laws of justice (*dinat misharim*) which Hammurapi the able king has established. . . . That the strong may not oppress the weak, to give justice to the orphan and the widow, I have inscribed my precious words on my stele and established it in Babylon before my statue called 'King of Justice'.

The statue, which was set up in Hammurapi's 21st year, is referred to again:

> Let the wronged man who is involved in a lawsuit go before my statue, the 'King of Justice', and let him have read out to him the writing on my stele, let him hear my precious words, and let my monument make clear his rights to him, let him see the law which applies to him, let his heart be set at ease.

50 Basalt stele inscribed with the Law Code of Hammurapi. The laws are carved in 49 vertical columns in an archaic style. This or a similar stele was set up in the temple of Marduk in Babylon and various copies were erected elsewhere in the kingdom. Found with other Babylonian booty at Susa. Ht 2·25 m. Louvre Museum. Cf. ill. 44.

Future kings are asked to 'give heed to the words which I have inscribed on my stele'. Yet among the thousands of court documents and contracts that survive from the Old Babylonian period, we know so far of only one in which reference is made to the code: the penalty clause in a contract from Ur, dealing with the cultivation of land and dated in the 5th year of Hammurapi's successor, provides that in the case of a breach of contract the cultivator shall be treated 'according to the wording of the stele'.[22] Whatever, if any, its legislative purpose, the Code of Hammurapi was much admired as a literary work, and copies found on tablets in Assurbanipal's library at Nineveh, dated over 11 centuries later, have served to restore the text of damaged portions of the original stele. Perhaps the true purpose of such a monument was justification rather than justice. If, as the prologue suggests, the inscription was addressed largely to the gods as a record of Hammurapi's accomplishments, and was intended to preserve for posterity the deeds of this just king, it could not have been more successful in its purpose.

Misharum-edicts

Although the Code of Hammurapi carried no force of law, other legal promulgations, known in Babylonian as *misharum*, clearly did. The *misharum* was a short-term measure, apparently proclaimed orally rather than inscribed on monuments, designed to alleviate social and economic distress. As measures of social reform these edicts are reminiscent of, and indeed probably descended from, Urukagina's famous document some 500 years before. References to *misharum*-edicts are found in texts from the reigns of kings of Isin and Larsa, but it was not until the time of Hammurapi that they became a regular institution, such proclamations normally being made in a king's first full regnal year and apparently also at intervals thereafter throughout his reign, presumably whenever economic conditions necessitated such action. Our main evidence for the content of a *misharum* proclamation comes from the Edict of Ammi-saduqa, which preserves in writing the text of a decree dating from the time of the penultimate king of the First Dynasty.[23]

A petition to one of Hammurapi's successors, appealing for a reversal of a decision resulting from a *misharum*, gives a rare glimpse of the practical effects of such royal decrees:

> When my lord raised high the Golden Torch for Sippar, instituting the *misharum* for Shamash who loves him, and convened in Sippar Taribatum the *shapir rede*, the judges of Babylon and the judges of Sippar, they reviewed the cases of the citizens of Sippar, 'heard' the tablets of purchase of field, house and orchard, and ordered broken those tablets in which the land was to be released by the terms of the *misharum*.[24]

We have seen that an appeal to the Code of Hammurapi carried only moral sanction, but this text leaves no doubt that the remission of debts and obligations legislated for in a *misharum*-edict, although such provisions would have been valid only for a short period, were very real measures, enforceable by the courts.

Old Babylonian cities

Unfortunately we know virtually nothing of Hammurapi's Babylon. Houses of this date have been excavated in the quarter of the city known as Merkes, but most of the 18th-century BC levels lie below the modern water-table, inaccessible to ordinary archaeological investigation. Other sites provide a wealth of information about this period, however, which is by far the best documented in the history of ancient Mesopotamia. Our most vivid picture of Old Babylonian life comes from Sir Leonard Woolley's excavation of private houses from the period of the Larsa domination of Ur. These 'Larsa' houses were destroyed in the time of Hammurapi's successor who, in the 10th year of his reign 'demolished the walls of Ur and Uruk', presumably after some local insurrection. Many show evidence of destruction by fire and it was this violent end that preserved in them large numbers of cuneiform documents as well as other artefacts of daily life. Even the householders' names are known: no. 1 Broad Street – Woolley's

51

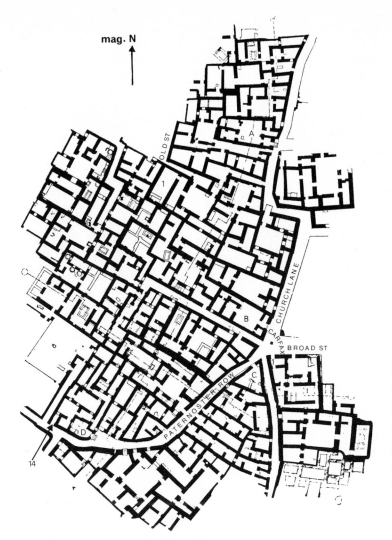

mag. N

51 Very few residential areas of Babylonian cities have been excavated. These houses and shops of the Old Babylonian Larsa phase, excavated at Ur by Sir Leonard Woolley, provide a rare glimpse of everyday life. Also found were a number of small wayside shrines (A: 'Ram Chapel', B: chapel of the goddess Hendur-sag, C: chapel of Nin-shubur, D: the 'Bazaar chapel'). After Woolley.

Oxford past is evident in his street plan! – belonged to the schoolmaster Igmil-Sin, and hundreds of his young pupils' exercise tablets were found in the ruins. No. 1 Old Street was the house of the *alik Tilmun* Ea-nasir, a major figure in the copper trade with Dilmun mentioned in the previous chapter. No. 14 Paternoster Row was a restaurant, with a wide window opening on to the street and a brick counter immediately inside, presumably for the display of cooked dishes in the manner of cook-shops in a modern bazaar. The kitchen contained a bread oven and a solid brick range in the top of which were troughs for the charcoal braziers on which the cooking of meat was done. The houses appear to have been two-storeyed, resembling the courtyard houses still to be seen in the older quarters of Iraqi cities; doors and windows were of reed set in wooden frames. A surprising discovery, representing a change from earlier periods when the dead were normally interred in

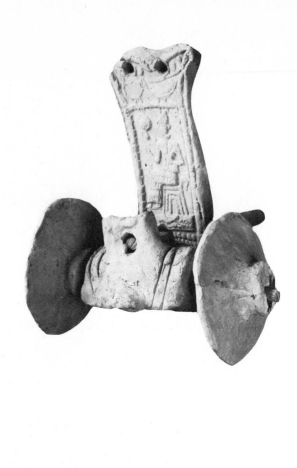

52 This unusually large bull-man clay plaque was found against the door of the Hendur-sag chapel at Ur (ill. 51). It was painted bright red with black on the beard and eyes. Ht 61 cm. Iraq Museum.

53 Model clay chariots were common in the Old Babylonian period. This example, decorated with the figure of a seated god, is now in the Louvre. A similar chariot was recovered from the Hendur-sag chapel at Ur (ill. 51), suggesting that these chariots, like the clay plaques, were cult objects. Ht 17 cm.

large cemeteries, was the presence of narrow paved areas at the backs of houses, each with a small domestic chapel and a corbel-vaulted family tomb. Several wayside shrines contained numerous clay and other votive objects.[25]

Tell Harmal, a small site in the suburbs of modern Baghdad, was as the ancient town of Shaduppum an administrative centre of a district under the rule of Eshnunna (some 30 km away) during the period before Hammurapi's conquest.[26] The name signifies the 'treasury, accountant's office', and it would appear that Shaduppum was originally built for this purpose. The tell's small size – 1.7 hectares, smaller than many prehistoric farming villages – has enabled the Iraq Antiquities Department to excavate large areas of the site, thus recovering unique evidence for Babylonian administration almost 4000 years ago. The town was heavily fortified, enclosed by a massive wall with buttressing towers. On either side of the main street were a temple, its entrance guarded by life-size terracotta lions, and what appears to have been the main administrative complex. A line of shops and several smaller shrines were situated along a nearby street, and a number of private houses, in plan not unlike those found at Ur, were also excavated. Tell Harmal is significant for two important reasons – as a warning to those archaeologists who would rank unexcavated sites in

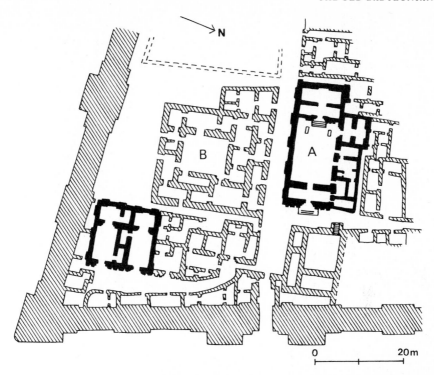

54 Southeastern corner of the Old Babylonian town of Shaduppum (modern Tell Harmal). In the main temple (A) both the principal and the subsidiary shrine (northern side) are constructed in the broad cella plan characteristic of the Old Babylonian period, while the smaller twin shrines in the southeastern angle of the town (solid black) are of the long-room type later more characteristic of Assyria. (B: administrative centre.) After Baqir.

55 Large guardian figures in baked clay are a feature of Old Babylonian temples. They have been found at Tell Harmal and at Isin. This is one of two lions, now in the Iraq Museum, which stood originally before the entrance to the antecella of the main temple at Tell Harmal (ill. 54).

56 Cuneiform tablet dated to the 19th century BC, found among the large archive recovered from Tell Harmal. It is a school exercise in surveying based on a right-angled 'Pythagorean' triangle. It depends for its solution on the Euclidean principle that 'In a right-angled triangle, if a perpendicular is drawn from the right angle to the hypotenuse, the triangles on either side are similar to the whole triangle and to one another'. Ht 10 cm. Iraq Museum.

order of importance by order of size, and by virtue of the large collection of cuneiform documents recovered from the site. These include administrative and literary texts, letters, a law code dated to the reign of Dadusha of Eshnunna (a contemporary of Shamshi-Adad), a number of lexical texts that contain long lists of geographical, zoological and botanical terms and, perhaps most fascinating of all, a group of mathematical texts. These, like a number of the other tablets, are school texts, copied by pupils in the scribal school that must have existed here. They display an extraordinary mathematical competence (see chapter 6); one text anticipates the right-angle theorem of Pythagoras by 1300 years.

There are a number of palaces in addition to the vast complex at Mari, which took its final form during the reign of Zimri-Lim (1782–1759). At Uruk, for example, a splendid palace has been excavated from the time of Sin-kashid, an independent Amorite ruler who married the daughter of Sumulael of Babylon.[27] But the most important palace of all, that of Hammurapi himself, remains undiscovered. Religious architecture is well-attested – at Ur, Harmal, in the temple of Ishtar-Kititum at Ishchali (ancient Neribtum, part of the kingdom of Eshnunna), but most impressively of all at the site of Tell al Rimah, ancient Karana, in northern Iraq, where we have already mentioned rare evidence for the building techniques of the Ur III period. At Rimah a monumental temple and ziggurat, occupying the whole of the

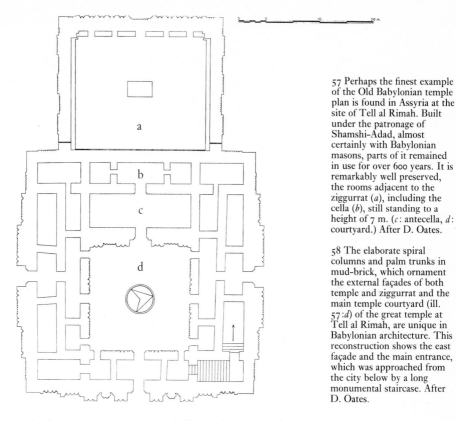

57 Perhaps the finest example of the Old Babylonian temple plan is found in Assyria at the site of Tell al Rimah. Built under the patronage of Shamshi-Adad, almost certainly with Babylonian masons, parts of it remained in use for over 600 years. It is remarkably well preserved, the rooms adjacent to the ziggurrat (*a*), including the cella (*b*), still standing to a height of 7 m. (*c*: antecella, *d*: courtyard.) After D. Oates.

58 The elaborate spiral columns and palm trunks in mud-brick, which ornament the external façades of both temple and ziggurrat and the main temple courtyard (ill. 57:*d*) of the great temple at Tell al Rimah, are unique in Babylonian architecture. This reconstruction shows the east façade and the main entrance, which was approached from the city below by a long monumental staircase. After D. Oates.

central mound of the ancient city, was built *c*. 1800 BC under the patronage of Shamshi-Adad, when Karana was a dependent state of Assur. The temple plan is wholly Babylonian in concept, and details of its construction even suggest the employment of Babylonian masons.[28] The attached ziggurrat, however, is a peculiarly Assyrian feature; those in the south, as can be seen at Ur and Babylon, were free-standing and self-contained structures. The most extraordinary aspect of the Rimah temple lies in its decoration. The central courtyard and the temple exterior and ziggurrat were ornamented with over 270 half-columns, 50 of which consisted of elaborate spirals and two types of palm-tree

27, 111

58

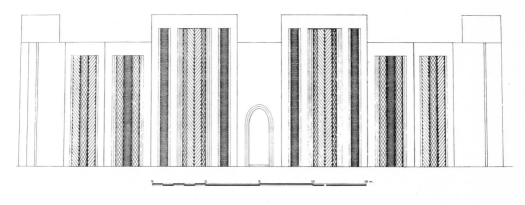

pattern. Most remarkable of all were the massive columns inset in the main gate towers, each consisting of 4 shafts of 2 opposed spiral and 2 palm-trunk columns.

This elaborate complex, with its ornamentation, was built entirely in mud-brick; the rooms, including the stairs, were constructed using radial vaulting with impressive expertise. Even the monumental staircase leading up from the town below was carried on a series of three vaults of increasing height. The whole structure was meticulously designed with a careful eye to the impact of its exterior elevations. The building owes its remarkable state of preservation to Karana's lack of resources after the death of its wealthy patron and protector. Not only was the original temple never completed, but thereafter this small kingdom could never afford to rebuild its main shrine in the manner of wealthier dynasties. The original sanctuary remained in use, though in a state of increasing neglect and dilapidation, for over 600 years, the extraordinary ornament preserved through the centuries by the continuous build-up of debris within the temple. A parallel for the palm-trunk decoration was discovered at Ur, in the 'bastion of Warad-Sin', but at no other contemporary site is there as yet any suggestion of the elaboration of ornament found in the great temple at Rimah. Here too is the first evidence in Mesopotamia for the decorative employment of carved stone orthostats which was to become so fashionable in the palaces of the later kings of Assyria and Achaemenid Iran.[29]

4
Kassites and Chaldaeans

The fall of Babylon

Hammurapi's political unification of the country together with the social and economic changes associated with this period mark an important turning-point in Mesopotamian history. In Babylonia the balance of power now lay firmly in the north. Henceforth no other city was seriously to rival Babylon in prestige. This development is the more surprising in view of the apparently pedestrian achievements of Hammurapi's successors. His son Samsu-iluna (1749–1712) was initially successful in emulating his father's policies but soon the south was in revolt – we have already had occasion to note Samsu-iluna's sack of Ur – and by the end of his reign the founder of a new dynasty in the marshlands of the south, one Iliman (Iluma-ilum), controlled Babylonia as far north as Nippur. This new dynasty, known as the Sealand, appears to have taken on the mantle of the earlier rulers of Isin, possibly even aspiring to a Sumerian revival; indeed its later kings assumed increasingly ponderous and fanciful Sumerian names. One authority has even suggested that in the declining years of Babylon's First Dynasty the Sealand provided in the south a refuge for those great centres of culture and learning, the 'universities' of Babylon and Nippur.[1] Not only did the Sealanders encroach on the immediate territory of Babylon in the years after Hammurapi's death, but in the early 16th century they appear to have succeeded, at least briefly, to the Babylonian throne. This we infer from the King-List which includes the Sealand Dynasty 'of Urukug', a city otherwise unknown.

Samsu-iluna's 9th year-name mentions the Kassite army. Unfortunately the text fails to reveal the context or indeed the outcome of this encounter. This is the first reference to the foreigners who some 150 years later were to inherit the hegemony of Babylon. The Kassites are thought to have come from the mountains to the east, although their names first appear on texts from western Babylonia in the region of the Euphrates. The period of the 17th–16th centuries BC was a time of great political change in Western Asia, and the Kassites were but one of a number of non-Semitic speaking peoples – the Hurrians and Hittites are others whom we shall meet shortly – who began to exert pressure from the north on the weakening kingdom of Babylon. The linguistic affinities of the Kassite language have yet to be established, but some features of their religion may suggest contact with Indo-European peoples. The Kassites appear first in Babylonia as agricultural labourers. During the 17th century the personal names on

Babylonian business documents illustrate their steady and apparently peaceful influx into the country; by the end of that century Kassite settlers were obtaining holdings even within the area of Babylon itself. Yet it is clear that from the reign of Samsu-iluna onwards the Kassites were also a military threat. Kassite tradition implies the founding of an independent state at this time somewhere on the borders of Babylonia, perhaps centred in or around the kingdom of Hana on the middle Euphrates. Indeed one of the independent and otherwise apparently Amorite kings of Terqa in the land of Hana bore the Kassite name Kashtiliashu.

Samsu-iluna maintained some control to the northwest, but the middle Euphrates was certainly lost to Babylon by the time of his son, Abi-eshuh (1711–1684), whose reign is notable for little more than his failure to catch the Sealand ruler Iliman by 'damming the Tigris'. Although there appears to have been no serious challenge to their authority from the cities of Sumer and Akkad, the last kings of Babylon's First Dynasty clearly presided over a kingdom dwindling steadily in both territory and prestige. Of far more interest than any of the minor events recorded from their reigns are certain texts preserved from this time, in particular the 'Venus tablets', which provide important, if unfortunately inconclusive, evidence for chronology,[2] and the well-known legal edict mentioned in the previous chapter. Literary and economic documents preserved from this period continue to reflect an apparently prosperous society in which the arts flourished – for example, the scribe who copied the only known Old Babylonian fragments of the epic cycle known as 'Atrahasis', which relates one version of the Flood legend, worked in Sippar at this time – while Ammi-saduqa's edict shows Babylon still in control of Uruk, Isin and Larsa. Certainly there is no hint of impending doom, and the fatal blow, when it fell, came not from the troublesome Sealanders or Kassites but from far to the north in Asia Minor, where the Hittites, an Indo-European speaking people, had created a rapidly growing kingdom. From its capital Hattusha, a king named Murshili I (Mursilis I, c. 1620–1595), a contemporary of Samsu-ditana of Babylon (1626–1595), attacked northwestern Syria and then swept down the Euphrates, apparently without opposition, towards Babylon. Murshili must have appeared to the apparently unsuspecting Samsu-ditana like a bolt out of the blue. Babylon was sacked, and its gods plundered. The famous First Dynasty was at an end (1595).

Murshili returned to Anatolia as quickly as he had come, though too late to crush a court conspiracy which ended in his assassination. To the victor may have belonged the spoils but the political vacuum left by Murshili's raid was filled not by the successful Hittite invaders but apparently by a king of the ever-threatening Sealand, who was quick to take advantage of the Hittite sack.

The history of Babylon immediately following upon the Hittite attack is far from clear. Indeed all documentary evidence ceases and Babylonia was engulfed in what our present state of ignorance leads us to term a Dark Age. There is no general agreement about the length of this period, a fact which has profound implications for 2nd-millennium chronology, but it would appear that not long after the fall of Babylon a

59 The earliest and finest example of a core-moulded glass vessel from Mesopotamia (Tell al Rimah, *c.* 1450 BC). The glass technology of 2nd-millennium Mesopotamia was already highly sophisticated. Strips of coloured glass, yellow, blue and white, were let into the still plastic surface of the dark blue vessel and then dragged with a pointed instrument to produce the pattern of festoons, technically a very difficult process. Ht 13·4 cm. Iraq Museum.

Sealand king by the name of Gulkishar took control of the city. We deduce this from the fact that his dynasty follows that of Hammurapi in the list which records successive claimants to the throne of Babylon; moreover, the colophon of an unusual and indeed enigmatic text recording recipes for the manufacture of two types of red glass claims that the tablet was inscribed in Babylon 'in the year Gulkishar became king'. Gulkishar remains a shadowy figure but the text itself is of great interest. Written with rare signs once thought to have been secret cryptograms, it contains the earliest glass recipe so far known. Its ascription to Gulkishar is now believed to be a scribal fiction,[3] largely because no other documents dated to the reign of this Sealand king have survived, but there is no inherent reason for rejecting the possibility that the recipe itself may date from this time. Words denoting various types of glass appear in lexical lists of the early 2nd millennium, rare references to glass occur even earlier in Ur III inventories, and already in the 15th century BC technically complicated core-moulded glass vessels are found. Whatever Gulkishar's role in the history either of glass or of Babylon, for the next 100 years the Sealand Dynasty was an effective political force, holding the south against the Kassites who were soon to supplant them on the Babylonian throne.

59

The Kassites

The number and order of the early Kassite kings has yet to be established. The first who can be identified with any certainty as ruling in Babylon is one Agum II (kakrime), thought to be the ninth king of his dynasty. Agum is said to have recovered the statues of the god Marduk and his wife after 24 years of Hittite captivity (thus *c*. 1570). A long inscription, known only from a later copy, possibly a scribal forgery, tells of the restoration of Marduk's shrine and how new clothes had to be made for the statue which had lost its gold finery.[4] With the reinstallation of the god in Babylon the Kassite kings were able to 'take the hand of Marduk', a symbolic gesture which if it did not actually serve to legitimize their rule in the eyes of native Babylonians undoubtedly commended them as a dynasty who respected and observed Babylonian traditions.[5] Though the rulers of this new dynasty were clearly of non-Mesopotamian origin, they can hardly be regarded as conquering foreigners. Like so many other intruders on the Mesopotamian scene they appear to have been totally absorbed into the seemingly inexhaustible sponge of Mesopotamian culture and tradition. Not only did they adopt local customs and even religion but also the Babylonian language; indeed, were it not for written sources that tell us these kings' outlandishly foreign names, there would be few clues to their non-Babylonian origin.

The period of Kassite rule has been much neglected by most Mesopotamian scholars: only some 900 tablets of Kassite date have so far been published while many thousands lie in museum collections unedited and largely ignored.[6] This period is often regarded – and not entirely without justification – as the least inspired in Babylonian history. Yet the Kassites reigned some four centuries, far longer than any native or for that matter any other dynasty. There is every reason to believe that Kassite domestic policies were both liberal and unoppressive; at the same time these rulers were to prove far more successful in administering Sumer than their better-known Agade and Old Babylonian predecessors. The Kassite conquest of the Sealand territories was effected by *c*. 1460 and thereafter the whole of Babylonia functioned as a single political unit, a state of affairs rarely achieved even under more distinguished rulers. Indeed, under Kassite hegemony, the old separatist policies of the Sumerian city-states seem to have been neutralized, an achievement almost certainly encouraged by the attention paid to these ancient centres by later Kassite monarchs who undertook major building operations in them.

Despite the apparent success of Kassite domestic policies, however, the most important single feature of this phase of Babylonian history was the shift of political initiative away from Babylonia and for the first time to lands outside Mesopotamia. We have already had cause to mention growing Hittite power; perhaps of even greater importance at this period were the Hurrians whom we encountered briefly at the time of the Agade kings. Little is known of the origins of these people, who first appear in the extreme north of Mesopotamia in the region of Diyarbakir, but by the end of the Old Babylonian period their names are found throughout the north, from Shemshara in Kurdistan to Alalakh in northwestern Syria. A number of small Hurrian states are known at this time, which by c. 1500 had been welded together into a new and ill-documented kingdom of Mitanni, in which the population appears to have been predominantly Hurrian but whose rulers were of Indo-European origin, worshippers of ancient Indian or Vedic deities such as Mitra, Varuna and Indra. The Mitanni aristocracy were a chariot-owning nobility known as *mariyanna*, almost certainly to be equated with *márya*, an Indo-European word for 'young man or young warrior'. The Mitanni capital, Washshukanni, so far unidentified and, like Agade, the subject of much fruitless search, is thought to lie somewhere in northeastern Syria or in the adjacent area of southern Turkey.[7]

Throughout the 15th and much of the 14th centuries the Mitanni state stretched from the Mediterranean to the Zagros, encompassing, as far as we know, much of the later state of Assyria, at least until the time of Assur-uballit (c. 1365). Mitanni military power, like that of the contemporary Kassites, owed much to new skills in horsemanship and the changes in military tactics consequent upon the introduction of the horse-drawn two-wheeled chariot, an instrument of war which the later Assyrians were to put to such effective use. Hurrian handbooks relating to the training and racing of horses survive. These contain various technical terms which have Indo-European cognate forms, a reflection of the eastern origin both of the Mitanni and the small Asiatic horse.[8] Perhaps the most important role of the Hurrians in the story of Babylon lies in the part they played as intermediaries in the transmission of Babylonian culture to the Hittites, to the Palestinians and Phoenicians, and, indirectly, to Greece and the western world.

Kara-indash and Kurigalzu

Although no contemporary sources for the early Kassite kings have yet come to light, by the time of Kara-indash (c. 1415) we find not only royal inscriptions but also a further and invaluable historical source in the Amarna letters.[9] These cuneiform documents, written largely in Babylonian, though in many instances of a rather illiterate variety, were first found in 1887 by a peasant woman digging for fertilizer in the ruins of Pharaoh Akhenaten's capital, now the site of Tell el-Amarna in Egypt. More than 350 tablets were eventually recovered by the local inhabitants and subsequently sold to a number of museums and private collections. The subject of these documents, which had formed part of Akhenaten's state archives, is international diplomacy, and they throw a unique and brilliant light on the political history of what is often for this reason termed the Amarna Age. Comparable documents have since been found in Palestine, Anatolia, Babylonia and Assyria.

Although this international correspondence begins some time after 1450, the surviving Amarna letters date largely from the reigns of the Pharaohs Amenophis III and Akhenaten (c. 1402–1347). Letters to and from the Kassite kings Kadashman-Enlil I (c. 1370) and Burnaburiash II (c. 1350) and mentioning their immediate predecessors were found at Amarna. None of the earlier correspondence has been recovered, but it is clear that by the time of Kara-indash Kassite Babylon had gained sufficient prestige to merit an exchange of ambassadors with the Egyptian court, and that thenceforth the dispatch of highly-prized commodities as 'presents' between the two courts became common. As early as 1431 Pharaoh Amenophis II recorded gifts from Babylonia following one of his campaigns in Syria; later in his reign Amenophis twitted his vizier for dalliance with 'a lady from Babylonia, a servant girl from Byblos, a young maiden from Alalakh and an old lady from Arrapha [modern Kirkuk]'.[10] By 1415 a regular exchange of messengers had been instituted between Egypt and Babylonia, and Babylonian caravans travelled widely to Syria, Egypt and Anatolia. In the tangled web of international intrigue and diplomacy which characterized the Amarna Age Egypt at first played the major military role, campaigning in Syria, but Babylon provided the lingua franca of diplomacy as did France in 18th- and 19th-century Europe.

60 The outer wall of the Innin (Inanna) temple of Kara-indash at Uruk (ill. 69) is decorated in relief with a frieze of deities holding flowing vases. The figures are made of moulded baked brick, a characteristic feature of architectural ornament of the Kassite period. Ht of brickwork, c. 1·8 m. Iraq Museum.

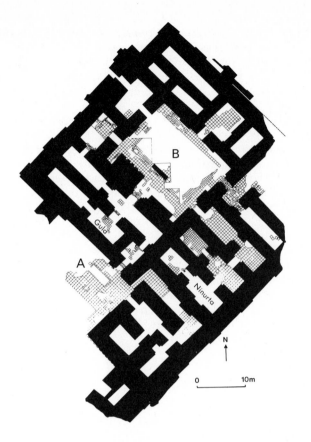

A

Gula

Ninurta

B

N

0   10m

61 The Kassite temple of
Gula, goddess of healing, at
Isin was entered through a
buttressed gateway on the
northwest. The main shrine,
of typical Babylonian 'broad-
room' plan, opened off the
southwest side of courtyard
B, and a second doorway on
the southeast led indirectly to
a chapel dedicated to Gula's
consort Ninurta. The
domestic quarters of the
temple probably surrounded
the inner courtyard A. After
Hrouda, Fritz, Haussperger,
Aziz, Strommenger and
Weidner.

Kara-indash is noted too for his successful domestic policies. The
Sealand had already been defeated, uniting Babylonia into a single
country for the first time in 200 years, and both Kara-indash and his
successor Kurigalzu carried out extensive building programmes in the
old Sumerian cities. At Uruk Kara-indash built a new temple dedicated
to Innin (Inanna), of which the façades were ornamented in relief with
a decorative frieze of deities, some 2 m in height, made of moulded
bricks and inset in narrow niches.

69

60

By the time of Kurigalzu I (*c.* 1390) Babylon was receiving large
quantities of gold from Egypt. Indeed gold seems at this period
temporarily to have replaced silver as the normal medium of
exchange.[11] Financed by Egypt Kurigalzu undertook an ambitious
building programme in a number of cities, including Ur, Eridu and
Uruk. Large quantities of Egyptian gold went also into the building of a
new fortified city, Dur-Kurigalzu, on the outskirts of modern Baghdad.
It is often assumed that this foundation was designed as a new capital,
but it is clear from contemporary documents that Babylon remained for
the Kassites the major city in the land, the seat of kingship and the most
important religious, political and commercial centre. Despite their
foreign origins Kassite monarchs rarely founded new buildings in the
old Sumerian cities – the Innin temple of Kara-indash is an exception –
but as a matter of deliberate policy reconstructed or restored those of

their predecessors. Kurigalzu's inscriptions often state, and indeed in ancient Sumerian, that his object was to restore the traditional sacred buildings.[12] Even the palace and the ziggurrat precinct at Dur-Kurigalzu, which have been described as 'of unique character which can only be considered as Kassite', display many similarities with conventional Mesopotamian plans, for example at Ur, while the

61   recently excavated Gula temple at Isin is entirely Babylonian in its architectural conventions. One of the very few hints that the Kassites did retain some of their own religious practices is to be found in a text of the time of the last Kurigalzu (1345–1324), which mentions the Kassite 'creator gods' Shuqamuna and Shimaliya in whose shrine in Babylon this Kurigalzu was invested with the trappings of royal office.[13]

The Amarna Age

Kurigalzu I's successors are perhaps best known for their part in the surviving Amarna correspondence. The Egyptian and Babylonian royal families were now linked by marriage, and the kings address each other as 'brother', a greeting implying equality of status. Protocol demanded an elaborate form of salutation, with enquiries after the royal household, including particularly the king's horses and chariots:

> Tell Napkhururiya [Akhenaten], the great king, the king of Egypt: your brother Burnaburiash, the great king, the king of Karduniash [the Kassite name for Babylonia], sends the following message:
>
> 'I and my house, horses, chariots, officials, and my country are well indeed. May everything be likewise well with my brother and his house, his horses, chariots, officials and his country.' (EA 7[14])

Gifts were exchanged – horses, chariots and lapis lazuli from Babylon for gold from Egypt, and also silver, bronze, ivory, furniture of ebony and other precious woods, garments and oil. Teams of horses were much in demand from the Kassites, who were noted not only for their horsemanship but also for their horses; indeed in a later letter to Kadashman-Enlil II, the Hittite king Hattushili III remarks that in Babylonia 'there are more horses even than straw' and, despite the fact that the well-watered Hittite homeland would seem more suited to the breeding of horses than the dry plains of Babylonia, demands 'fine horses' from Babylon.[15]

The general tone of the surviving Amarna correspondence between Babylon and Egypt suggests a decline in relations between the two countries, possibly a reflection of growing weakness in Egypt under Amenophis III and Akhenaten. Both Kadashman-Enlil I and Burnaburiash complain of the ill-treatment of their messengers and the meanness of Pharaoh. 'Twenty minas of gold' sent to Burnaburiash 'were not complete, for when they were put in the furnace, 5 minas did not come forth' (EA 10). In the letter to Akhenaten Burnaburiash asks that Pharaoh seal and dispatch the gold himself and not leave this task to some 'trustworthy official' (EA 7). This same letter reveals an extraordinary naïvety on the part of Burnaburiash who complains querulously that the Egyptian king has failed to enquire about his health and, on being told that Egypt is too far away for Pharaoh to have

62 Impression of an agate cylinder seal belonging to an official of the Kassite king Burnaburiash. The scene of worship shows a kneeling suppliant and, in the corner, a dog, symbol of the goddess Gula. Other common Kassite symbols include the cross, bee, rosette and lozenge. Ht 4 cm. Vorderasiatisches Museum, Berlin.

heard of the Babylonian king's indisposition, asks of his own messenger whether this is really true.

Marriage arrangements were made between the two families, Burnaburiash promising to send a daughter to Egypt. But he complains to Pharaoh that the delegation who came to fetch her had only five carriages and imagines what his courtiers would say if a daughter of the great king were to travel with such a paltry escort (EA 11). A satisfactory arrangement seems to have been reached, however, as letters 13 and 14 record in interminable length presents exchanged between the two kings, presumably as the marriage settlement.

Although connections at this time between Egypt and Babylonia appear to decline, Babylonian influence elsewhere in the 14th century remained undiminished. Evidence from ancient Dilmun (Bahrain), the presence of a Mycenaean 'ox-hide' ingot at Dur-Kurigalzu, and Kassite seals in Greece (Thebes) testify to an active and far-reaching Kassite commercial policy.[16] To the north relations with the Hittites were cordial, while the collapse of the Mitanni empire encouraged Babylonian interference in Assyria and at the same time gestures of independence on the part of that northern kingdom. The presumption of the Assyrian king Assur-uballit I (1365–1330) in sending envoys to Pharaoh (Tutankhamun) provoked a stiff note from Burnaburiash:

> Now it was not I who sent to you the Assyrians, who are my subjects. Why have they been allowed to come to your land of their own free will? If you love me they must not carry on any business; let them accomplish nothing. . . . (EA 9)

Whether Assyria was politically subordinate to Babylonia, as this letter suggests, remains uncertain. There is no doubt, however, that with the decline of Mitanni hegemony Babylon extended its horizons northward, and under most of the later Kassite kings we find Kirkuk (Arrapha) reckoned as part of Babylonian territory.[17] Babylonian cultural dominance is beyond dispute, and can be seen in the increasing use of 'Marduk' in Assyrian personal names and even the presence – so the evidence suggests – of a shrine to Marduk in Assyria at this time.[18]

From the reign of Assur-uballit I onwards Assyria was established as a major power, but close ties with Babylon are still evident in the marriage of a Babylonian prince to Assur-uballit's daughter, whose son, Kara-hardash, succeeded to the throne after the death of Burnaburiash II. The Assyrian connection was to prove unpopular in Babylon, however, and Kara-hardash was deposed and probably assassinated in a local revolt. The Assyrian king now intervened in Babylon and installed another member of the Kassite royal house on the throne, a son of Burnaburiash known as Kurigalzu *sehru* ('the younger') (*c*. 1345). This intervention represents the high point of Assyrian influence in the 14th century. Even Kurigalzu, who owed his throne to Assur-uballit, was to turn on his erstwhile ally, doing battle with a later Assyrian king Enlil-nerari at Sugagu, just south of Assur. Surviving chronicles disagree as to the outcome, but the very fact that the battle was fought near Assur suggests that the Babylonians were not on the defensive.[19] From this time onwards the fortunes of Assyria and Babylonia remain closely linked; dynastic marriages and treaties alternate with breaches of the peace and 'adjustments' to the common boundary.

The younger Kurigalzu was clearly a gifted monarch. His reign is notable particularly for a successful attack against the Elamites, who were causing trouble, as so often in the past, on the eastern frontier of Babylonia. This campaign ended with the capture of the Elamite capital Susa, where Kurigalzu dedicated a statue recording his victory. When he returned to Babylon Kurigalzu brought with him from Susa an agate tablet, once a votive offering 'for the life of' the famous Shulgi of Ur's Third Dynasty, which he presented, with a new dedication, to the goddess Ninlil at Nippur.[20]

Babylonians, Hittites and Assyrians

Towards the end of the 14th century Egypt re-entered the Asiatic scene. Both Seti I and Ramesses II campaigned in Palestine and Syria, the latter pausing to record his progress on the cliffs at the mouth of the famous Dog River (Nahr el-Kelb), now a well-known archaeological attraction near Beirut. Here in antiquity the narrow passage between sea and headland formed an important defensive barrier, and among later armies who followed pharaonic precedent in recording their passing were those of Nebuchadrezzar II of Babylon, the Roman emperor Caracalla and even Allenby and Gouraud in World War I. Ramesses' army met the Hittites at Qadesh (modern Tell Nebi Mend) on the Orontes in northern Syria (*c*. 1300 BC). The result, despite glowing and certainly exaggerated accounts from Egyptian sources – indeed the long-winded compositions and pictures on the walls of Ramesses' temples have made Qadesh one of the best-known battles in antiquity – was undoubtedly a strategic victory for the Hittites.

A renewal at this time of relations between the Hittites and Kassites (under Kadashman-Turgu, 1297–1280) can be seen as a measure of the apprehension with which these kingdoms now viewed the growing power of Assyria, freed of the Mitanni yoke and ruled in the 14th and 13th centuries by a succession of unusually able monarchs. A treaty of friendship was concluded and the royal houses of Babylon and Hattusha appear again to have been linked by marriage. However, Kadashman-Turgu died while his son and heir was still a child, leaving effective power in Babylon in the hands of his anti-Hittite vizier, Itti-Marduk-balatu. According to a lengthy letter later addressed to the young Kassite monarch, Kadashman-Enlil II (1279–1265), the Hittite king (Hattushili III) had tried to ensure his succession, an intervention which was clearly unwelcome in Babylon:

> While the gods have kept me alive and preserved my rule, your father passed away and I mourned him as befits our brotherly relationship. When I had done what is proper after the death of your father, I dried my tears and dispatched a messenger to the land Karduniash [Babylonia] and sent the following message to the high officials of Karduniash: 'If you do not keep the son of my brother as ruler, I shall become your enemy, I will go and invade Karduniash; but if you do, send me word if an enemy rises against you or if any difficulty threatens you, and I will come to your aid.' In those days my brother was a child and so I assume no one ever read these tablets to him; now these old scribes are not alive any more, and none of the tablets are even kept in archives so that they could be read to you now.

The Hittite king's motives become clear in a later passage in which he assures Kadashman-Enlil that Assyria is far too weak to threaten Babylon:

> And I have still more to say to my brother: I have heard that my brother has grown into a man and often goes out to hunt. I am very pleased that the god Adad has thus made famous the name of the offspring of my brother, Kadashman-Turgu. And so I say: 'Go ahead now, and make a raid into the land of the enemy [Assyria]', and I would like to hear how many of the enemy my brother has slain. And I would like to say to my brother: 'They used to call your father a king who prepares for war but then stays at home. Go out into enemy country and defeat the enemy!'

The letter concludes with a request for fine horses (see above), lapis lazuli and a carver of stone reliefs from Babylon.[15]

After the death of Kadashman-Enlil (c. 1265) relations between the Babylonians and Hittites seem to have waned, perhaps owing to disruption of communications by Aramaean tribes, a situation commented upon in Hattushili's letter. Little is known of Babylon now until the reign of Kashtiliashu IV (1242–1235), when the powerful Assyrian king Tukulti-Ninurta I (1244–1208) attacked Babylonia, sacked the capital and, according to his own inscription,

> captured Kashtiliashu and trod with my feet upon his lordly neck as though it were a footstool. Bound I brought him as a captive into the presence of Assur, my lord. Thus I became lord of Sumer and

63, 64 Kassite art is noted for the realism of its clay figurines. Two of the best-known were found in the palace at Dur-Kurigalzu. The small bearded head (ht 4 cm) is decorated with red ochre and black paint; the feline head is a detail from a figurine of a lioness (length of head *c*. 3 cm). Iraq Museum.

Akkad in its entirety and fixed the boundary of my land as the Lower Sea in the east.[21]

The precise causes of this war are not clear, although an Assyrian epic celebrating Tukulti-Ninurta's victory charges that Kashtiliashu had broken his oath and had plundered Assyrian territory. Babylon was devastated: Babylonian Chronicle P records that the walls of the city were destroyed, the Babylonians 'put to the sword', Marduk's temple (Esagila) plundered and his statue carried to Assyria. Assyrian governors were installed in Babylonia and for several years (*c*. 1235–1228) Babylon had its first taste of Assyrian rule.[19]

Who was to prove the ultimate victor in this encounter, however, is a moot question. The motives for Assyrian expansion remain obscure, though it is clear at least in later periods that there was an element of *folie de grandeur*. One probable and more practical factor was economic,

and it would seem that many Assyrian campaigns were directed towards not only sources of raw materials but the very profitable control of trade routes along which such goods flowed. This motive may in part explain Assyrian attempts to dominate northern Babylonia, but on balance the heavy and continuous military effort now required for its occupation and control almost certainly diverted Assyrian attention from more profitable enterprises elsewhere. This dichotomy of interest – for Assyria was essentially, by tradition and resources, a northern power – diluted its energies and probably contributed to the catastrophic end of its empire in 612 BC. At the same time the cultural impact of Babylon upon Assyria was henceforth such that Tukulti-Ninurta's conquest can be argued, paradoxically, as a victory for Babylon. Even large numbers of Babylonian cuneiform tablets were removed as booty by the Assyrians, hungry for Babylonian culture.[22] This Assyrian obsession with, and ambivalence towards, Babylon was to trouble the northern kingdom for the next 600 years.

Tukulti-Ninurta's military successes mark him as a leading figure of the 13th century. At home he claimed virtually divine honours, together with the Babylonian titulary: 'King of Karduniash, King of Sumer and Akkad, King of Sippar and Babylon, King of Dilmun and Meluhha [perhaps a claim to Babylonian rights in these distant regions], King of the Upper and Lower Seas.' He built a new capital, named after himself, on the bank of the Tigris opposite Assur, in which, interestingly, the main temple plan is Babylonian, though the mural decoration is north Mesopotamian in style. But in these excesses he seems to have aroused increasing enmity, according to later tradition, oddly, for his sacrileges against Babylon and Marduk. Local insurgents, led by Tukulti-Ninurta's own son and heir, imprisoned the king in his new palace and set fire to it. Garbled accounts of Tukulti-Ninurta's reign may possibly be preserved in the later Greek legends of 'King Ninos' and his new capital.

The fall of the Kassites

The history of events during and immediately following upon the Assyrian interregnum in Babylon is confused.[23] Several 'kings' who can have been little more than puppets are named in the King-List; there is also evidence for an Elamite intervention. Eventually a son of Kashtiliashu IV, Adad-shuma-usur (1218–1189), was enthroned, apparently with both popular acclaim and Elamite approval. Two further kings, Meli-Shipak (1188–1174) and his son Marduk-apla-iddina I (1173–1161) ruled in relative peace and prosperity. This is the period of the Painted Palace at Dur-Kurigalzu (see below), from which have been recovered records of Assyrian merchants.[24] After the death of Marduk-apla-iddina, however, the Kassite kingdom disintegrated, suffering first a raid by Assur-dan I of Assyria, then an attack by the Elamite Shutruk-Nahhunte in which the powerless Babylonian king was deposed (c. 1159). Babylonian sources tell us little of these events, but Elamite records – unfortunately still imperfectly understood – are more informative. A son of Shutruk-Nahhunte was appointed governor in Babylon, but Kassite resistance was fierce and the struggle continued a further three years. Babylonian tradition remembers this as a time of extraordinary violence:

> [The Elamite's] crimes were greater and his grievous sins worse than all his fathers had committed . . . like a deluge he swept away all the peoples of Akkad, and cast in ruins Babylon and all the noblest cult-centres.[25]

Among the trophies carried away to Susa were two of Mesopotamia's most famous surviving monuments: the stele of Naram-Sin, on which Shutruk-Nahhunte caused his own victory inscription to be carved, and Hammurapi's famous laws, both probably looted from Sippar. Shutruk-Nahhunte died before completing his victory dedications: a space cut out on Hammurapi's stele still awaits the Elamite's inscription. Other trophies included a number of statues of the Agade king Manishtushu plundered from Eshnunna, Kish and Agade. The

24

50

65 The remains of the ziggurrat at Aqar Quf (Dur-Kurigalzu) were often mistaken by early travellers for the Tower of Babel. This view shows the lower stage now reconstructed by the Directorate-General of Antiquities, Baghdad.

statue of Nana of Uruk was also among the loot taken to Susa, where it waited over 500 years for its release by the army of the 7th-century Assyrian king Assurbanipal. Marduk too was carried away and remained in Susa until the reign in Babylon of the first Nebuchadrezzar (1126–1105).[26] For this act of sacrilege the Elamite Kudur-Nahhunte, Shutruk-Nahhunte's son, was to remain forever infamous in the memory and poetic tradition of the Babylonians. Thus ended the dynasty of the Kassite kings, who with more than modest success had reigned in Babylon, according to Mesopotamian tradition, an unprecedented 576 years 9 months.

Kassite archaeology: Dur-Kurigalzu

The existing ruins of Aqar Quf, just west of Baghdad, mark a new Kassite foundation, 'the Fortress of Kurigalzu', almost certainly built as an outer line of defence against Assyria and Elam. Reference to the city in a tablet dated to the reign of Burnaburiash (*c.* 1350) suggests its founding by the first of the two known Kurigalzus (*c.* 1390). The site is noted today for its unusually well-preserved ziggurrat, which still stands some 57 m above the plain and was often mistaken by early travellers for the biblical Tower of Babel. The ziggurrat's distinctive profile is due to layers of reed matting and plaited ropes – still remarkably preserved after more than 3000 years – which run horizontally through the

65

66 In the doorways of the latest phase of the palace at Dur-Kurigalzu (12th century) were found painted dadoes showing processions of courtiers or officials entering and leaving the palace. This is the best preserved of a group of bearded figures wearing a fringed garment and a fez-like hat. The figures were painted in black, white and red on a 'yellowish wash'. Ht of figure *c.* 50 cm. After Baqir.

67

structure. Their purpose is uncertain, but they were possibly intended as levelling and bonding agents during construction and the subsequent drying-out of the brickwork. Fronting the ziggurrat is a complex of courtyards, surrounded by long, narrow chambers, only excavated in part but very similar in their overall plan to comparable structures at Ur, founded under the Third Dynasty but restored on the same basic plan by a Kurigalzu, probably also the first. Although in both cities the dependencies of the ziggurrat, which stands in isolation in its own courtyard, are described as 'temples', on neither site is there any single room that can be identified as a shrine of the common Babylonian type. At Aqar Quf there is also an unusual low platform, approximately on the axis of the central ziggurrat stair, which may have carried a small temple or offering-place. Building inscriptions attribute the Aqar Quf ziggurrat and adjoining complex to a Kurigalzu.[27]

A vast palace was also investigated by the Iraqi excavators, about a kilometre northwest of the ziggurrat. Four building levels were identified, of which the upper two can be securely attributed, on the basis of associated tablets, to a time later than Kurigalzu II.[28] An inscribed door-socket assigns at least one of the two earlier palaces to a Kurigalzu. The most interesting feature of the palace appears in its latest phase (I), when in one wing long narrow galleries were entered from a courtyard through multiple doorways with painted dadoes depicting processions of human figures. Wall painting has a long history in Mesopotamia, from the early 6th millennium BC onwards, and there is evidence for its employment in earlier palaces, for example at Mari, Nuzi and Aqar Quf itself, but this is the first instance of the procession motif that was to become so characteristic of later Assyrian architectural ornament. One Aqar Quf group indeed wear the fez, later to become the royal headdress in Assyria, worn at this time by the nobility, apparently also in Babylonia – unless these courtiers are meant to represent Assyrian subjects. The best-preserved wall paintings are from the very latest phase of level I (IA), in which, elsewhere, have been found tablets of Marduk-apla-iddina I (1173–1161).

Both the latest palace (levels IC—IA) and the ziggurrat dependencies are constructed in a very unusual and distinctive building technique, in which some courses of bricks are laid alternately flat and on edge. The earlier palaces (II—IV) are built in the more customary 'English bond', in which all the bricks lie flat. The general pattern of development on the palace site seems clear, but it is impossible to relate it to the sequence in the ziggurrat area, where the use of horizontal and vertical brickwork and the occurrence of two destruction levels are closely paralleled only in phases IC to IA of the palace. Certainly the striking differences in construction make it difficult to believe that the ziggurrat courts, apparently founded by a Kurigalzu, are contemporary with the earliest palaces, at least one of which was also built by a Kurigalzu. Only two kings of this name are securely attested, reigning some 50 years apart in the 14th century, long before the building of palace I.

These conflicting archaeological data led the excavators of Aqar Quf to postulate yet a third Kurigalzu, builder of the apparently contemporary ziggurrat complex and the latest palace. But it seems unlikely that the earlier palaces were in use for so long before the foundation of the religious precinct. Nor does the King-List allow room for a Kurigalzu between the two Kassite monarchs whose tablets were found in the level II palace (Kudur-Enlil, 1264–1256, and Kashtiliashu IV, 1242–1235) and Marduk-apla-iddina whose tablets occur in the latest phase.[29] One can only reiterate that the archaeological evidence is irreconcilable with the King-List and hope that further excavations or inscriptions may illuminate this complex problem.

Kassite art and architecture: southern cities

Regrettably little is known of the most important Kassite city, Babylon, where occupation of this period for the most part lies inaccessible below the modern water table. However, in Merkes (the central commercial area of the later city) some Kassite levels were reached and in them were found a number of well-built houses, graves and a group of fire-pits which were interpreted as kilns for the manufacture of objects in faience ('frit'),[30] a material consisting of finely ground crystalline quartz held together by a vitreous matrix and coated with a glassy surface. True glasses, which as we have seen are also known at this period, have a homogeneous non-crystalline structure throughout. Faience was highly fashionable, more common and presumably cheaper than glass in the 2nd millennium BC, when it was used for a variety of objects, including beads, cylinder seals, plaques and decorative masks (ill. 68).

For Kassite material generally we must turn to sites other than Babylon. Aqar Quf is perhaps the most informative, while Kassite levels have also been excavated in the old cities of Sumer, such as Nippur, Isin, Larsa and Ur which we know to have been honoured and respected by the Kassite kings. The earliest known Kassite building has already been mentioned – the small but unusual temple of Kara-indash (ill. 69) noted for its moulded brick frieze and its very 'Assyrian' *langraum* plan. Although the use of unbaked brick for exterior architectural decoration can now be traced back to the Old Babylonian period, the Kassites were the first to employ baked bricks and to include minor deities in human form among the repertoire of motifs. Fragments of moulded brick ornament have been found at Ur, Nippur, Aqar Quf and Larsa. At the latter site a recently excavated temple, built at least as early as the 14th century, was decorated with spiral columns superficially resembling those found on the façade of the Old Babylonian temple at Rimah, but identical in construction with some unpublished columns at Aqar Quf.[31] At the time of the Elamite sack of Babylon, Kara-indash's new decorative technique was carried by Kudur-Nahhunte to Susa, where the moulded bricks of his temple to In-Shushinak[32] were possibly made by Babylonian prisoners. This form of ornament is perhaps best known in the remarkable glazed-brick friezes of Nebuchadrezzar's Babylon and Darius' palace at Susa, where it is recorded that the brickwork was indeed executed by Babylonians.

Undoubtedly the most distinctive type of object from Kassite Mesopotamia – indeed it was among the very first to attract antiquarian

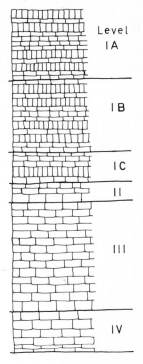

67 Schematic diagram illustrating the abrupt change in building technique which takes place between the first three (IV–II) and the latest palaces (IC–IA)) at Dur-Kurigalzu. The unusual and very distinctive brick work of the latest phase, in which the bricks are laid alternately flat and on edge, is characteristic also of the ziggurrat precinct. After Baqir.

102, 104,
108

interest – is the 'boundary-stone' or *kudurru*, a term new in Kassite times and designating a particular type of royal grant, generally inscribed on an oval or pillar-shaped stone. These were official charters issued by kings, or occasionally high officials, to proclaim publicly the granting to a particular person of a particular piece of land, together with the remission of certain taxes and the imposition of certain duties. The *kudurru* itself was apparently set up in the field or other holding involved; copies on clay tablets were deposited in temples to ensure their preservation.

Over 80 such monuments are known, from the time of Kadashman-Enlil I (*c.* 1370) to the 7th century. One especially fine example records a grant by Meli-Shipak in favour of his son Marduk-apla-iddina I. Characteristic of these boundary-stones is the type of relief sculpture 70 seen here, in which a variety of divine symbols, sometimes placed on 'stands' or 'seats', representing the 'enthroned deity', serve to protect the monument. On some the carving depicts the king himself, either alone or with the recipient of the grant; in certain instances the recipient is shown worshipping before the deity. Additional protection was ensured by elaborate curses and blessings inscribed on the *kudurru* to prevent its removal or destruction.

62 Kassite cylinder seals also display an unusual variety of symbols, including the 'Kassite cross'. Another innovation was the long

68 Objects made of glazed frit or faience were common in Kassite times. Among the most attractive are a number of small masks, one of which was found in the tomb of a high priestess in the Gipar-ku at Ur. Undoubtedly the finest is this unusually large and elaborately inlaid example from the great temple at Tell al Rimah. The coloured frit and glass inlays (black, white and yellow) are set in bitumen. 14th/13th century. Ht 11·8 cm. Iraq Museum.

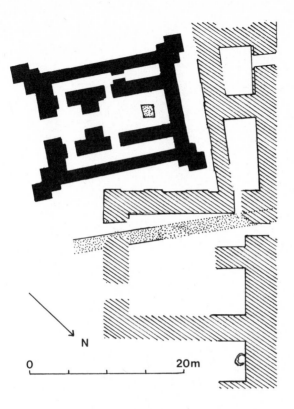

69 The earliest known Kassite temple is this small shrine (solid-black walls) built at Uruk by King Kara-indash (15th century), dedicated to the goddess Inanna. The outer wall has a recessed socle of moulded bricks (ill. 60). The outer precinct wall (hatched) is of much later date (Sargon II). After Jordan.

inscription in Sumerian, which often filled most of the seal's surface. This was generally a prayer to some tutelary deity and often obscure in expression, perhaps a manifestation of the learned interests which characterized this period.

Kassites in retrospect

The Kassites are often dismissed as conservative in their attitudes, rulers of a 'static' Babylonia noted only for its peaceful mediocrity and enlivened only by its diplomatic correspondence. The paucity of sources, other than the virtually ignored administrative archives (largely from Nippur), has resulted in a general neglect of this period in Babylonian history, not merely by Assyriologists but also by archaeologists who have tended to seek sites occupied at periods generally considered to be of greater significance. Yet the Kassites ruled a unified Babylonia far longer than any other Mesopotamian dynasty, and the emergence of Babylon as the political and cultural centre of the ancient world took place under their aegis. Politically the period is noted for the intensification of the conflict with Assyria which was to last until the 7th century.

The period of Kassite rule was a time of social if not cultural change. The king as 'law-giver' disappears with the dynasty of Hammurapi while the Kassite *kudurru* reveal an administration reminiscent of feudalism, although to use this term *sensu stricto* would be misleading.

Kassite law governing transfers of land marks a notable departure from Old Babylonian practice, and there is evidence for land tenure by 'households' or territorial districts defined as the property of tribes, that is land owned collectively by tribal communities, a feature characteristic also of Babylonian society later in the 1st millennium.

A highly conservative attitude was shown towards language and literature, but this conservatism almost certainly reflected the conscious attempt by a foreign dynasty to become in every sense Babylonian and to preserve the traditions and culture of the past. With the Kassite period the Babylonians began to use ancestral names, a practice previously unknown. Indeed, the names of a number of famous scribes and scribal families have survived from this time.[33] Although the body of literature which emerged from Kassite schools is often referred to as 'canonical', there is no suggestion of any systematic selection of literary works, nor of a conscious attempt to produce authoritative editions. Much Akkadian literature did assume a fixed form, but by no means all. New works were still composed, and for the first time in Babylonian history we have a number of texts of which the authorship can be established. Of interest, indeed unusual, is the 'signature' on the slightly later Babylonian 'Theodicy' which occurs in the acrostic form of the poem.

The period which saw the end of Kassite rule was one of general unrest and upheaval in the eastern Mediterranean. This was the time of the Fall of Troy and the widespread migrations of groups identified in Egyptian sources as the 'Sea Peoples'. Babylonia was not directly affected but these widespread movements, of which the Philistine entry into Palestine was a part, brought about the collapse of the Hittite empire, thus temporarily depriving Mesopotamia of vital Anatolian metal. These events must have contributed to the decline of Assyria after the time of Tukulti-Ninurta. The border skirmishes along Babylonia's eastern frontiers at this time reflect the increasing importance to Babylon of the eastern trade routes.

One of the effects of the Hittite collapse was the wider availability of iron, and the period archaeologists designate the Iron Age begins in the Near East *c*. 1200, although a small number of iron objects are found in Western Asia well before this time, roughly from 2000 BC onwards. Iron technology is highly complex, and unlike that of any other ancient metal. The spread of iron working, in consequence, was extraordinarily slow, and indeed there is some evidence to suggest that in the early centuries of iron manufacture the Hittites exploited this metal under monopolistic conditions. In an often-quoted letter a Hittite king writes to one of his contemporaries:

> As for the good iron which you wrote about to me, good iron is not available in my seal-house in Kizzuwatna. That it is a bad time for producing iron I have written. They will produce good iron, but as yet they will not have finished. When they have finished I shall send it to you. To-day now I am dispatching an iron dagger-blade to you.[34]

This passage is sometimes interpreted to imply that the Hittites did not manufacture their own iron, but obtained it from elsewhere. But the

70 (*Opposite*) Boundary-stones (*kudurru*) are perhaps the most characteristic surviving monuments of Kassite Babylonia. This particularly fine example records a grant of land to Marduk-apla-iddina I by his father Meli-Shipak (12th century). The symbols represent various deities and include the dragon and spade of Marduk (3rd register). At the top are the moon (Sin), planet Venus (Ishtar), sun (Shamash), horned crowns representing Anu and Enlil and the goat-fish of Ea. Ht 65 cm. Louvre Museum.

71 This lively drawing on clay was found at Babylon in a house said to be of Kassite date. It shows a lion attacking a wild boar.

statement is ambiguous, and, whether or not there is any truth in the myth of Hittite monopoly, early sources of iron were undoubtedly confined to some part of Asia Minor. By the 14th century iron was in extensive use for weapons, but it was not until the destruction of the Hittite empire that this apparent monopoly was broken and iron-working brought into Palestine by the Philistines. Indeed the Bible recalls the advantage it was thought to give the Philistines over the Israelites in the 11th century (I Sam. 13, 19 ff.).

The inherent superiority of iron over bronze has been much exaggerated by students of the ancient world. Early iron, because of its rarity, had a high prestige value, but in later periods when iron was readily available many weapons continued to be made of bronze despite the fact that iron ores are by far the most common among the metals employed in antiquity. Indeed it seems likely that when iron became widespread it was as a substitute for bronze. As one scholar recently phrased it, 'The early adoption of iron was not so much an advance as a response to straitened circumstances.'[35] By far the greatest impact of iron technology was not on weaponry, as is often supposed, but on the more peaceful world of the craftsman and farmer. By about the 10th century iron ploughs, sickles and cutting tools had come into common use. Chisels and saws are much better made of iron, which takes a sharp edge more easily, than of bronze, and this single fact was to revolutionize working methods, especially among such crafts as those of stonemason and carpenter.

Post-Kassite Babylon

With the death of its last Kassite king Babylon entered a long phase of political instability. From now until the period of Assyrian supremacy in the 8th century BC the country was ruled by some six politically unimportant dynasties. 'Babylonia for the Babylonians' has been proposed as a motto appropriate to the next few centuries[36] which, oddly, constitute the only period in the history of Babylon when native Babylonians dominated the scene. The first of these native dynasties was associated with the city of Isin and is recorded in the King-List as the second dynasty of that city, where native resistance to the Elamites had centred and a local shaikh assumed the title King of Babylon (?1158). Its most important monarch was the first Babylonian ruler to bear the distinguished name of Nebuchadrezzar (1126–1105).

This Nebuchadrezzar was remembered by succeeding generations for his success in avenging the infamous Elamite sack of Babylon. A first attack on Elam failed disastrously when Nebuchadrezzar's troops were struck down by a plague and the king himself nearly killed in the panic and retreat which ensued. Success came, however, in a later campaign, perhaps owing to its unexpected timing in high summer. An inscription on a contemporary *kudurru* – one of the finest examples of this genre – describes the gruelling march to Susa, across desert where today summer temperatures often exceed 50°C.: 'The axes in the soldiers' hands burnt like fire and the road-surfaces scorched like flame. In the wells there was no water . . . the strength of the powerful horses gave out, and the legs of even the strongest warrior weakened.'[37] According to the same inscription 'the face of the sun was darkened by the clouds of dust' raised by the battle. Nonetheless Nebuchadrezzar was victorious and it was many years before any Elamite invader set foot again in Babylonia (ill. 72).

An important consequence of this campaign was the restoration of national morale in Babylonia effected by the recovery of the Marduk statue, removed to Susa by Kudur-Nahhunte several generations before. Since the time of the Old Babylonian kings, Marduk – once an insignificant minor deity – had played an increasingly important role. Indeed we have already had cause to note the spread of his cult to Assyria. His triumphant restoration by Nebuchadrezzar I, however, has been seen as the decisive factor in the elevation of this minor god to the position of supreme deity and, perhaps, an early step in the direction of monotheism.[38] Nebuchadrezzar's crushing defeat of the Elamites made him a national hero whose deeds were celebrated in contemporary and later poetic tradition. 'The pious prince' was assiduous in his attention not only to Marduk but also to the ancient shrines of Sumer. At Ur he dedicated objects of gold and silver and in the Gipar-ku (chapter 3) erected a stele depicting the *entu* priestess of the moon-god in her ceremonial dress and inscribed with her duties and rituals. This votive dedication suggests that Nebuchadrezzar, following the ancient tradition of the Agade and Old Babylonian kings, installed his own daughter as *entu* at Ur.

Relations with Assyria at this time are obscure, highlighted only by occasional border skirmishes. A much later copy of a letter alleged to originate from this period, addressed to an Assyrian from a Babylonian king (perhaps but not certainly Nebuchadrezzar[39]), takes an abusive and taunting tone, but there is little evidence to suggest that the Babylonian was in any position to carry out his threats. Indeed with the

72 The lengthy inscription on this white limestone boundary-stone, records the granting by Nebuchadrezzar I of certain privileges to one Lakti(?)-Marduk, captain of the right-wing chariotry in the victorious campaign against Elam. It vividly illustrates the variety of magical symbols by which such charters were protected. In the 3rd register are the spade and dragon of Marduk, and the stylus and goat of Nabu. The 4th register appears to depict purely Kassite deities, the horse in its shrine symbolizing the Kassite goddess of horsemanship. In the last register are the bull and lightning of Adad and the lamp of Nusku, god of light. Above sits Gula with her dog. The significance of the scorpion-man is uncertain. Ht 56 cm. British Museum.

73 Black limestone boundary-stone recording the conveyance of a field acquired by a royal official, Marduk-nasir. Payment consisted of a chariot, 6 saddles, 2 asses, 2 asses' saddles, one ox, grain, oil, clothing etc. Probably of the time of Marduk-nadin-ahhe (11th century). Ht 53 cm. British Museum.

accession of Assur-resha-ishi I, 'the avenger of Assyria' (1133–1116), and his talented and energetic son Tiglath-Pileser I (1115–1077), Assyrian fortunes rapidly improved. While the latter part of Nebuchadrezzar's reign and that of his successor passed in relative obscurity, Tiglath-Pileser extended Assyrian hegemony further than ever before, even into Lebanon where the Egyptian king sent him a crocodile as a present. The record of his military, hunting and building activities is preserved on clay prisms found at Assur,[40] the text of which in 1857 achieved fame in Assyriological circles through its selection by the Royal Asiatic Society for translation by representative scholars in order to test the validity of early solutions to the decipherment of cuneiform. Tiglath-Pileser's military campaigns are recorded in the extraordinarily bloodthirsty style that was to become the Assyrian custom, but the text also mentions more mundane matters, for example one of the first known botanical gardens, stocked with specimens 'not found in my own land', and the hunting of elephants which still survived at this time in northern Syria. Lions and wild bulls were also hunted, with the bow or the king's own 'iron spear', the first written documentation of the ritual royal hunt attested elsewhere in Western Asia at this time and which can be traced back to the very dawn of Sumerian history.[41]

While Tiglath-Pileser was occupied with the foreign conquests enumerated in this lengthy inscription, Nebuchadrezzar's younger brother and second successor, Marduk-nadin-ahhe (1100–1083) seized the initiative, attacked Ekallate, an Assyrian city not far from Assur, and carried off two cult statues which were to remain in Babylon until the 7th century. The exact sequence of events at this time is uncertain, but Tiglath-Pileser retaliated in a raid on northern Babylonia in which Dur-Kurigalzu, Sippar, Opis and Babylon were captured and the royal palaces of Marduk-nadin-ahhe burnt. Nonetheless, records show the Babylonian king to have remained firmly in control until his 18th year when a terrible famine struck, the inhabitants of the cities of Babylonia were reduced to eating human flesh and, in the words of an Assyrian chronicle, Marduk-nadin-ahhe simply 'disappeared'.[42]

A major disruptive force in Babylonia at this time came from the increasing pressure of Aramaean tribes. Towards the end of Tiglath-Pileser's reign Assyria too was harassed by Aramaeans, and there followed in both countries a period of national decline. The presence of these tribes from the western desert is first recorded towards the end of the 2nd millennium. Repeating the pattern of Amorite and earlier incursions they settled on the agricultural land whenever local authority was too weak to prevent them; those who settled were themselves plagued by their nomadic brethren. On the Mediterranean coast and in northern Syria Aramaeans were successful in establishing local kingdoms. In Babylonia a ring of minor tribal states or 'houses' (*bitu*) was established, at times extending to the very gates of major cities such as Babylon, Nippur and Uruk, and by the 8th century Aramaean tribesmen had begun to settle in Babylonian villages and towns. Their language, Aramaic, like Amorite, was a dialect of West Semitic. In Babylonia it gradually replaced Akkadian as the spoken language, becoming the *lingua franca* until the Arab conquest. It was the first Mesopotamian language to be written not in cuneiform but in a cursive alphabetic script, and its simpler style encouraged its increased adoption. Aramaic is, of course, the language of New Testament Palestine; modern Arabic as well as Hebrew characters derive from its cursive script.

In the 11th century the pressure of Aramaean tribes on the western borders of Babylonia and Assyria was especially severe. This Aramaean threat seems to have encouraged the Babylonians and Assyrians to forget their differences, and we find the new Babylonian king Marduk-shapik-zeri (1082–1070) travelling to Assur in order to seek aid from Assur-bel-kala. On his return to Babylon, however, he found the city in the hands of Adad-apla-iddina (1069–1048), identified by a Babylonian chronicle as 'Aramaean'.[43] The Assyrian king appears to have recognized this 'usurper' – or perhaps was even responsible for his accession – and sealed the bargain by marrying his daughter. Contemporary inscriptions, however, reveal the 'Aramaean usurper' as a dutiful monarch, mindful of his obligations to the ancient shrines of Sumer. Nor did his presence on the Babylonian throne serve to protect the country against further depredations by his marauding brethren.

The raids and devastation of this time are thought to form the background of a literary composition known as the Erra Epic, in which a catastrophe at Babylon is blamed on the inept fumblings of minor gods during the absence of Marduk, depicted as an old 'fuddy-duddy' who leaves Erra in charge while he 'goes off to have his crown jewels cleaned'.[44] The text details the havoc wrought: cities are ravaged, the inhabitants weep for their ruined shrines. The actual destruction caused in Babylonia at this time by the Sutu, a tribal group in some way connected with the Aramaeans, accords well with that narrated in the epic, which relates also that the citizens of Babylon rebelled against their king who sent troops against them; Uruk fell, Der and Dur-Kurigalzu were sacked. It has been suggested that the 'Aramaean usurper', a king who remained unpopular in later tradition, is the most likely candidate for this unnamed epic king, but there is no contemporary evidence for civil war in Babylon during his reign. Although the Sutu raids seem to have died down before the end of the 11th century, the disruption both of the country and of external trade led to extensive economic difficulties and general unrest. For over a century the history of both Babylonia and Assyria is once again obscure.

The Fifth to the Eighth Dynasties of Babylon

Of the last kings of the Fourth Dynasty of Babylon (the Second Dynasty of Isin) we know little: even their names are uncertain. About 1026 a second Sealand Dynasty, presumably from the south but bearing Kassite names, achieved brief control. These Sealanders were shortly succeeded by the Sixth Dynasty, known as the House of Bazi, a family which had held high office under Marduk-nadin-ahhe. The third 'dynasty' of this unstable period consisted of a single king of Elamite descent who, as an outsider, was relegated by the compilers of the King-List to dynastic solitude (c. 985–980). The dynastic affiliations of the succeeding rulers of Babylon (Eighth Dynasty) also remain uncertain, but these monarchs are usually grouped together with five who appear in the King-List as members of 'Dynasty *E*', *E* perhaps simply signifying Babylon.[45] This rather indeterminate dynasty ruled for some two centuries, during the period that was to see the rise of Assyria as the greatest power in the Middle East.

At the accession of Nabu-mukin-apli (979–944) the country was still weak after the unstable politics of the previous half century; conditions were such that at times the New Year Festival could not be held. This constituted a serious deprivation in Babylonian eyes, for not only was the Festival the most important religious event of the year, when the king 'took the hand of Marduk', but the god's blessing, received in this symbolic ritual, was considered essential to the continued well-being of the country. The importance to the Babylonians of the physical presence of the god's statue, without which the ceremony could not be celebrated, derives from this concept, which explains also the preoccupation of Mesopotamian chroniclers not only with the New Year Festival but with the theft and return of the statue itself. A chronicle relating to *c*. 960 BC records that 'for nine years in succession Marduk did not go forth, Nabu did not come'. From this it is clear that even in the immediate neighbourhood of the capital security was so poor that the New Year procession, which passed outside the city, could not take place, nor could the god's son Nabu come from his shrine in nearby Borsippa.

With the accession of Shamash-mudammiq (*c*. 905) there began a century of close, though not always friendly, contact with Assyria. An exchange of royal brides concluded a treaty between the northern power and Shamash-mudammiq's successor. The resultant peace, which lasted with only minor unpleasantries for some 80 years, may well have owed something to the presence of enemy queens in each respective court. Under Tukulti-Ninurta II (890–884) Assyrian military might was paraded blatantly in northern Babylonia: the Assyrian king marched down the Tigris, pausing to hunt wild cattle along the desolate Wadi Tharthar, camped with his army at Dur-Kurigalzu and Sippar, and proceeded back up the Euphrates 'beating the bounds' of his empire. There is no hint of actual Assyrian suzerainty, however, nor indeed of any Babylonian opposition. The continuing success of Assyrian expansionist policies under Tukulti-Ninurta's son Assurnasirpal II (883–859) marks the real beginning of the Late or Neo-Assyrian Empire, which by the 7th century BC was to control much of the Middle East, even as far as Egypt.

Assurnasirpal, however, seems to have caused little trouble to his Babylonian contemporary Nabu-apla-iddina. The latter is perhaps best known for his restoration of Ebabbar, the temple of the sun-god at Sippar which had been ravaged two centuries earlier by the Sutu. This restoration is recorded on a well-known stone tablet now in the British Museum, on which Nabu-apla-iddina is depicted worshipping before the sun-god's shrine with its fine 'Ionic' palm-trunk column. The inscription tells of the restoration of the statue to Ebabbar, and provides an amusing instance of ancient forgery. According to Babylonian convention it was not normally possible to carve a new

74 The 'sun-god tablet' from Sippar, on which Nabu-apla-iddina records his restoration of the ancient image of the sun-god and of his temple (*c.* 870 BC). The king is shown being led towards an altar on which rests the sun-disk of Shamash. Ht 28 cm. British Museum.

statue of a deity; the old one was always renovated with special ceremonies. The statue of Shamash had been plundered from Sippar, but a priest of Ebabbar 'found' a clay model of the original, from which, it was alleged, a new statue could properly be made. In this suspiciously fortuitous circumstance there must remain a strong suggestion of pious fraud. Some 250 years later another Babylonian king, Nabopolassar, father of the famous Nebuchadrezzar II, again restored Ebabbar, recording that he came across Nabu-apla-iddina's tablet in the course of his work.[46]

The reign of this 9th-century Babylonian monarch seems to have been both lengthy and prosperous; literature flourished – it is likely that the Erra Epic was written at this time – while Nabu-apla-iddina's final years saw a new treaty with Assurnasirpal's son Shalmaneser III (858–824). This treaty was soon to be invoked by the succeeding Babylonian king, Marduk-zakir-shumi, who was forced to ask for Assyrian aid in quelling a revolt instigated in Babylon by his younger brother. A massive throne base, discovered in 1962 in the palace of Shalmaneser's great arsenal at his capital Kalhu (modern Nimrud), depicts the Assyrian king clasping the hand of Marduk-zakir-shumi; the accompanying inscription records the reinstatement of the Babylonian monarch.[47] Again, there is no evidence to suggest Assyrian suzerainty over Babylon and on the throne base the two kings are shown as equals. Indeed Shalmaneser personally visited the principal cult centres of northern Babylonia, offered sacrifices, presented lavish gifts and endowments, fêted the citizens of Babylon and Borsippa, 'gave them food and wine, clothed them in brightly coloured garments

75

and presented them with gifts',[21] hardly an Assyrian king's usual behaviour towards subject peoples and once again evidence of the remarkable cultural dominance exercised by Babylon upon her northern neighbour. By contrast, from the Chaldaean tribes who at this time controlled much of southern Babylonia, Shalmaneser extorted vast tribute in a campaign illustrated both on the Nimrud throne base and on the famous bronze gates from Balawat, now in the British Museum. Here we see the beginning of a pattern which was to recur throughout the period of Assyrian supremacy: on the one hand, Assyrian propitiation of the Babylonian gods and recognition of the special rights of the citizens of certain Babylonian cities; on the other, a continuing effort to control the tribes who were to prove a constant thorn in the flesh, feuding among themselves and preying upon those cities.

The final years of Shalmaneser's long reign were marked by a great rebellion, during which the old king died. His son Shamshi-Adad V (823–811) was assisted by Marduk-zakir-shumi in putting down the revolt, which had by then spread throughout Assyria. Thus did the Babylonian repay a debt to his former benefactor, but the terms of the treaty now imposed were humiliating to Shamshi-Adad, an error of judgment that was to prove costly to the Babylonians. The Assyrian king was not slow to exact revenge, and within a short space of time two of Marduk-zakir-shumi's unfortunate successors were carried off to Assyria, and Babylonia was reduced to a state of total anarchy. The Assyrian royal annals record these events in typically bloodthirsty fashion: in Dur-Papsukal, an island fortress to which the Babylonian armies had fled,

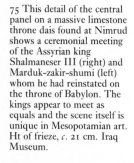

75 This detail of the central panel on a massive limestone throne dais found at Nimrud shows a ceremonial meeting of the Assyrian king Shalmaneser III (right) and Marduk-zakir-shumi (left) whom he had reinstated on the throne of Babylon. The kings appear to meet as equals and the scene itself is unique in Mesopotamian art. Ht of frieze, c. 21 cm. Iraq Museum.

13,000 of their warriors I cut down with the sword. Their blood like the waters of a stream I caused to run through the squares of their city. The corpses of their soldiers I piled in heaps . . . His [the

76 One of the finest Assyrian stelae ever recovered portrays King Adad-Nirari III, son of the famous Semiramis. Among the symbols of the gods shown in the background are the winged disk of Assur, the spade of Marduk and the stylus of Nabu whose worship in Assyria Adad-Nirari and his mother did much to encourage. The defaced portion of the inscription relates to the donor of the stele who appears to have caused offence by exceeding his prerogative as a local governor. From Rimah. Ht 1·30 m. Iraq Museum.

Babylonian king's] royal bed, his royal couch, the treasure of his palaces, his property, his gods and everything from his palace, without number, I carried away. His captive warriors were given to the soldiers of my land like grasshoppers. The city I destroyed, I devastated, I burned with fire.[21]

A Babylonian chronicle records that after the capture of the two unfortunate kings, for at least the next 12 years 'there was no king in the land'. Meanwhile Shamshi-Adad laid claim to the whole of the country under the ancient title 'King of Sumer and Akkad'.

We cannot leave the reign of Shamshi-Adad without reference to his wife, one of the few Orientals the Greeks remembered. Her name was Sammu-ramat, better recognized in its Greek form Semiramis. For five years after the death of Shamshi-Adad, this Assyrian queen ruled as regent for her young son, later Adad-Nirari III. She clearly held real power, making dedications in her own name, which was placed before that of her son. A memorial stele to her was found at Assur along with those of the kings and high officials of the country, an honour quite exceptional for a woman.

76

The Chaldaeans

In Babylonia the period that follows the conquests of Shamshi-Adad is obscure. After the death of Adad-Nirari III (783) Assyrian power too seems to have declined. In Babylon the resulting political vacuum was filled by the Chaldaeans, first encountered in the 9th century annals of Shalmaneser III, and one of whose shaikhs now claimed the throne.

3 The Chaldaeans lived among the swamps and lakes along the lower courses of the Tigris and Euphrates. Their organization was tribal, and each Chaldaean *bitu* ('house') was under the leadership of a shaikh who at times called himself a 'king'. But the tribal regions were ill-defined and the political strength of each individual shaikh was largely a matter of personal ability and prestige. The largest of the tribes, the Bit-Dakuri, was located south of Borsippa, not far from Babylon. Further south were the Bit-Amukani, and along the Tigris to the east bordering on Elam the Bit-Yakin. Contemporary evidence shows beyond any doubt that these people were far from being impoverished nomads. The Assyrian reliefs portray them living in an area of flourishing date palms and other evidence indicates that some were even city-dwellers. The Chaldaeans kept large herds of horses and cattle, and to judge from the tribute exacted from them were, if not themselves merchants, at least in control of the southern routes along which travelled such exotic luxuries as ebony, ivory, sissoo (a kind of valuable Indian timber), elephant hides and gold.

No direct evidence indicates that the Chaldaeans spoke a language other than Babylonian. Certainly most of those mentioned in letters and historical texts are the possessors of good Babylonian names. The presence of a few possibly Aramaean names is sometimes taken as an indication that the Chaldaeans spoke a local dialect of Aramaic, but ancient sources distinguish carefully between the Chaldaeans and Aramaean tribes to the north. Little is known of the first Chaldaean king of Babylon, but he was succeeded by another 'Sealand' shaikh, Eriba-Marduk (*c.* 770), who seems to have had some success in ridding the immediate neighbourhood of Babylon and Borsippa of the ever-encroaching Aramaeans and is remembered by later Chaldaean kings as the true founder of their dynastic line. Under his immediate successors, however, anarchy and civil war were once again rife.

With the accession of Nabonassar (Nabu-nasir) in 747 we enter a new era in the history of Babylon. Henceforth precise records of historical events were systematically kept, and both the Babylonian Chronicle and the 'Ptolemaic Canon' begin their accounts with the accession of this king. Indeed, according to later Ptolemaic reckoning the Nabonassar Era began precisely at midday on 26 February 747 BC! Tradition relates that highly accurate astronomical observations were also kept from this time onwards. Astronomical 'diaries', a number of which have been preserved, were now compiled, and it would appear that these documents may have comprised the sources followed by various later chroniclers.[48] In these Babylonian diaries were listed monthly astronomical observations together with fluctuations in such matters as commodity prices, river levels and the weather. Such records provide a striking, and of course much earlier, parallel for the Pontifical Tables of the Roman Republic, the yearly entries made by the Pontifex Maximus chronicling the names of consuls and other officials, wars and disturbances, plagues and pestilence, and the price of grain. The Roman tables were kept on 'whitened boards', and it would seem that some of the Babylonian records too may have been inscribed

77 Reconstruction of part of the earliest known set of hinged writing boards. Each leaf was recessed to receive a coating of beeswax on which the text was inscribed. This particular example was a special edition of the astrological omen series *enuma Anu Enlil*, prepared for King Sargon II of Assyria (721–705 BC). From Nimrud. After Howard.

on wax-covered boards. One Mesopotamian chronicle actually relates that 'historical' records were now kept on such hinged boards, while the earliest known examples date from a time not long after Nabonassar's reign.[49]   77

One authority has suggested that the intensive astronomical activity noted from this time onwards may have been inspired by a spectacular conjunction of the moon and planets in Nabonassar's first regnal year, but the increasing political stability from this time onwards must also have been a factor in the greater preservation of records. Hellenistic tradition has a somewhat bizarre explanation for the Babylonians' new devotion to history:

> From the time of Nabonassar the Chaldaeans accurately recorded the times of the motion of the stars. The polymaths among the Greeks learned from the Chaldaeans that – as Alexander Polyhistor and Berossus, men versed in Chaldaean antiquities, say – Nabonassar collected together the records of the deeds of the kings before him and destroyed them so that the reckoning of Chaldaean kings might start with himself.[50]

In Hellenistic astronomy the Nabonassar Era was indeed recognized as a turning point in the history of science and the very term Chaldaean came to signify 'astronomer'.

In Assyria too this period was to mark a change in the country's fortunes. In 746 a revolt led to the murder of the royal family, bringing to the throne Tiglath-Pileser III (744–727), Pul of the Old Testament, an Assyrian general and the country's most able monarch for over a century. Under his guidance Assyria was to recover and consolidate its position as the pre-eminent military power in the Middle East. Much of this achievement was the direct result of Tiglath-Pileser's administrative reforms. In particular the Assyrian provinces were reorganized, providing an effective imperial government for the powerful empire of the next 100 years, while a system of posting-stages was introduced for rapid communication. The name Pul

or Pulu is often assumed to have been this king's official name in
Babylon, but there is no contemporary evidence for its use; it appears
only in later sources such as the Bible, Berossus and Josephus. Nor is its
derivation certain.

Early in Nabonassar's reign trouble once again broke out among the
tribes in Babylonia. Tiglath-Pileser intervened on his behalf,
campaigning extensively in areas nominally under Babylonian control,
demanding tribute from various Chaldaean tribes and even assuming
'kingship' over Aramaean shaikhs in northern Babylonia. Although at
the same time Tiglath-Pileser assumed the ancient title 'King of Sumer
and Akkad', undoubtedly implying suzerainty over Babylonia, he
seems not to have interfered directly with Nabonassar's position in
Babylon, and under the shadow of his Assyrian protector the
Babylonian king appears thereafter to have enjoyed a peaceful and
prosperous reign. On his death, however, trouble broke out once more.
A rebellion in Babylon led to the murder of Nabonassar's son and heir,
and Tiglath-Pileser was again forced to intervene in southern affairs.

The conflict of loyalties within the cities of northern Babylonia at
this time is clearly revealed in a series of letters found in 1952 at the
Assyrian capital Kalhu (Nimrud). These documents tell of intrigue and
conspiracy among pro- and anti-Assyrian factions. One letter reports a
public debate between official representatives of the Assyrian king and
the citizens of Babylon while an official of the Chaldaean usurper
Mukin-zeri stood by. The Babylonians are reminded that their
privileges as citizens are recognized by the Assyrians, to which they
reply that they would submit to the Assyrian monarch if he came in
person, though 'they did not believe the king would come'.[51] This
Tiglath-Pileser proceeded to do, and after a successful campaign in
which many Babylonian cities, and indeed many tribes as well, chose to
side with the Assyrians, Tiglath-Pileser placed Babylonia under
Assyrian administrators. In the New Year ceremony at Babylon in 729
the Assyrian king 'took the hand of Bel' (Marduk). Tiglath-Pileser also
offered sacrifices in a number of major shrines elsewhere in northern
Babylonia, a policy clearly calculated to increase Assyrian popularity.
The period from now until 626 was one of Assyrian supremacy in
Babylonia, but a supremacy plagued by the curious love-hate
relationship which had flowered in reaction to the conflicting demands
of Babylonian cultural dominance and Assyrian military hegemony.

The dual monarchy inaugurated by Tiglath-Pileser III set a
precedent which was followed by most of his successors for the next
century. Yet the 'Babylonian problem' remained unsolved. The
Assyrians expended energy and resources their small country could ill
afford in repeated attempts to control the troublesome southern tribes,
while the Chaldaeans fought alternately among themselves and to
maintain their independence from Assyria. Thus the Chaldaeans, with
Elam to the east ever ready to supply both moral and military support,
came to symbolize the anti-Assyrian movement and became the
unwitting champions of Babylonian nationalism. The citizens of
Babylonia's northern cities preferred peace and security at any cost and
remained strongly pro-Assyrian even in the last years of Assyria's
decline.

5

Assyrians, Babylonians, Persians and Greeks

The year 722 BC saw a significant change in Babylonian fortunes. In the confusion following the death of Tiglath-Pileser's son Shalmaneser V (726–722), a Chaldaean shaikh of the powerful Yakin tribe, a man whom the Assyrians had already recognized as King of the Sealand, seized the throne in Babylon. He was Marduk-apla-iddina II, the first Babylonian mentioned by name in the Bible (as Merodach-Baladan) and the only one to become king on two occasions, according to the traditions preserved in the King-Lists (721–710 and 703).[1] A man of great ability and an astute political leader, Merodach-Baladan is first encountered as one of the Chaldaean rulers who came to terms with Tiglath-Pileser III at the time of the Mukin-zeri rebellion (chapter 4). It is clear that he was regarded by the Assyrians as the most important of the Chaldaean shaikhs and much space in the official annals was devoted to the recital of his submission and the itemizing of his wealthy tribute: expensive gifts of gold, gold ore in quantity ('the dust of his mountains'), precious stones, exotic woods and plants, brightly coloured garments, frankincense, cattle and sheep.[2] Worthy of record also was the fact that he had never before submitted to any Assyrian king. At no point, however, do the Assyrian annals suggest that Merodach-Baladan was either conquered by or made subject to Tiglath-Pileser. Indeed his 'submission' would seem to have been little more than a political stratagem to protect his territory.

A large number of documents have been preserved from the period of Merodach-Baladan's rule in Babylon. These show that he followed tradition in repairing major shrines, that – contrary to Assyrian propaganda – he recognized and respected the hereditary privileges of the ancient cities of Akkad, and that he saw himself as saviour of the country, the agent through whom Marduk defeated the enemies of the Babylonian people. Later tradition reveals him as a collector of exotic garden plants and tells of the functioning of an astronomical observatory in Babylon during his reign. The new king seems initially to have been successful in welding together the previously divided Chaldaean tribes into an anti-Assyrian alliance. At the same time he used the very considerable wealth of the Bit-Yakin to buy the assistance of the Elamite army to campaign against Assyria on Babylon's behalf. Such measures set the tone for Babylonian policy for the next century, though throughout this period many city-dwellers, particularly in Akkad, continued to voice a preference for Assyrian rule and the relative order and prosperity they believed it to ensure.

78

In Assyria the events of 722 also brought to the throne an unusually able and energetic ruler, an apparently minor member of Tiglath-Pileser's family who on his accession assumed the illustrious name of Sargon (Sharru-ken, the 'true or legitimate king'), a choice perhaps as significant of his ambition as of his uncertain ancestry.[3] Sargon campaigned widely throughout the now extensive empire, in Palestine as the Bible tells us, indeed even to the gates of Egypt which for the first time was defeated and forced to pay tribute. In Babylonia, however, the economy seems to have suffered as, despite the efforts of Merodach-Baladan, tribesmen interfered with trade routes and practised various extortions upon the cities. This situation led Sargon to march in 710 against the Chaldaeans whose Elamite allies were then inconveniently preoccupied at home. If the Assyrian account can be believed Merodach-Baladan fled to the marshes where his Sealand territory was overrun and his principal fortress 'burned with fire, devastated, even its foundations torn up'. The cities of northern Babylonia are alleged to have welcomed the Assyrian king, throwing open their gates 'with great rejoicing'. Assyrian governors were appointed throughout Babylonia and, following the custom of Tiglath-Pileser III and Shalmaneser V, Sargon took the hand of Bel and assumed the kingship of Babylon (709–705). It would seem that Merodach-Baladan then made yet another diplomatic submission. At least Sargon appears to have re-instated him as king of the Bit-Yakin.

In 705 Sargon was killed, apparently in battle on the northern frontier, a death rare for a Mesopotamian monarch. His son Sennacherib (704–681) inherited the dual monarchy but the Babylonian problem persisted unsolved. Sennacherib did little to assert his authority in Babylonia and c. 703 an otherwise little-known upstart by the name of Marduk-zakir-shumi II seized the throne. This was too much for Merodach-Baladan, whose loyalty to Sargon did not extend to his son. Yet again the Chaldaean made a bid for power, at the same time apparently attempting to encourage rebellion among Sennacherib's vassals in Palestine in order to divert Assyrian attention westwards, or so the biblical account of the Babylonian mission to Hezekiah, King of Judah, would suggest. Sennacherib marched south nonetheless, defeating Merodach-Baladan's Elamite allies near Cutha in the plain of Kish. Again Merodach-Baladan fled into the marshes while Assyrian troops looted his palace. Sennacherib claims to have captured 75 of the Babylonian king's strong walled cities and 420 smaller towns; 208,000 people are said to have been carried off to Assyria as booty. The Chaldaean tribal areas were left under Assyrian officials and in Babylon Bel-ibni, a Babylonian noble who had been educated at the Assyrian court – according to Sennacherib he had 'grown up like a puppy in my palace' – was installed as king. Hezekiah's rebellion broke out in 701, too late to save Merodach-Baladan.

Bel-ibni (702–700) proved an ineffectual monarch, unable to maintain any semblance of government in Babylonia, and yet again Sennacherib was forced to campaign against the Bit-Yakin. On his way south he paused to subdue a local chieftain, Shuzubu, who seven years later was to reappear on the scene as king in Babylon under his full name Mushezib-Marduk. At the approach of the Assyrian army

78 Black marble boundary-stone of Merodach-Baladan (712 BC). The Babylonian king is shown making a grant of land to the governor of Babylon. Ht 46 cm. Vorderasiatisches Museum, Berlin.

Merodach-Baladan fled by sea, apparently abandoning members of his family but taking with him his national gods and the bones of his ancestors (700 BC). This seemingly bizarre behaviour can perhaps be explained by evidence from the Chronicles which points to a particular Sealand veneration for ancestral bones and concern for their proper care. In the so-called Dynastic Chronicle, the one fact that is faithfully recorded about each of the kings of the second Sealand and Bazi dynasties is his place of burial, while a much later mortuary inscription reveals that the Assyrian king Assur-etel-ilani (626–623) returned the body of one of his officers, a member of the Bit-Yakin, to his tribal territory for burial 'in the house of the fortress'.[4] The eldest son of Sennacherib, Assur-nadin-shumi (699–694), was now installed in Babylon where he ruled in relative peace for six years. Shortly after his accession the aged Merodach-Baladan, who lived in later memory as the most astute tribal champion of Babylonian independence, died.

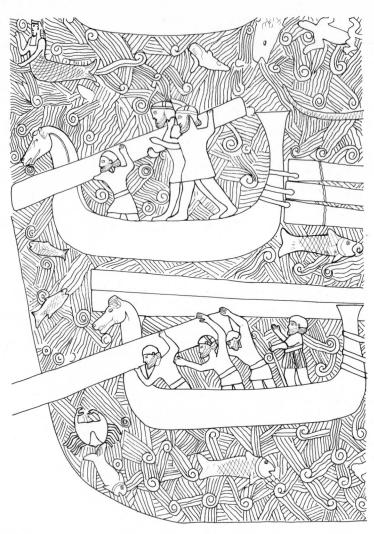

79 Detail from a stone relief from the palace of the Assyrian king Sargon II at Khorsabad (721–705 BC). It shows the transport of timber, destined for Assyria, along the Phoenician coast. Louvre Museum.

Elam continued to be a threat, and Sennacherib now decided upon a direct assault by sea. Syrian craftsmen were brought to Nineveh to construct a great fleet of ships which were then ferried by sailors from Sidon and Tyre down the Tigris to Opis, where they were transferred on rollers some 40–50 km to the Euphrates. Sennacherib's annals record a great storm: 'The mighty waves of the sea came up and entered my tent. They completely surrounded me, causing all of my men to remain in the mighty ships as in cages for five days and nights.' On finally reaching the Gulf the Assyrian king offered sacrifices: 'To Ea, king of the deep, I cast into the sea a golden fish together with a ship of gold.' The assault on Elam was a success and the remaining Bit-Yakin and their gods were taken prisoner. While the Assyrian forces were thus occupied in the south, the Elamites, in a bold raid across the Tigris, captured Sennacherib's son at Sippar; an Elamite puppet, Nergal-ushezib, was set upon the Babylonian throne (694). Within a few

months, however, the latter was taken prisoner near Nippur by the returning Assyrian troops and carried in chains to Assyria. Sennacherib's annals make no further mention of Babylon at this point, and it was now that Mushezib-Marduk, with Aramaean support, seized the throne. The new king and his Elamite allies – paid for with gold taken from the treasury of the Marduk temple – raised a mighty army which marched 'like the onset of locust swarms' against Assyria. Sennacherib met them at Halule, on the Tigris near its confluence with the Diyala. According to the Assyrian annals a terrible slaughter ensued. Sennacherib's troops are said to have killed 150,000 enemy soldiers and among their captives was a son of Merodach-Baladan. The Babylonian Chronicle, however, records an 'Assyrian retreat', and indeed it would seem that the Assyrians, despite their boasts, must have suffered severe losses, if not defeat. At least Sennacherib appears not to have taken further action against Mushezib-Marduk, although a recently published letter shows Babylon again under siege in the following year (690).[5]

In 689 the Elamite king was 'stricken by paralysis and his mouth was so affected that he could not speak'. With this royal stroke Mushezib-Marduk lost a powerful ally. The Chaldaean forces in Babylon held out against the Assyrians for a further nine months, finally succumbing to famine and disease. Exasperated by his difficulties in the south and the loss of his son, Sennacherib now abandoned the long-standing Assyrian

80 Detail from a stone relief from the palace of Assurbanipal at Nineveh (7th century BC) which provides one of the few ancient representations of a ziggurrat. Of particular interest is the 'horned' shrine. The scene is in Elam, city uncertain, although we know that the ziggurrat at Susa had horns of burnished bronze. The drawing is after the 19th-century artist William Boutcher. The original slab was lost in 1854 when a raft carrying a large number of Assyrian sculptures from Baghdad to Basra was sunk by bandits near Qurna.

81 Black basalt memorial stone of Esarhaddon, inscribed with an account of the restoration of the walls and temples of Babylon. At the top of the stone are sculptured the Assyrian 'sacred tree' and a horned crown resting on an altar. In the lower register is one of the clearest representations of a Babylonian plough with seed-drill (cf. ill. 132). Ht 21·5 cm. British Museum.

policy of leniency towards the city they viewed as the cultural capital of the world. The Assyrian king allowed his troops an unrestrained hand in its sacking, and Babylon was systematically destroyed and burned, the rubble thrown into the Euphrates. A deliberate flooding was engineered and the city's 'very foundations were destroyed'.

> I made its destruction more complete than that by a flood, that in days to come the site of that city, and its temples and gods, might not be remembered; I completely blotted it out with floods of water and made it like a meadow.[2]

The statue of Marduk was removed to Assyria, and those statues which Marduk-nadin-ahhe had seized in Ekallate 418 years before were returned to their rightful place.

Sennacherib left Babylon believing he had eliminated forever all thought of competition from the south. He himself assumed the ancient title 'King of Sumer and Akkad', while his son Esarhaddon (Assur-aha-iddina), who was now Crown Prince, was put in charge of the administration in Babylonia. For the next eight years no further trouble ensued, but in 681 Sennacherib was murdered by his sons, possibly in Babylon.[6] Esarhaddon's term as governor had left him with a sympathetic appreciation of Babylonian affairs, and on his accession he adopted a policy of reconciliation. He clearly recognized the futility of his father's destructive policies and, when the omens were shown to be favourable, the rebuilding of Babylon was undertaken on a lavish scale. The ancient rights and privileges of Babylon's citizens were restored

81

and an efficient administration established. Good relations were encouraged by the king's wife, who was a Babylonian, and who, with his mother Zakutu, encouraged in Assyria the worship not only of Marduk but also of his son Nabu, whose cult had enjoyed increasing popularity there since the end of the 9th century. Peace and prosperity reigned, and by 676 Esarhaddon was able to use Babylonia as a base for an expedition far into Persia.

With Babylon secure Esarhaddon now undertook the conquest of Egypt, a kingdom long coveted by the kings of Assyria. Unsuccessful in his first expeditions (675, 674) and remembering his own contested succession, the now aging king decided before setting forth again to invest his son Assurbanipal with full powers. Thus in 672 in a great ceremony at Nineveh Assurbanipal was proclaimed Crown Prince and heir to the Assyrian throne. At the same time the title Crown Prince was given to Assurbanipal's (?twin) brother Shamash-shuma-ukin, this second title being tied to the Babylonian throne. Governors of provinces and vassal rulers were required to take an oath recognizing the settlement and promising, on the death of Esarhaddon, to assist the two brothers to assume their co-equal thrones.[7] In 671 Esarhaddon returned from a spectacular triumph in which Memphis had been captured and Egypt placed under Assyrian administration. Like Ramesses II long before he paused to record his victory by the Dog River near Beirut.

In Egypt the Pharaoh Tarqu (Taharqa) soon retook Memphis. Yet again the aging Esarhaddon set out westwards (669), but this time his good fortune failed him, and he fell sick and died en route. The carefully arranged double succession came into effect, though even in this instance there were threats of rebellion. At the instigation of the 'Queen-Grandmother', Sennacherib's wife Naqia-Zakutu, a formidable and clearly powerful royal lady, all opposition was quelled and the oath of loyalty enforced. The statue of Marduk – removed to Assur by Sennacherib 20 years before and to whom Assurbanipal, rather surprisingly, attributed his safe accession in Assyria[8] – was now returned to Babylon in a great ceremonial procession.

The double monarchy was not a success. Although in theory Shamash-shuma-ukin's kingship was equal to that of Assurbanipal, in practice the Assyrian king maintained a garrison at Nippur loyal to him alone. At the same time other garrisons in the south seem to have felt responsible to him rather than to the king in Babylon; texts from Ur show clearly that the governor there (Sin-balassu-iqbi), though nominally under the jurisdiction of Babylon, was more concerned with courting the favour of Assurbanipal. Many dedications show the Assyrian king to have been active in the restoration even of Babylon itself: one stele, now in the British Museum, depicts the young Assurbanipal as the restorer of Esagila, while another in the same museum records his rebuilding of Ezida, Nabu's shrine in Borsippa; the latter shows him bearing on his head a basket of 'earth' for the moulding of the first brick,[9] a symbolic representation of the royal responsibility for the proper housing and care of the gods which can be traced back at least to the 3rd millennium, an ancient ritual made explicit in Esarhaddon's Esagila inscription:

82

81

I summoned all of my artisans and the people of Karduniash [Babylonia] in their totality. I made them carry the basket and laid the headpad upon them. In choice oil, honey, butter, wine, wine of the shining mountains, I laid its foundation walls. I raised the headpad to my own head and carried it. In brick-mould of ivory, maple, boxwood and mulberry, on which was an inscription, I moulded a brick. Esagila, the temple of the gods, together with its shrines, Babylon . . . I built anew.

Assurbanipal's dedications repeat a pious prayer for Shamash-shuma-ukin – 'may his days be long', but growing friction between the two brothers led in 652 to open revolt. The king in Babylon was joined not only by the usual southern allies, Elam and the persistently anti-Assyrian Chaldaean tribes, but also by 'kings of the Guti, Amurru and Meluhha', tribes in the western desert and even Arabia. After two years of bitter fighting (650) Babylon and Borsippa were besieged. At the same time Assyrian successes to the south and civil war in Elam left Babylon with no effective military support. By 648 all hope for the city had gone and appalling famine compelled surrender. Conditions were so bad that the survivors had been forced to resort to cannibalism and the streets were piled high with corpses. Just before the city surrendered, Shamash-shuma-ukin threw himself into the flames of his own palace, an event remembered in the Greek legend of Sardanapalus. The Assyrians looted what remained of the palace, hunting down and destroying rebel leaders.

As for those men . . . who plotted evil against me, I tore out their tongues and defeated them completely. The others, alive, I smashed with the very same statues of protective deities with which they had smashed my own grandfather Sennacherib – now finally as a belated burial sacrifice for his soul. I fed their corpses, cut into small pieces, to the dogs, pigs, *zibu*-birds, vultures, the birds of the sky and to the fish of the ocean.[6]

The terrible slaughter over, Assurbanipal cleansed and purified the city, and resettled there the survivors of the carnage. A mysterious ruler by the name of Kandalanu now appears as king of Babylon (647–627), but it is generally accepted that this was a throne-name adopted in Babylonia by Assurbanipal himself, who thus reverted to the practice of direct rule and reigned in Babylon until his death.[10]

To the rest of the world the Assyria of the 7th century BC must have seemed invincible. Yet Assyria's resources had been seriously weakened by constant struggles not simply to resolve problems in Babylonia but to maintain control of the far-flung provinces on which this small nation depended for the many luxuries to which it had become accustomed and essential imports such as metal and timber. The invasions of Egypt, though prestigious, had not been born of common sense, while the repetition of campaigns against the powerful kingdom of Urartu and lesser states to the north and west had proved an unacceptable drain on Assyrian manpower and resources. Indeed, this small country had simply overreached itself and within two decades of the death of Assurbanipal the greatest empire the world had then known was no more.

82 (*Opposite*) Sandstone stele commemorating Assurbanipal's rebuilding of Esagila in Babylon. The king carries on his head the basket of earth for the ritual moulding of the first brick. Ht 37 cm. British Museum.

83 Assyrian seal impression
showing a worshipper before
various symbols of the gods
and a temple-tower or
ziggurat. 9th/8th century BC.
Ht 7·2 cm Vorderasiatisches
Museum, Berlin.

Post-Kassite art and architecture

The period from the end of Kassite rule to the collapse of the Assyrian
Empire in 612 BC is in all respects the least documented in Babylonian
history. Virtually no archaeological data have been recovered, though
ill-preserved levels of this period have been excavated at both Ur and
Babylon. New evidence will soon be forthcoming from recently
excavated sites such as Isin, but at the moment even the ordinary
everyday pottery, of which hundreds of thousands of fragments
lie scattered over many Mesopotamian tells, is so little known that the
specific identification of archaeological sites between the Kassite period
and the end of the Assyrian Empire remains impossible. A number of
stone stelae and *kudurru* have survived, especially from Sippar and
71   Babylon, and a variety of attractive small objects have been found in
houses and graves of the period. But in general the archaeological
information available from Babylonia is minimal.

From Assyria, on the other hand, come some of the most impressive
84   monuments of the ancient world. The stone reliefs and colossal winged
animals which adorned Late Assyrian palaces and temples are well
known to most museum-goers, while thanks to the continuing efforts of
the Iraq Directorate-General of Antiquities, who are today excavating
and restoring the gates and palaces of Nineveh and Nimrud, many of
these massive monuments can now be seen in their original splendour.
Indeed the major sources for the political history of Babylon at this
time come not from Babylonia but from the Assyrian royal annals
carved upon these stone monuments and from cuneiform documents
recovered in the excavation of the Assyrian royal cities. This has led
inevitably to the viewing of the events of this time with an Assyrian
bias. Before the 8th century official Babylonian records exhibit a
profound lack of interest in most military and political events, and
rarely, even in later periods, do they provide the wealth of detail found

in the Assyrian annals and illuminated by the extraordinary narrative reliefs.

Assurbanipal left a further and perhaps more important legacy to the modern world. A library, collected at Nineveh under his personal direction and discovered there by British excavators in 1853, has provided modern scholars with undoubtedly the world's single most important collection of cuneiform tablets. Copies of a number of literary masterpieces, including the Epic of Gilgamesh and the Creation Epic, the 'Babylonian Genesis', were among the enormous number of texts found. Assurbanipal was that rare phenomenon, a 'scholar-king', though the level of his literacy may perhaps be questioned. At a time when few but the scribes could read or write he took great pride in his academic accomplishments. In a famous inscription he tells of his school-days when he learned 'the hidden treasure of all scribal knowledge. I solve complex mathematical reciprocals and products with no apparent solution; I read abstruse tablets whose Sumerian is obscure and whose Akkadian is hard to construe . . .' He was instructed also in archery, the javelin, chariot-driving and 'royal decorum'.[11]

84 Very few pieces of stone carving in relief are known from the Neo-Babylonian period, by contrast with Assyria where large numbers of stone reliefs have survived. This unfinished fragment of unknown provenance is probably Babylonian in origin and depicts the goddess Ishtar on her lion. Ht 40 cm. Metropolitan Museum of Art, New York.

85 85 Babylon's only well-preserved surviving monument is the famous Ishtar Gate, built by Nebuchadrezzar II (604–562), which leads through the inner town wall beside the royal palace. Only the earliest unglazed part of the structure, later filled in, can now be seen at the site. It is ornamented with bulls and dragons in brick relief.

Although inscriptions show that both Assurbanipal and his father undertook extensive building programmes at Babylon, little has yet been found of the great city of which they were the patrons. At Ur, however, Woolley did recover evidence of the work of the pro-Assyrian governor Sin-balassu-iqbi who rebuilt the public monuments of that city on a scale grander than at any time since Kurigalzu. Like Assurbanipal Sin-balassu-iqbi took an interest in ancient texts; he had his own building inscriptions written in ancient Sumerian and a copy, dated to his time as governor, of a text of the Ur III king Amar-Sin was apparently designed for display in a temple museum.[12]

Babylonian cultural dominance persisted even at the peak of Assyrian power. At both Nimrud and Khorsabad, a new capital built by Sargon northeast of Nineveh, the largest temple was dedicated to the god Nabu, the son of Marduk, whose worship had been popularized in Assyria by Semiramis and her son Adad-nirari III. Sargon's new capital boasted too a free-standing ziggurat as in Babylonia, while the Nabu temple façade was decorated not in the Assyrian style but with individual motifs in the Babylonian fashion, recalling the later friezes on the famous Ishtar Gate in Babylon itself.

The Neo-Babylonian Dynasty

Although under Kandalanu metropolitan Babylonia was politically unimportant, the Chaldaeans remained strong and after the death of Assurbanipal yet another Chaldaean shaikh seized the throne. With Assyrian power nearing the point of collapse this new king, Nabopolassar (Nabu-apla-usur, 625–605), was to succeed where

Merodach-Baladan had failed in establishing the wealthy and politically astute Chaldaeans not only as successors to the Assyrians but briefly as the principal political power in Western Asia. With the accession of Nabopolassar was founded a new dynasty, generally known to modern scholars as Neo-Babylonian or 'Chaldaean', under which Babylon was to achieve its greatest fame.

Nabopolassar's path to power, however, was far from smooth. On the death of Assurbanipal (627) fighting had broken out between contending factions in both Babylonia and Assyria. In Babylon the struggle for control went on for over a year, during which time no king was recognized. According to the Neo-Babylonian Chronicle Nabopolassar finally seized the throne in November 626, but his early years as king were disrupted by the continuing struggle with Assyria. The course of affairs in Babylon at this time is confused and the surviving sources often contradictory. Assyria succeeded in maintaining control of the Nippur garrison throughout most of the early years of Nabopolassar's reign, and two Assyrians, a general Sin-shumu-lishir and the penultimate king Sin-sharra-ishkun, were both briefly recognized in Babylon (?623–622).[13] Several archives attest long sieges, in particular at Nippur and Uruk; indeed in 620 the inhabitants of Nippur were reduced to selling their children in order to buy food. Contemporary letters reveal that during this unstable period control in various Babylonian cities passed from one party to another as much by political coup as by military action.[14]

By 616 Nabopolassar's position was more secure, and his army marched up the Euphrates into territory long under Assyrian control. Although less than 50 years had passed since Assurbanipal's sack of Thebes, such was the new Babylonian threat that Egypt now joined her former enemy in an alliance, of which the immediate effect was the withdrawal of Nabopolassar to Babylon. In 615 the Babylonian king made a bold attack upon the ancient capital, Assur, but was again forced to withdraw southwards, taking refuge in Tikrit where he was besieged by the Assyrian army. A new power now entered the Mesopotamian scene, the Medes, heirs to Elamite power in western Iran. Originally but one of a number of associated yet separate Indo-European tribes, they had been welded into a single kingdom by an able ruler, Huvakshatra, known to Herodotus as Cyaxares. In 614 Cyaxares marched on Nineveh; Nimrud was sacked, the walls of Assur breached and that city captured and looted. Nabopolassar, wishing to be in at the kill, marched north, but failed to arrive until after Assur had fallen. Near the ruined city he and Cyaxares met. A formal treaty was drawn up and ratified, so later tradition tells us, by a marriage between Nebuchadrezzar, Nabopolassar's son, and Amyitis, a granddaughter of the Median king.

It is clear that the Assyrians had no foreboding of disaster; in 613 they again took the offensive, marching south against the Babylonians who were occupied at home with yet another tribal revolt. The extent of their confidence is revealed by the fact that at this time the defences of Nimrud, damaged in the Median attack of 614, had been dismantled for repair.[15] In 612 a coalition of Babylonians, Medes and Scythians laid siege to Nineveh. After three months the city fell; Sin-sharra-ishkun is said to have perished in the burning city, further fuel to the Sardanapalus legend. At this single blow the great empire of Assyria collapsed, never to revive.

A nominal Assyrian kingdom survived briefly in Harran, in southern Turkey, but Harran too soon fell to the Babylonians who established a garrison there (610). Nabopolassar now undertook several campaigns into the hill country north of Assyria, while the last Assyrian king (Assur-uballit II, 611–609) fled southwards to await his Egyptian allies, who now constituted Babylon's main opposition. Under Pharaoh Necho II Egyptian troops marched into Syria, having defeated the small army of Josiah at Megiddo (*c.* 608), and joined the remnants of the Assyrian army at Carchemish. In the spring of 605 the Crown Prince Nebuchadrezzar attacked. The slaughter was heavy on both sides ('for the mighty man hath stumbled against the mighty, and they are fallen both of them together,' Jeremiah 46, 12), but the Egyptians were decisively defeated, their troops bolting in disorder, pursued through Syria by the Babylonian army. This victorious chase was cut short, however, by the death of Nabopolassar. Nebuchadrezzar and a few supporters hastened to Babylon to claim the throne, a moment which marks the beginning of the most illustrious reign in Babylon's history. Carchemish saw the direct confrontation of the two remaining great powers, Egypt and Babylon. Babylon's victory was decisive, and in the struggle Assyria disappeared without trace.

Nebuchadrezzar

Nebuchadrezzar (Nabu-kudurri-usur, 604–562) needs no introduction as one of the most famous figures in ancient history. A statesman and general of exceptional talents, he was also a builder of ambition and imagination whose surviving monuments are without rival in Mesopotamia. The Babylon of Herodotus, indeed that seen by the modern visitor today – if he can exercise his imagination over and above the depressing mounds of ruined brick – is largely the work of Nebuchadrezzar's architects. This Babylonian king is perhaps best known from biblical accounts, though his campaigns against Jerusalem were of only minor importance in the wider arena of Middle Eastern affairs. After his accession Nebuchadrezzar moved into Syria for a lengthy campaign which was little more than an unopposed display of military might, designed no doubt to facilitate the collection of tribute. Beating the bounds of the empire was to become an annual event, not only for the collection of tax and tribute but for the punishment of recalcitrant towns or territories. In this the Babylonian was emulating a highly successful Assyrian policy. At this time Jehoiakim, King of Judah, made a voluntary submission to Nebuchadrezzar and a number of Jews, probably including the prophet Daniel, were taken as hostages to Babylon.

In 601 Nebuchadrezzar marched against Egypt, but both sides incurred heavy losses in a battle somewhere near the Egyptian frontier; Nebuchadrezzar was forced to withdraw to Babylon and re-equip his army, while Necho made no further attempt to advance into Syria. However, the news of Babylonian losses was sufficient to encourage

86

Jehoiakim, undeterred by the warnings of Jeremiah, to stop payment of tribute to Babylon and return his allegiance to Egypt. Events were to prove Jeremiah the wiser man, and in 597 Nebuchadrezzar sent troops to besiege Jerusalem. Jehoiakim died, perhaps in the siege but certainly before the main Babylonian army arrived,[16] and his son Jehoiachin, together with his family, leading state and military officials, craftsmen and troops, were taken captive to Babylon. Hebrew records place the total number of captives at this time at 10,000.[17] Jerusalem was spared, but 'heavy tribute' was taken, including treasure from Solomon's temple and the royal palace. An uncle of Jehoiachin, his name changed to Zedekiah, was appointed to rule over the surviving population. The Jewish exiles were settled in Babylonia. Jehoiachin and his family were detained in the palace at Babylon, where tablets recording the rations issued to them have been found.[18] Some, like the prophet Ezekiel, were settled in the region of Nippur.

Despite Nebuchadrezzar's popularity with later generations of Babylonians, the Chaldaean claim to the Babylonian throne seems still to have been contested. In his tenth year (595) there was a serious rebellion which appears to have been suppressed only after the slaughter of many of his troops. Meanwhile, renewed Egyptian activity in Palestine persuaded Zedekiah to change sides. Nebuchadrezzar reacted strongly and dispatched a powerful army westwards. The Egyptians quickly abandoned their erstwhile vassals; Lachish and a number of other towns were recovered by the Babylonians, who then

86 General view of Nebuchadrezzar's Southern Palace at Babylon, looking northeast towards the 'Hanging Gardens' and the Processional Way, taken after excavation by the Deutsche Orient-Gesellschaft and before its recent restoration by the Directorate-General of Antiquities, Baghdad.

87, 88 Contest scenes are common on Neo-Babylonian seals. An earlier group often show a winged hero attacking an animal or monster. (*Above*) Carnelian seal, ht 3·9 cm, now in the Pierpont Morgan Library, New York; the inscription contains a prayer to Nabu for the life of the owner. (*Opposite*) On later seals a symmetrical group is often shown, with a winged hero grasping two beasts. Ht 3·2 cm. Vorderasiatisches Museum, Berlin.

laid siege to Jerusalem. After 18 months, with severe famine rampant in the city, the Babylonians breached the walls (586). Zedekiah escaped but was captured near Jericho and brought to Nebuchadrezzar's headquarters on the Orontes in Syria. There his sons were killed before his eyes, and he himself was blinded and taken captive to Babylon. Jerusalem was looted, its walls dismantled and the temple and palace burned to the ground. The leaders of the anti-Babylonian faction were executed, and a large portion of the surviving population deported to Babylonia.

Nebuchadrezzar seems to have maintained friendly relations with the Medes, as there is little mention of trouble on the eastern frontier. Cyaxares had overrun Urartu and pushed westwards into Asia Minor towards the kingdom of Lydia, a flourishing centre of trade which had grown considerably in importance with the elimination of Assyria. The bitter struggle between these two states ended in the famous battle interrupted by an eclipse (28 May 585), after which an armistice was agreed. According to Herodotus (I, 74) the mediator who represented the Medes in this settlement was the Babylonian Labynetus, possibly Nabonidus, one of Nebuchadrezzar's generals who was later to succeed to the throne. Although Babylonian relations with the Medes continued ostensibly to be friendly, before the end of his reign Nebuchadrezzar must have become suspicious of Median intentions. A great defensive wall was built north of Babylon which ran from Sippar to Opis, the famous Median Wall, designed to keep out barbarian tribes and to make attack from the north more difficult.[19]

Unfortunately almost no historical information survives concerning the latter part of Nebuchadrezzar's reign. The Book of Kings speaks of the murder, possibly at the instigation of Egypt, of the Babylonian-appointed governor of Jerusalem, and a fragmentary text indicates an

invasion of Egypt by the Babylonian king, but no details are known.[20] Nebuchadrezzar died in 562 and was succeeded by his son Amel-Marduk (Evil-Merodach), of whom little is known beyond his unpopularity in Babylon. Berossus says of him that he was restrained neither by law nor by decency. In his favour it can be said that he treated kindly the exiled Jehoiachin of Judah, who was released from prison and for the remainder of his life dined at the king's table. After a brief reign Amel-Marduk was killed in a revolution. His successor was Nergal-sharra-usur (559–556) (biblical Neriglissar), an experienced Babylonian general who had held the high military office of *rab mag* at the siege of Jerusalem, and had married a daughter of Nebuchadrezzar. Little is known of his reign beyond his restoration of temples in Babylon and Borsippa; in addition a single chronicle text gives details of a campaign in Cilicia[21] which shows that he must have pursued an active military policy. He died in 556, in circumstances which are obscure. His young son Labashi-Marduk attempted to assume the throne but found widespread opposition. A rebellion of the chief officers of state brought about his removal after only three months and placed on the throne Nabu-na'id (Nabonidus).

Nabonidus

Nabonidus (555–539) is often regarded as little more than an aging antiquarian. Certainly his concern with the past and with the restoration of the proper rituals and embellishments of the ancient shrines of Sumer and Akkad bordered on the obsessive, yet this king was probably the distinguished general who negotiated the peace between Lydia and the Medes some 30 years before his accession (above), while the chronicle of his early years records an effective

89 Baked-clay cylinder with a long cuneiform inscription of Nabonidus (555-539) in which is recorded his famous dream concerning the restoration of the temple of the moon-god in Harran. Nabonidus also describes how he rebuilt the temple of the sun-god at Sippar, finding during the course of his work an inscription of Naram-Sin of Agade, the original founder of the temple. 15·6 × 9·2 cm. British Museum.

military policy. The new ruler was not of the family of Nebuchadrez-zar: 'I am Nabonidus who have not the honour of being a somebody – kingship is not within me.' His mother was Adda-Guppi, a long-lived votaress of the god Sin at Harran. Her biography is known from a stele found in 1956 preserved as a paving stone, inscription side down, in the Great Mosque at Harran.[22] Her career would be quite extraordinary even in modern times: not only did she survive four reigning monarchs in Assyria but her life encompassed the whole of the Neo-Babylonian Dynasty down to the 9th year of its last king, her son, when she died at the ripe old age of 104.

Harran had long been an important commercial and religious centre and was, as we remember, the final seat of Assyrian power; indeed there is some reason to suppose that Adda-Guppi's position derived from her relationship to the Assyrian royal family. One of Nabonidus' early acts was to begin the restoration of his mother's temple, which had been destroyed in the sack of Harran by the Medes and Babylonians and was, apparently, still in Median hands. An interesting text records a dream 89 in which Marduk instructed the new king to undertake the work at Harran:

> At the beginning of my reign the gods let me see a dream: in it there stood both Marduk, the Great Lord, and Sin, the light of heaven and earth. Marduk said to me: 'Nabonidus, King of Babylon, bring bricks on your own horse and chariot and build the temple of Ehulhul [the moon-god's shrine, lit. 'the house of joy'] that Sin, the Great Lord, may take up his dwelling there.' I replied to Marduk, the chief of the gods, 'The *Umman-manda* [barbarian hordes, in this instance the Medes] are laying siege to the very temple you have ordered me to build and their armed might is very great.' But Marduk said to me, 'The *Umman-manda* of whom you spoke, they, and their country and all the kings who march at their side, shall cease to exist!' And indeed, when the third year came to pass, Marduk made rise against them Cyrus, King of Anshan, his young servant, and Cyrus scattered the numerous *Umman-manda* with his

small army and captured Astyages, King of the *Umman-manda* and brought him in fetters into his [Cyrus'] land. That was the doing of the Great Lord Marduk, whose command cannot be changed.[23]

Nabonidus' restoration of Ehulhul may have been motivated solely by filial piety, but his increasing devotion to the god Sin – the dream references to Marduk were obvious propaganda for Babylonian consumption and are totally absent from the local Harran inscriptions – constituted a religious innovation which proved exceedingly unpopular with conservative elements in Babylonia, an unpopularity which the 'young servant' of the dream text was later to exploit. The Harran inscription records rebellion in Akkad:

The sons of Babylon, Borsippa, Nippur, Ur, Uruk, Larsa, priests and people of the capitals of Akkad, against his great divinity offended . . . they forgot their duty, whenever they talked it was treason and not loyalty, like a dog they devoured one another; fever and famine in the midst of them . . .

Clearly Nabonidus' religious and administrative reforms provoked great resentment, while the wars and extensive building programmes of his predecessors had proved a severe burden on the country's resources. Large numbers of economic texts reveal severe inflation, a situation now made worse by the spread of plague. Between 560 and 550 prices rose by up to 50%, and from 560 to 485 the total increase amounted to some 200%.[24]

Nabonidus now made an extraordinary move that has yet to be satisfactorily explained. Installing his son Bel-shar-usur (Belshazzar) as regent in Babylon, he led an army through Syria and Lebanon and finally on to the oasis of Taima in northwest Arabia where he was to remain for the next ten years.

But I hied myself afar from my city of Babylon . . .
ten years to my city Babylon I went not in.[25]

Despite the king's unpopularity in Babylon, his departure seems to have been voluntary. A number of motives for this seemingly inexplicable behaviour have been put forward, but none has proved entirely convincing. Perhaps Nabonidus feared the growing power of Persia, perhaps he was driven by his preoccupation with religious reform and the disgust, expressed in his dedications, at what he considered the impiety and lawlessness of his subjects. A passage in the Harran inscription implies divine direction – perhaps another 'dream' – 'in ten years arrived the appointed time, the days were fulfilled which Sin, king of the gods, had spoken'. The verses in the Book of Daniel (4, 28–33) which attribute to Nebuchadrezzar a period of madness are clearly a corruption of the stories about Nabonidus; indeed a fragment from the recently discovered Qumran scrolls shows that other Jewish traditions assigned this long sojourn in the desert to the correct Babylonian king, ascribing to him a seven-year illness brought on by divine wrath.[26]

It is possible that Nabonidus' motives were saner than Babylonian tradition later recognized. At Taima met caravan routes from

Damascus, Sheba, the Arabian Gulf and Egypt: the city was a natural centre for Arabian trade, and the acquisition of a new trading empire in southern Arabia would have been an achievement worthy of a king who saw himself in the mould of Nebuchadrezzar. Yet to impute such a motive to the now aging Nabonidus is certainly to exceed extant evidence. One fact is certain; Nabonidus cannot have hoped to increase his popularity in Babylon by a prolonged absence during which the New Year Festival could not take place.

The reasons for the king's return to Babylon are as obscure as those which led to his departure. After 10 years, and now certainly approaching 70 years of age, he left Taima. The work at Harran was completed and that city survived for many centuries as a centre of the worship of the moon-god whose crescent symbol still appeared on Roman coins minted there down to the 3rd century AD. Yet for Babylon the writing was on the wall. While the Babylonian king was 'weighed in the balance and found wanting', the young servant of Nabonidus' dream was engaged in the conquest of an empire that was soon to exceed even the greatest aspirations of the Babylonians. This young servant was Cyrus, a Persian of the royal line of Achaemenes, the 7th-century founder of the dynasty known by his name and to whom by tradition the modern Iranian royal house traces its authority.

The Persians were an Indo-European tribe who settled in the territory of ancient Elam, their name deriving from Parsua (modern Fars), one of their first strongholds. One of their princes Cambyses had married the daughter of the Median king Astyages, perhaps a recognition by the latter of the rising strength of the Persians. Of this union was born Cyrus who was to become the subject of legends recorded by Herodotus and reminiscent of those circulated about the Akkadian Sargon. One well-known story relates Astyages' dream of the spreading vine, which was interpreted to signify that the child then carried by his daughter Mandane was destined to rule all Asia. Fearful for himself Astyages ordered the death of the newborn child, but his kinsman Harpagus handed the baby to a shepherd who substituted for it his own wife's still-born son. Ultimately the fraud was discovered by the dramatic if apocryphal story of the young Cyrus playing at being king. Astyages relented and Cyrus became his 'young servant', presently to revolt successfully with Harpagus against his grandfather (c. 550). According to the Babylonian Chronicle the Median army rebelled against Astyages and handed him over to Cyrus who was welcomed in the capital Ecbatana (modern Hamadan) as the new and rightful king.

In 547 Cyrus crossed the Tigris and led his army westwards across the Khabur River and into Asia Minor. An indecisive battle was fought against Croesus of Lydia at the Halys. Croesus returned to his capital Sardis, and called on both Nabonidus and the Egyptians for aid. Needless to say there was no response from Taima. In an immediate and unexpected attack Cyrus took Sardis and Lydia was made into a Persian province, Cyrus now also gaining the support of the Greek colonies in Asia Minor. Cyrus was busy too with a blatant propaganda campaign throughout the Babylonian Empire, winning support for what were presented as his liberal policies. The Greek historians tell us that he treated Croesus with kindness and respect, and certainly his generosity in his treatment of local priests in Asia Minor won him a reputation for clemency and religious tolerance. This deliberate propaganda, no doubt accompanied by more monetary methods of persuasion, seems to have been successful in Babylon too; when that city finally fell, Cyrus is said to have been hailed as a liberator, freeing the people from the tyranny of Nabonidus. To be fair, however, it must be remembered that the Greek accounts are based on Persian sources, which all betray an understandable bias against Nabonidus.

In 539 the New Year Festival was celebrated in Babylon, apparently for the first time since Nabonidus' retirement to Taima; the Persian account ascribes to the Babylonian king various sacrilegious actions during the festival.[27] During the ceremony a plentiful supply of wine was distributed, and to judge from the accounts of Herodotus, Xenophon and the author of the Book of Daniel, not only were the revels prolonged but the memory of them remained fresh for many years. Already, however, Cyrus was advancing on Babylonia. Nabonidus ordered the collection of the country's gods in Babylon to secure their protection, but the Persian king's propaganda had accomplished its purpose and the measure raised much local opposition, Borsippa, Cutha and Sippar refusing to comply. In the month of Tishri Cyrus successfully assaulted Opis on the Tigris and then marched on Sippar which was taken without opposition. Nabonidus fled, and two days later 'Ugbaru, governor of the Guti, and the army of Cyrus entered Babylon without a battle.'[28] Herodotus attributes the uncontested fall of the city to the diverting of the Euphrates into the depression near Aqar Quf, thereby permitting the Persian troops to enter the city along the river bed. There is no particular reason to doubt this story, although it may refer to the altering of the course of the Tigris for the assault on Opis. It seems certain, however, that the Babylonians put up no effective resistance:

> As it was, the Persians came upon them by surprise and so took the city. Owing to the vast size of the place, the inhabitants of the central parts, as the residents of Babylon declare, long after the outer portions of the town were taken, knew nothing of what had chanced, but as they were engaged in a festival, continued dancing and revelling until they learnt the capture but too certainly. (Herodotus I, 191)

It would appear that Cyrus' liberal religious views were welcomed after the discontent aroused by the heresies of Nabonidus. Indeed an inscription of Cyrus from Babylon relates how Marduk, whom Nabonidus had neglected, marched with him and his army 'as a friend and companion'.[29] Nabonidus was later captured in Babylon where, according to Xenophon, he was killed. Cyrus entered Babylon in triumph, forbade looting and appointed a Persian governor, leaving undisturbed the religious institutions and civil administration. Thus came to an end the last native dynasty to rule the city. At the beginning of the following year Cambyses appears to have represented his father in the New Year ceremonies, legitimizing the new Persian rule.

The Persians in Babylon

90, 91 Large numbers of
carved ivories have survived
from 8th/7th century Assyria,
but very few are known from
contemporary Babylon. This
rare and very attractive small
head was found at Babylon in
a richly furnished child's
grave, probably of
Achaemenid date. Ht 3·5 cm.
Vorderasiatisches Museum,
Berlin.

Before the time of Cyrus Babylon had seen many foreign dynasties
come and go, and had in turn successfully assimilated each of them.
Now, however, new forces were at work in the Middle East and new
religious and political ideas were gradually replacing those of ancient
Mesopotamia. Social institutions were also changing, and even the
system of writing, long a unifying force, was being superseded by the
more efficient Aramaic alphabet of only 22 letters. Cuneiform
continued to be employed, however, especially for religious and
astronomical treatises; a number of the latter are known from as late as
the 1st century AD. Cuneiform also remained in use for at least some
economic documents, and we have numerous records in this script of
prosperous merchants and 'banking houses' in Babylon and Nippur.[30]
Indeed on the surface the private lives of Babylonian citizens appear to
have changed very little under Persian rule. Religious forms were
preserved and commercial activity prospered.

Cyrus offered peace and friendship to all, and compensated those
who had suffered under Nabonidus, or so he tells us. Simultaneously a
campaign was instituted to blacken the name and reputation of the last
Babylonian king. Wherever he went Cyrus called on the support of the
local gods, a policy which proved highly successful. Equally acceptable,
apparently, was the new Persian administration. For the most part local
officials were retained in office, but governors known as satraps were
installed in the various provinces. Their power was effectively
restrained by holding the treasurer and garrison commander in each
capital city responsible solely to the king, a system which had been tried

92 Seals of the Persian period often reveal in their style and ornament the widespread Persian contacts with Egypt and the eastern Mediterranean, seen here in the falcon and the Wedjat eye (border), symbols of the Egyptian god Horus and, interestingly, of Kingship. Ht 2·6 cm. British Museum.

93 Impression of a chalcedony cylinder seal showing a king and a lion, and a hero and an ibex, an Achaemenid version of the well-known Mesopotamian 'contest scene'. Ht 4·8 cm. British Museum.

94 Stamp seals are found in prehistoric Mesopotamia and return to popularity in the Neo-Babylonian and Persian periods. This impression is of an Achaemenid rock crystal seal. 2·0 × 1·5 cm. Fitzwilliam Museum, Cambridge.

with success in Babylonia as early as the 3rd millennium. There was, moreover, an annual visit of the royal inspector, the notorious 'King's Eye'.

Cyrus was killed in battle in 530, and his body brought back to Pasargadae, near Persepolis, for burial in the tomb still to be seen there. Cambyses II (529–522), who succeeded his father, added Egypt to the Persian Empire, which now surpassed any the world had yet seen. Events in Babylon, however, were far from peaceful and in a series of local coups and revolts two spurious 'Nebuchadrezzars' briefly claimed the throne. Order was eventually restored by Darius (521–486) who completed the organization of the empire into 20 satrapies, imposed a uniform system of law throughout and created a carefully maintained road system. Darius undertook an extensive building programme including the construction of the new capital at Persepolis and the digging of a canal from the Nile to the Red Sea. The closing years of his reign saw the outbreak of the Graeco-Persian wars, with the Persians suffering defeat at Marathon (490).

In Babylon trade and commerce continued unimpaired, but rapidly rising prices and increased government interference suggest an unstable economy. Darius was accustomed to winter in Babylon and when Xerxes was designated his heir and successor, the king made his son his personal representative in the ancient city. Darius now directed the building of a new palace there (of which a columned hall with glazed brick ornament was excavated in the early years of this century) and installed Xerxes in it. When Darius died, Babylon loyally accepted the new king who had resided in the city so long as Crown Prince. Under Xerxes (485–465) the famous repetition of his father's unsuccessful expedition to Greece took place, culminating in Thermopylae and Salamis (480), the Babylonians making their contribution in the form of detachments of troops as well as heavy taxes. Indeed, a series of repressive measures directed against Babylon by the Great King had served to inflame the ever-present rebellious elements. The facts are not altogether clear, but it would seem that in a series of revolts at least two local usurpers were proclaimed (482). Classical authors describe Xerxes' capture of the rebellious city after several months' siege, and state that it was then sacked, its fortifications demolished; the great temple of Marduk and others were burnt to the ground and the statue of Marduk carried away as a spoil of war. Xerxes dealt severely with the Babylonians: the satrapy was abolished and incorporated with that of Assyria, the portions to the west being made into a separate unit. Great estates were confiscated and handed over to the Persians, and henceforth the country was ferociously taxed.

In 465 Xerxes was assassinated and succeeded by his younger son, Artaxerxes (464–424), who seems to have held a more sympathetic attitude towards Babylon. To the priests of Marduk he restored their lands and their position, but it is doubtful whether much of their temple was standing at this time. However, the detailed descriptions of Herodotus (*c.* 450) show that despite its harsh treatment, the city was far from destroyed. Herodotus gives too some indication of the tax burdens now supported by Babylon, by far the highest of any province in the empire. Thirty tons of silver a year together with the 'gift' of 500 boys to be made eunuchs are said to have been exacted, over and above the duty of provisioning the Persian army and court for four months each year. The daily collection to cover satrapal expenses is said to have been sufficient to fill a 13-gallon jar with silver, while four villages were exempted from taxation in exchange for feeding and looking after the satrap's large number of hunting dogs. The result of these policies was an increasing scarcity of silver and severe inflation.

The period after the death of Artaxerxes I was marked by further contested successions and intrigues in Babylonia, culminating in the march of his grandson Cyrus the Younger with a force of 13,000 Greek mercenaries from Asia Minor, where he was satrap, down the Euphrates against his elder brother Artaxerxes II. The two brothers met at Cunaxa, not far from Babylon (401), but Cyrus was killed at the moment of victory. The story of the return march of the surviving 10,000 Greeks to the Black Sea is well known from Xenophon's famous account. With an adroit use of gold Artaxerxes II nearly achieved in Greece what his predecessors had failed to accomplish by force, but just as the world seemed quiet under a Persian-imposed peace, the lands west of the Euphrates again revolted. At the same time in Macedonia a new power was emerging that was soon briefly to create an empire even greater than that of the Achaemenid Persians.

In 331 Alexander, having made himself master of the entire eastern Mediterranean, including Egypt, set forth to do battle with the Persians, led by Darius III (335–331). Advancing with 7000 cavalry and 30,000 infantry Alexander crossed the Euphrates at Thapsacus, on two pontoon bridges. Darius, expecting the Macedonian to follow the obvious course down river to Babylon, stationed his troops beyond the upper Tigris whence he could cut off Alexander's line of supply. Alexander outwitted him, however, and moved eastwards, crossing the Tigris unopposed above Nineveh. Darius now drew his battle lines at Gaugamela, modern Keramlais, not far east of the Assyrian capital, where the plain had been levelled to permit the Persian chariots to manoeuvre freely. The ensuing struggle was Alexander's, and Darius fled ignominiously, thus bringing to an end the greatest and most efficient imperial organization the ancient world had then known.

Babylon under Macedonian rule

Alexander received a warm welcome from the citizens of Babylon, who were rewarded with an order for the restoration of Esagila. The new king resolved to make Babylon his eastern capital, and lingered there a month before proceeding east to Persepolis and thence on his well-known campaigns to Bactria and India. In 324 Alexander's great friend Hephaestion died in Ecbatana. A funeral pyre was prepared in his honour at Babylon, at a cost of 10,000 talents; part of the city wall east of the royal palace was demolished to provide rubble for the platform. The remains of the latter with its scorched and reddened surface still discernible were discovered by Robert Koldewey, who excavated at Babylon early in this century.

In the spring of 323 Alexander returned to Babylon amidst a number of disquieting signs and omens. A passage from Plutarch illuminates too the confrontation of Greek and Oriental thought that was one of the major consequences of Alexander's conquest:

> And one day after he had undressed himself to be anointed, and was playing at ball, just as they were going to bring his clothes again, the young men who played with him perceived a man clad in the king's robes with a diadem upon his head, sitting silently upon his throne. They asked him who he was, to which he gave no answer a good while till at last coming to himself, he told them his name was Dionysius, that he was of Messenia, that for some crime of which he was accused he was brought thither from the seaside, and had been kept long in prison, that Serapis appeared to him, had freed him from his chains, conducted him to that place, and commanded him to put on the king's robe and diadem, and to sit where they found him, and to say nothing. Alexander, when he heard this, by the direction of his soothsayers, put the fellow to death, but he lost his spirits, and grew diffident of the protection and assistance of the gods, and suspicious of his friends.

It is clear that what the young ball players had blundered into was the ancient Mesopotamian ritual of the substitute king, enthroned when the omens foretold danger to the true king, a custom apparently still fully alive at the time.[31]

The work of clearing the site of Esagila had not proceeded far but was now taken up again in earnest. Strabo says that it took 10,000 workmen two months to clear the rubble; this was deposited near the site of Hephaestion's pyre, where it too was found by Koldewey. On 2 June 323, just before he was due to leave on his projected Arabian expedition, Alexander fell ill, and on 13 June he died, at the age of only 32. Babylon, which had looked like regaining its former greatness under his rule, was now to suffer under his squabbling successors. Indeed the conflicts among his generals, the Diadochi ('Successors'), were finally to result in the creation of two new empires, that of the Ptolemies in Egypt and of the Seleucids in Asia Minor. The events of these years are recorded in a very fragmentary Babylonian chronicle in which there is a reference to 'weeping and mourning in the land' and 'the plundering of the city and the countryside'. In 312 Seleucus, a former satrap of Babylon, gained control of the Asian province, returned to Babylon and seized the citadel. Although the fate of Babylon was to be contested yet again Seleucus obviously considered the events of 312 crucial in his bid for power. His 'official reign' begins in the autumn of that year, which was subsequently taken to mark the advent of the Seleucid era and of a chronological system that is to this day employed in Western Asia. His successors continued to rule in Syria until Pompey made it a Roman province in 64 BC.

Hellenistic Babylon

By this time the city of Babylon had suffered severe physical damage, first at the hands of Xerxes, and then in the struggle for its control among Alexander's generals. The victorious Seleucus took a decision that was to have far-reaching effects. This was to found a new city,

95 Many objects of the Hellenistic and Parthian periods were recovered from the upper levels excavated in Merkes, the central residential area of Babylon. Among them was this green glazed rhyton or drinking vessel in the shape of a calf's head. Length 36 cm. Vorderasiatisches Museum, Berlin.

Seleucia-on-the-Tigris, about 90 km to the north of Babylon, on a site already occupied at least in Neo-Babylonian and Achaemenid times and thought by some to have been the ancient port of Opis. It is possible that this decision was made simply in order to rehouse the homeless inhabitants of Babylon, but Seleucus may equally have been persuaded by economic considerations, the Tigris providing better access to the Arabian Gulf and thence India than the Euphrates. Although it is unlikely that this was a deliberate move to reduce Babylon's prestige, it was to have this effect, and the Babylonians cannot have reacted favourably to the increasing desolation and isolation of their once-great capital.

Under Seleucus' successor Antiochus I (281–261) Seleucia officially became the Royal City (c. 275), and the civilian population of Babylon was ordered to move there. By these two decrees Antiochus effected the end of Babylon's civil existence. At the same time he ordered the rebuilding of Esagila, thus providing the Babylonians with a sacred centre and rallying point which was to survive until the 1st century BC. His motives in this are unfortunately not clear: perhaps it was a kind of compensation, possibly he possessed a true sense of history, or perhaps no Babylonian ruler could afford to ignore Marduk. Ezida, the temple of Nabu, the second great Babylonian god, was also re-erected in Borsippa, Antiochus, although he was in Syria, performing the ancient ritual of moulding the first brick.[32]

A revival of interest in cuneiform literature seems to have taken place at this time. The library of Esagila is known to have contained extensive historical records, and these documents seem frequently to have been copied and studied. During this period there is evidence for a particular interest among the scribes in astronomy and astrology. These academic pursuits were perhaps actively encouraged by Antiochus; certainly

Berossus, who was at this time a priest of the temple of Marduk, dedicated his history to the Seleucid monarch. This famous work, written in Greek, recorded the history of Babylonia from before the Flood until the time of Alexander; unfortunately it is known only from fragments transmitted by Josephus, Eusebius, and others. Antiochus seems to have been proud of his work in Babylon, for among his titles he used 'King of Babylon' and 'Restorer of Esagila'.

Antiochus II (261–246) and Seleucus II (246–225) continued their predecessor's policy of cultivating favour with the inhabitants of Babylon. In 237 the latter presented to Babylon, Borsippa, and Cutha a great gift of landed property and other valuables. Esagila is mentioned in the deed which stresses that the gift is to be Babylonian temple property eternally.[33] The fact that the deed was re-copied under Antiochus IV Epiphanes in 173 BC would suggest that the Seleucid ruler wished to emphasize that it was still valid, and that Esagila remained the sacred centre of Babylonia. Under this later Antiochus a Greek colony was founded at Babylon and an attempt was made to Hellenize the city, perhaps even as a new capital.[34] Unique among Seleucid foundations the city retained its ancient name. Cuneiform texts hail Antiochus as 'Founder of the City' and 'Saviour of Asia', and it would appear that Babylon achieved a new prosperity during his brief
96 rule. A theatre and gymnasium were built; laws were enacted regulating business transactions and currency.

Seleucid power was now to be challenged from the east where a new Iranian state, founded in Turkestan by one Arsaces (c. 256) and now based in Parthia, southeast of the Caspian, was gradually extending its sovereignty westwards at the expense of its Seleucid neighbours. Between 161 and 122 BC a struggle for Mesopotamia itself ensued, during which Babylon suffered numerous changes of ruler and continuing depredation. Indeed the city must have been a desolate ruin by the time Mithradates II finally established Parthian authority there (c. 122 BC). We know, however, from a text dated late in the Seleucid era that the religious functions of Esagila were still maintained. We read of the temple itself, its steward, and its college of priests, 'the Anu-Enlil priesthood'; surprisingly there is now no mention of Marduk.[35] A text of 93 BC reveals that at least parts of Esagila were at that late time still used for religious services.[36] Hereafter all primary cuneiform sources concerning the city and its temple cease.

Classical authors continue to give a picture of the desolation of Babylon. Their accounts do not always agree, however, and Nineveh, which was considered by them to have been a ruin after 612 BC, we know to have been the site of a considerable city during both the Seleucid and Parthian periods. At Babylon traces of a large Parthian building with pillared halls have been found near Esagila, and the theatre appears to have been rebuilt and enlarged at this time. About AD 24 merchants from the caravan city of Palmyra founded a trading colony there, but half a century later this colony was transferred to a new settlement across the river from Seleucia. With this move Babylon seems finally to have been abandoned.

After almost 2000 years as the cultural and political centre of the ancient world, little was left but the city's reputation and its vast

defensive walls. Babylonian cuneiform continued in use in the 1st century AD, but only as the learned language of mathematical and astronomical documents. The latest known of these comes from Babylon and is dated AD 75.[37] Diodorus Siculus, who wrote late in the 1st century BC, says that Esagila had sunk into ruins as had the royal palaces and other buildings (II, 9); only a small area of the city was still inhabited and the greater part of the space within the walls had been transformed into arable land. Strabo (24 BC) describes Babylon as for the most part empty and desolate. Only the walls remain as a witness to the city's former greatness; these he counts among the seven wonders of the world (XVI, 5). Yet Pliny, writing in the 1st century AD, suggests that Esagila was still in existence (VI, 30). In AD 116 Trajan wintered in Babylon during his campaign against the Parthians. He too found nothing except ruins, but with a sense of history he offered a sacrifice in the room where Alexander had died. A 2nd-century AD dialogue by Lucian harps on the vanity of human endeavour. Nineveh, he says, has vanished without a trace, and soon men will search in vain for Babylon (XII, 23): 'Why, as to Nineveh, it is gone, friend, long ago, and has left no trace behind it; there is no saying where it may have been.'

The site of Nineveh, a city which survives in modern Mosul, was in fact never forgotten, but Lucian was right about Babylon; after its mention by Zosimus with reference to an attack on Ctesiphon by Septimius Severus, the city was lost until the 17th century, and even as late as the last century the ziggurrats of Birs Nimrud (Borsippa) and Aqar Quf (Dur-Kurigalzu) continued to be mistaken for the Tower of Babel. Nevertheless, the name persisted in *Tell Babil*, the city's northernmost mound, and the area of the site was known locally as *ardh Babil*, the soil or land of Babylon. Today, despite the restoration of its major buildings, its desolation remains complete; once the centre of the

96 The Greek theatre in Babylon was first built at or not long after the time of Alexander and was reconstructed under his Seleucid successors. This view, from the north, shows the theatre after excavation, with the palaestra beyond. The theatre has now been restored by the Directorate-General of Antiquities, Baghdad.

world it now serves as a moving reminder of the impermanence of life and, along its once busy river, a quiet picnickers' haven.

The site of Babylon

Is not this great Babylon, which I have built for the royal dwelling place, by the might of my power and for the glory of my majesty? (Dan. 4, 30)

The Babylon visible to the tourist today is largely 'this great Babylon', the work of the Neo-Babylonian kings Nabopolassar and Nebuchadrezzar. As we have seen, much of the city was restored and indeed rebuilt under several Achaemenid and Seleucid monarchs, but far less is preserved of their monuments than those of Nebuchadrezzar, during whose reign Babylon achieved the architectural eminence for which it is remembered. There is relatively little in cuneiform sources to tell us how the ancient city looked, but we have the authority of a number of Classical writers,[38] in particular Herodotus, who probably never visited the city although he clearly relied on first-hand reports, and Ctesias, physician to Artaxerxes II Memnon, who was present at Cunaxa, where he was credited with saving the king's life. Unfortunately Ctesias' original works are now lost, but several later authors, including Diodorus Siculus and Plutarch, made extensive use of them.

97 Most of our direct information about Babylon comes from the work of Robert Koldewey, who between 1899 and 1917 excavated there on behalf of the Deutsche Orient-Gesellschaft. Since 1958 the Iraq Directorate-General of Antiquities has carried out further archaeological investigations and considerable restoration. During this same period the late Professor Heinrich Lenzen and Dr J. Schmidt of the German Archaeological Institute have also directed a series of brief excavations at the site.[39]

98 The ruins of Babylon extend over an area of some 850 hectares and constitute the largest ancient settlement in Mesopotamia. Greater Nineveh, by comparison, is some 750 hectares in area and the mound of Ur only 55. The excavation of a city of the size and complexity of Babylon presents formidable problems to the archaeologist. Koldewey worked the year round, in itself a gruelling task with summer shade temperatures often as high as 50°C. After 13 years he wrote in the preface to his comprehensive summary of his discoveries that he considered only half the necessary work completed.[40] Thus his projected labours were far from finished when in March 1917 the approach of the British Expeditionary Force under General Maude compelled him abruptly to close down the excavations.

99 The air photograph shows the general layout of the city, with Tell Babil, Nebuchadrezzar's Summer Palace, in the very northeastern corner and the citadel and palace areas clearly visible in the centre. At the time of Nebuchadrezzar the Euphrates flowed east of its present 100 position, dividing the inner city into two sectors. Excavation has been largely concentrated in the older eastern sector, where most of the principal buildings were situated, and little is known of the area that originally lay west of the river and is now partly beneath its bed. During the period of the Achaemenid Persians the river altered its course to

flow even further to the east around the citadel, thus materially affecting not only the form but ultimately the fortunes of the city. During Seleucid and Parthian times the excellent burnt bricks of the Neo-Babylonian royal buildings were robbed and re-used, thus initiating a process of demolition that has ceased only in the present day under the careful supervision of the local Antiquities Department.

Two sets of fortification walls enclose the city, of which traces of the innermost alone are visible on the eastern portion of the air photograph. This great defensive system was conceived and begun by Nabopolassar and completed by his son; the excavators found nothing of the original city walls of Sumu-abum, nor indeed of those of Kassite Babylon. The outer wall enclosing the inner city and the summer palace to the north was constructed on the east bank only. Nebuchadrezzar records:

> In order to strengthen the defences of Esagila that the evil and the wicked might not oppress Babylon, that which no king had done before me, at the outskirts of Babylon to the east I put about a great wall. Its moat I dug and its inner moat-wall with mortar and brick I raised mountain-high. About the sides of Babylon great banks of earth I heaped up. Great floods of destroying waters like the great waves of the sea I made to flow about it; with marsh I surrounded it.[41]

97 This photograph was taken on the first day of the excavation of the Ishtar Gate in Babylon (1 April 1902). The visible portion is on the east side of the second doorway of the outer gate and stood just below the pavement level of the latest (glazed) gate. Only the uppermost bricks are glazed; the bull is the highest preserved animal on the earliest unglazed structure.

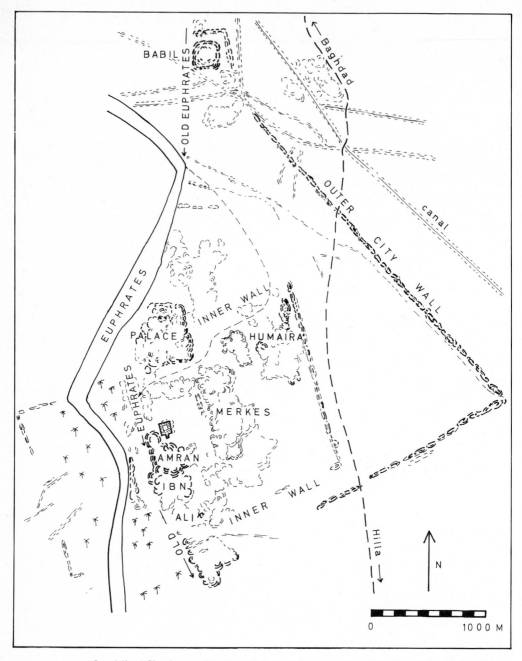

98,99 (*Above*) Sketch map of the site of Babylon before excavation. After Wetzel. The outline of the ziggurrat, the 'Tower of Babel', can be seen clearly (above Amran) where the excellent ancient baked brick of the casing has been robbed for re-use, leaving only an insignificant stump of mud-brick in the middle. The air photograph (*right*), taken from 6000 feet (*c.* 2000 m), shows approximately the same area.

Esagila

Procession Street

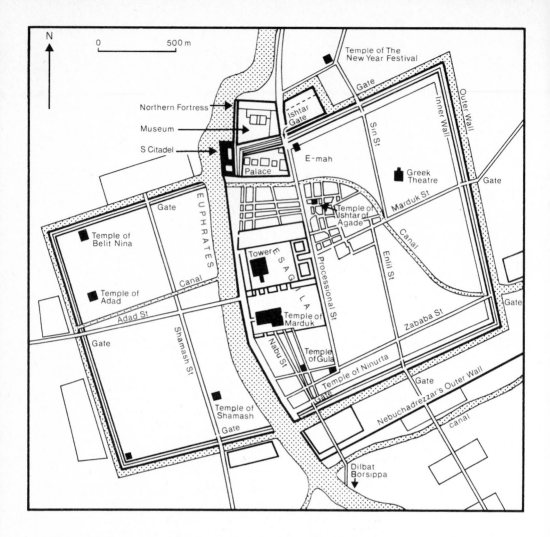

N

0   500 m

Temple of The
New Year Festival

Gate

Ishtar
Gate

Northern Fortress

Museum

S Citadel

Palace

E-mah

Sin St

Inner Wall

Outer Wall

Greek
Theatre

Gate

Marduk St

Temple of
Belit Nina

Gate

E
U
P
H
R
A
T
E
S

Temple of
Ishtar of
Agade

Canal

Enlil St

Tower

S
A
G
I
L
A

Processional St

Temple of
Adad

Canal

Temple of
Marduk

Adad St

Shamash St

Nabu St

Temple
of Gula

Zababa St

Gate

Gate

Temple of Ninurta

Gate

Gate

Gate

Temple of
Shamash

Gate

Nebuchadrezzar's Outer Wall

canal

Dilbat
Borsippa

100 Schematic plan of the
inner city of Babylon in the
Neo-Babylonian period. The
excavations have been
concentrated largely in the
western portion of the older
part of the city, east of the
Euphrates. After Unger.

This outer wall in fact comprised three separate walls: the innermost,
some 7 m thick, was constructed of sun-dried mud-brick; 12 m beyond
this was a second slightly thicker wall of baked brick; while outside and
against this was a further baked-brick wall about 3 m thick, forming the
scarp of a moat perhaps as much as 100 m in width. Astride the inner
wall at regular intervals were projecting towers; similar towers must
have protected the outer enceinte also, but no trace of these survives.
The space between the walls was filled with rubble, presumably as a
base for a protected roadway of sufficient width to permit Herodotus'
'four-horse chariot to turn round'. The length of these eastern walls is
over 8 km. Oddly, it is the less durable inner wall that has survived and
is visible now as one approaches the site. This is because the baked
bricks from the outer wall, as elsewhere on the site, were of such
excellent quality that they were long ago robbed.

100   The inner fortifications consisted of two sun-dried mud-brick walls,
the inner known as *Imgur-Enlil*, some 6.5 m thick, and the outer
Nimitti-Enlil, just under 4 m thick. The space between them, a width
of just over 7 m, was apparently unfilled and used as a military road. A

berm 20 m wide separated the outer wall from the baked-brick scarp of the inner moat, some 50 m across, which was linked at both ends with the Euphrates. Nebuchadrezzar adds,

> In order that no pillaging robber might enter into this water sewer, with bright iron bars I closed the entrance to the river, in gratings of iron I set it and fastened it with hinges. The defences of Esagila and Babylon I strengthened and secured for my reign an enduring name.[41]

Along the river were bulwarks of masonry to strengthen the banks, and at intervals steps led down to landing platforms. It was not until the time of Nabonidus that fortification walls were built along this, the weakest side of Babylon's defences. In the towers and courtines of his river wall were gateways opening towards the quay. Thus Greater Babylon, excluding its western suburb, had become a triangular fortified island, 12–13 km in circumference, with about a third of its area an inner fortress, elaborately defended and containing the old town with the royal palace, the temple of Marduk and a considerable residential area.

The palaces

The principal palaces at the time of Nebuchadrezzar were the so-called Northern, Southern and Summer Palaces, the latter occupying the mound known as Babil at the northern limit of the site, the only area where the original name has been preserved. Little was left of the Summer Palace beyond substructures some 18 m high; the name derives from the presence of vertical ventilation shafts of a type still used today for cooling Oriental houses. This palace in its surviving form was built by Nebuchadrezzar; it was remodelled and added to

101 The main or Southern Palace at Babylon lies between the Processional Way to the east, from which it was entered, and the thickly walled citadel to the west. Part of the inner city wall can be seen to the north of the palace adjoining the famous Ishtar Gate (*a*). Nebuchadrezzar's throne room (*c*) is situated on the southern side of the third or central courtyard, approached through a monumental gateway to the east. To the east of the Processional Way lies *E-mah*, the temple dedicated to Ninmah (*b*). After Koldewey.

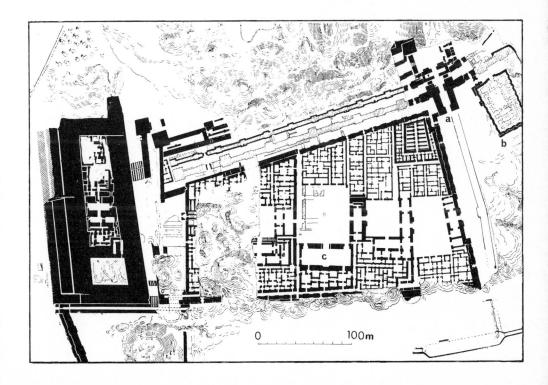

0   100m

102 Reconstruction of the glazed-brick frieze on the façade of Nebuchadrezzar's throne room (ill. 101, *c*), now in the Vorderasiatisches Museum, Berlin. The background colour is dark blue, the columns and lions appearing in yellow, white, blue and red, now weathered to green. (See also *MDOG* 99, 1968.) Ht 12·40 m.

during the Persian and Seleucid periods. Babylon's principal palace was the Southern Palace. In the time of Nebuchadrezzar, and presumably under the Persian kings who often used it as their winter residence, this palace contained five great courtyards surrounded by many apartments and suites of rooms. The entrance was from the east into the first small courtyard; nearby were rooms belonging to the palace guard and other members of the household, including at one time a maker of alabaster vases. From this court one passed into a second, presumably occupied by administrative officials. A monumental doorway on the east side led to the third and most important court (60 × 55 m), on the south side of which was situated the king's throne room, perhaps the scene of Belshazzar's feast and Alexander's death and still easily identified at the site. The façade of the court was once richly ornamented with multi-coloured glazed bricks, a noted feature of late-Babylonian palace architecture. To the west lay the original palace of Nabopolassar, later presumably the domestic wing. Beyond it Nebuchadrezzar also built a huge fortified citadel with walls 25 m

101

102

THE SITE OF BABYLON

thick, elaborately constructed to protect it against damp from the adjacent river.

At the very northeast corner of the great southern palace the excavators found an underground 'crypt' consisting of a series of 14 vaulted rooms surrounded by an unexpectedly thick wall, the vaults clearly having been constructed to support some enormous weight. This massive and unusual building together with the presence of a type of well unknown elsewhere in ancient Babylonia, with three shafts laced together in a manner suggesting a hydraulic lifting system with an endless chain of buckets drawn up in continuous rotation, led the excavators to conclude that they had found here the remains of the renowned Hanging Gardens, considered by Classical writers, together with the walls of Babylon, one of the seven wonders of the ancient world. It must be noted, however, that it was here that the lists of rations for the Jewish exiles were found,[42] and the plan itself suggests that this odd structure might have served as a warehouse and administrative unit. Classical tradition attributes the famous gardens to Semiramis, but Berossus credits them to Nebuchadrezzar, who is said to have built them for his Median wife, Amyitis, to remind her of her mountain homeland.

In the latter part of his reign Nebuchadrezzar built a second palace just to the north of his principal residence. The moat between the two palace-citadels was filled in and at the same time a large bastion was erected to form a complementary fortified area across the roadway to the east. The northern palace has not been completely excavated but in

103 Perhaps the most famous landmark at Babylon is this unfinished basalt figure of a lion trampling on a man who lies beneath him. Found by local villagers in 1776, in the ruins of the Northern Palace where it comprised part of the Neo-Babylonian royal museum, it was re-excavated in 1784 by Joseph de Beauchamp, the first instance in Mesopotamia of local workmen and a local foreman (from Hilla) being employed to excavate an archaeological site. Length of lion 2·60 m.

104 The Processional Way, leading from the north to the Ishtar Gate, was bordered with high defensive walls (ill. 112), ornamented with some 120 lions in glazed-brick relief, of which this is one example. The lions appear on a blue ground in white with yellow manes or yellow with red manes, now weathered to green. This example is now in the Metropolitan Museum of Art, New York. Ht 1·05 m.

the ruins were found a large number of 'antiquities' where Nebuchadrezzar and his successors had maintained a museum. Among the collections were the famous lion (ill. 103), statues of governors of Mari, stelae of Assurbanipal (ill. 82) and his twin brother Shamash-shuma-ukin, a stele of an 8th-century governor of Mari, Shamash-resha-usur, who introduced the keeping of bees into Mesopotamia (ill. 133), a basalt stele of a Hittite weather-god, and countless other fragments and inscriptions from times as early as the Third Dynasty of Ur; a number of clay tablets attest to the presence also of a royal library. We know that the museum was still in existence in Persian times, since a stele of Darius I was found there.

Immediately to the north of this palace was another great defensive structure, its outer bastion strengthened by large limestone blocks in front of which now ran the moat. The scale of these buildings is truly grandiose and difficult to imagine from the plans alone. It may perhaps help comparison to note that the whole of the great walled acropolis of Tiryns in Greece could be contained comfortably within the Southern Palace, while Nebuchadrezzar's throne room (52 × 17 m) compares in size not unfavourably with the Gallery of Mirrors at Versailles (73 × 10.4 m).

The Processional Way and the Ishtar Gate

The inner city was magnificently laid out, the main streets running roughly parallel with the river and at right angles, terminating in great bronze gates in the city wall. A cuneiform text which describes the topography of Babylon, of Seleucid date but presumably a copy of an earlier document, reveals the names of eight gates, together with those of numerous temples, streets and quarters of the city.[43] The most famous of these streets was the 'Processional Way' which ran along the eastern side of the Southern Palace, through the massive Ishtar Gate and outside the inner town to a special festival house, the *Bit Akitu*, located to the north. It was along this street, known in Babylonian as *Aibur-shabu*, 'the enemy shall never pass', that the images of the gods were carried during the New Year Festival.

105

As one approached the Ishtar Gate from the north, one passed along *Aibur-shabu*, at this point a broad paved road which ran for 200 m between high walls, respectively the eastern wall of the Northern Palace and the western side of the eastern outer bastion, lined with figures of some 120 lions, symbols of Ishtar, in moulded glazed brick. On the road itself, which climbed gently upwards towards the gate, are still preserved the great 6th-century paving stones, over which Nebuchadrezzar, Daniel and Darius must frequently have passed. The centre of the roadway was laid with huge flags of limestone; on either side were slabs of red breccia veined with white. On the edge of each paving stone is still inscribed Nebuchadrezzar's dedication, visible only to the god.

The gate itself was double, encompassing both fortification walls. It had been frequently rebuilt, three times by Nebuchadrezzar, and the level of the street within the gate had been raised on each occasion. The ruins now visible at the site were left entirely underground when Nebuchadrezzar constructed the latest (glazed) phase. On the earlier gate can still be seen some 150 bulls and dragons, symbols of Adad and Marduk, in plain moulded brick. The latest gate was brilliantly decorated with similar animals, this time in glazed brick of which the background colour was a vivid blue, the animals appearing alternately

112

104

105 General view of the Ishtar Gate, Babylon, which leads through the inner city wall, seen from the southeastern corner of the Northern Palace. It shows the earliest unglazed portion of the gate, still visible at the site, before the reconstruction of the temple to Ninmah (cf. ill. 109). The walls of the gate still stand to a height of some 12 m.

106, 107 Details of the unglazed moulded brick animals from the earliest phase of Nebuchadrezzar's Ishtar Gate, *in situ* (cf. ill. 85). The bull is the symbol of the god Adad; *below* is the dragon of Marduk. Ht 1·30 m.

108 This reconstruction of the latest phase of Nebuchadrezzar's Ishtar Gate, ornamented with glazed-brick animals and rosettes, can be seen in the Vorderasiatisches Museum, Berlin. Ht 14·30 m; the original gate was much higher, perhaps over 23·0 m. According to Nebuchadrezzar the gate was also guarded by 'mighty bronze colossi of bulls and dragons'. A half-size reproduction of this gate now stands at the entrance to the site itself.

in yellow and white. The original glazed gate can now be seen in the East Berlin Museum, while a half-size reproduction has been constructed for tourists to view near the official entrance to the site. On leaving the gate, the Processional Way proceeds past the Southern Palace, sloping downwards, and then, some 900 m to the south, turns west between the ziggurat enclosure and the Marduk temple towards the Euphrates bridge built by either Nabopolassar or his son.

The temples

109–10

On entering the city along *Aibur-shabu* the visitor passes, on his left opposite the Southern Palace, *E-mah*, the temple of the mother-goddess Ninmah, which has recently been restored by the Directorate-General of Antiquities. A number of other temples have been excavated, including the ancient shrine of Ishtar of Agade, situated in Merkes. These temples follow the traditional Babylonian plan, with a broad cella on one side of the inner court and, in its rear wall facing the door, a niche containing a platform, presumably for the statue of the god.

Babylon's most important temple was, of course, Esagila, the dwelling-place of the city-god Marduk. This was situated almost 1 km south of the royal palaces. Unfortunately its remains, beneath the later mound of Amran ibn Ali, lay at such a depth that Koldewey was unable to excavate them properly. By a happy chance, however, his test pit struck a paved floor (at a depth of 21 m!) with inscriptions stating that it had been laid in Esagila by the Assyrian kings Assurbanipal and Esarhaddon. The outlines of the temple were recovered by tunnelling;

109, 110 View of the Ishtar Gate at Babylon and, in the distance, the reconstructed temple *E-mah*, dedicated to the mother-goddess Ninmah. By Babylonian standards this is a small temple, but a particularly fine example of the broad-cella plan. *Opposite* is a view, taken in the temple courtyard, looking from the antecella toward the towered entrance chamber. The temple well can be seen in the courtyard, foreground.

the main building proved to occupy an area of some 78 × 86 m with, to the east, two outer courts, 90 × 116 m overall. In the main temple were a number of chapels, including one on the north side believed by Koldewey to be the sanctuary of Marduk's father, Ea, in Greek times identified with Serapis. Presumably it was here that the generals of Alexander sought counsel of the god with regard to the king's illness, whether he should be brought to the shrine to be cured. The principal shrine, that of Marduk, lay to the west, entered through a monumental towered façade. Of this inner cella Nebuchadrezzar says that he 'covered its wall with sparkling gold, I caused it to shine like the sun'. Here, according to Herodotus, was the

> great sitting figure of Marduk, all of gold on a golden throne, supported on a base of gold, with a golden table standing beside it. I was told by the Chaldaeans that to make all this more than 22 tons of gold were used. Outside the temple is a golden altar, and there is another, not of gold, but of great size . . . on the larger altar the Chaldaeans offer some two and a half tons of frankincense every year at the festival of Bel [Marduk].

Second only to the Hanging Gardens Babylon's most famous monument was undoubtedly the great staged tower or ziggurrat, Etemenanki, 'the house that is the foundation of heaven and earth', situated in a vast enclosure to the north of Esagila. Although the latter is

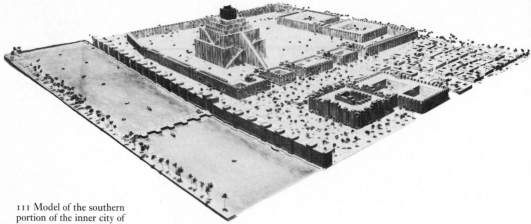

111 Model of the southern portion of the inner city of Babylon, as reconstructed in the Neo-Babylonian period. The Euphrates bridge is in the foreground (left), Esagila, the temple of Marduk, in the foreground (right), and beyond lies Etemenanki, the ziggurrat of Babylon, in its great enclosure. Babylon Museum.

112 Model of the Ishtar Gate and the Procession Street, from the north. This is the latest phase of the gate of Nebuchadrezzar (glazed), beneath which lies the unglazed earlier portion still visible at the site. A procession of striding lions (ill. 104) lines either side of the heavily fortified street. Babylon Museum.

attested in cuneiform texts as far back as the First Dynasty, the ziggurrat, which must be of a comparable age, is not referred to until the 7th century BC, after Sennacherib in 689 demolished both monuments.[44] Its subsequent rebuilding is mentioned by the Assyrian kings Esarhaddon and Assurbanipal and later by Nabopolassar and Nebuchadrezzar, who completed his father's work and built the 'high temple', the shrine on its uppermost stage. Nothing but the foundation of the tower was left when Koldewey began his excavation. Indeed the outline of the lowest stage with its monumental stair to the south is clearly visible on the air photograph in the deep and broad brick-robbers' excavations. The actual thickness of the baked-brick facing of the ziggurrat was some 15 m, which explains the great breadth of these illicit trenches. Much controversy has been centred on the reconstruction of this Tower of Babel, which is described not only in Greek sources but also in a Babylonian text, the so-called Esagila tablet, in which its actual dimensions are given.[45] For the lowest stage these do

not differ significantly from those established in the excavations (approximately 91 m square), but the number of stages and the arrangement of the staircases remain in dispute. There is also some doubt about the actual date of the outer precinct walls of Koldewey's plan. Much of this area of the site was built over in Parthian times and even later, while a number of Seleucid objects were actually recovered from the pavement of Esagila.[46]

Private houses

A number of private houses have been excavated, especially in the sector known as Merkes which we have already noted is the sole area in which ruins of the city of Hammurapi remain accessible above the present water table. The later houses, like those known already at the time of the Old Babylonian kings, were of the courtyard type. A unique feature of the later period, found not only at Babylon but also at Ur, was the 'saw-toothed' façade, an ingenious structural device to permit the proper bonding of walls askew to the general layout of the rest of the building.[47] A large number of both utilitarian and decorative objects were recovered from these houses (ills. 71, 95, 113, 125).

113 Small clay plaque of a seated woman wearing a turreted crown, found at Babylon and now in the Istanbul Museum. Early 2nd millennium. Ht 11 cm.

The Babylon of Persian and Greek times

Persian occupation of Babylon is evident in a number of areas. Of particular interest is the *apadana* or columned hall found at the northwest corner of the principal palace. This is possibly the palace built by Darius and used by the Crown Prince Xerxes, who was later to be responsible for the destruction of the city. Following Neo-Babylonian tradition this Persian palace was decorated with glazed bricks, a contemporary description of which survives in Diodorus (ii, 1), quoting Ctesias who ascribed these ornaments not to Darius but to Semiramis, whose form he professed to see in a woman on horseback, part of a chase of wild beasts depicted on the palace walls. Among the fragments of glazed brick found here by Koldewey was indeed 'the white face of a woman', almost certainly a fragment of that very figure seen by Ctesias.[48] Also recovered from the Persian version of the palace were floral designs and columns with double volute Ionic capitals and fragments of other human figures, apparently depicting members of the royal guard, the Ten Thousand Immortals.

Hellenistic influence in Babylon is even more evident. Close to the inner city wall east of the palace lies a group of mounds which because of their reddish colour are called by the local inhabitants 'Humaira'. The southernmost of these contains the remains of a Greek theatre, now restored by the Iraq Directorate-General of Antiquities, and an adjoining Palaestra or gymnasium. First built early in Seleucid times, perhaps even under Alexander, the theatre was in ruins when rebuilt in its present form during the Parthian period. A dedicatory inscription in Greek was found on the site. The central mound consists of debris of broken bricks, among which an artificial platform was found, marked by traces of a great conflagration. These ruins are believed to mark the site of the funeral pyre erected by order of Alexander for the funeral of Hephaestion. The northernmost mound, c. 16 m high, consists of nothing but brick rubble, artificially heaped up. Some of the brick

96

114 A variety of Greek-inspired figures in both stone and terracotta has been found at Babylon. This reclining lady in alabaster is one of the most attractive. Said to come from Hilla, but almost certainly found in one of the many Parthian graves in the mound of Amran, it is now in the Louvre Museum. Length 21 cm.

fragments bear Nebuchadrezzar's name and record the building of Etemenanki. Indeed it would seem that this is the actual debris removed by Alexander when he decided to rebuilt the ziggurrat, which was in ruins when he reached Babylon. Alexander is said to have employed 10,000 men for two months in order to clear the site (Strabo xvi, 1), that is, 600,000 daily wages. Koldewey, in noting this, remarks that in eleven years' continuous excavation of the site he had paid only the slightly larger total of 800,000 working days.

The large mound, Amran, which conceals the ruins of Esagila, marks the longest-inhabited part of Babylon. Indeed there was probably a village here until the founding of nearby Hillah in the 11th century AD. Considerable traces of Greek and Parthian occupation were revealed in the excavations, including a massive columned building and a nearby stoa. Large numbers of graves were also discovered, in which were 114 many Hellenistic figures in alabaster and clay.

Neo-Babylonian remains outside the capital

The last native kings of Babylon carried on an active building policy in several of the ancient cities of Sumer and Akkad, and ruins of this period have been found at almost every important excavated city – Sippar, Ur, Borsippa, Nippur, Uruk, Isin, and indeed Kish where the 115 impressive remains of a large Neo-Babylonian temple built by Nebuchadrezzar can still be seen. We know that Nabopolassar restored the temple of Shamash at Sippar where he also 'dug the course of the Euphrates to the city', the river having by this time moved away from its former course. Nebuchadrezzar rebuilt the temple of Nabu and the great ziggurrat of Borsippa, and both he and Nabonidus were active at Ur. As the major Babylonian centre for the worship of the moon-god Ur was, of course, a particular attraction to the fanatical Nabonidus, who rebuilt the ziggurrat and restored a number of the city's major monuments. Of especial interest is his restoration of the official residence of the high priestess of the moon-god, during which work he was overjoyed to discover 'the inscriptions of former ancient kings', including a cylinder of Enanedu, daughter of Kudur-mabuk and the last recorded high priestess or *entu* (chapter 3). 'As of old' Nabonidus built its shrines and appurtenances, and in dedicating his own daughter, En-nigaldi-Nanna (formerly read Bel-shalti-Nannar), as *entu* the last Babylonian king and antiquarian revived an ancient but apparently long-neglected custom. During his restoration Nabonidus also found 'an ancient memorial tablet of Nebuchadrezzar [I], a royal predecessor, upon which he had fashioned the likeness of an *entu*, her insignia, her clothing, and her ornaments'.[49]

This pleasure in archaeological discovery was shared too by Nabonidus' predecessor Nebuchadrezzar II, who records that in restoring a temple in Marad (not far from Nippur) he searched for the ancient foundation – an essential part of such an undertaking – and to his delight discovered that of 'an ancient ancestor', the great Naram-Sin: 'the inscription of my name I placed with the inscription of his name and upon the foundation [*temennu*] of Naram-Sin, king, I established its [new] foundation'.[49] At Larsa Nebuchadrezzar rebuilt the temple of the sun-god, the ruins of which had been swept clean of sand by a great storm, an act of god that would have been much welcomed by recent excavators of this now wholly sand-enshrouded site! In searching for its foundations Nebuchadrezzar discovered the *temennu* of Burnaburiash, only to be outdone by Nabonidus whose later efforts yielded here an inscription of Hammurapi.[50] Perhaps the most interesting archaeological exercise of all is revealed in the same text, which records the search for the foundation of Eulmash, the temple of Ishtar in Agade. Nabonidus notes that a number of kings before him had searched unsuccessfully – Kurigalzu, Esarhaddon, Assurbanipal and even Nebuchadrezzar – and indeed Nabonidus himself had excavated in vain for three years when a heavy downpour of rain opened a great gully in which the *temennu* of Naram-Sin of Agade was soon revealed, a discovery which 'made the king's heart glad and caused his countenance to brighten!' It is clear that the location of the long-

115 These unusually well-preserved ruins of two adjoining Neo-Babylonian temples can still be seen at the southeastern mound of Kish (Hursagkalama; the historical site of Kish includes two city mounds). The temple complex was built by Nebuchadrezzar II and shows clearly the recessed façades with which such mud-brick buildings were ornamented. The walls still stand to a height of 5·6 m.

deserted Agade was no mystery to the Neo-Babylonians and the synonymous use of Agade and Babylon at this time[51] lends credence to the theory that the two cities lie close together, if indeed Sargon's capital is not to be found somewhere directly beneath the very extensive ruins of Greater Babylon.

Although the archaeological activities of the Neo-Babylonian kings were essentially religious in their motivation, there was undoubtedly a genuine interest both in the traditions and history of the past and in the actual objects to be found in the ancient mounds of Mesopotamia. We have already mentioned museums in Babylon and Ur; at Nippur too there was recovered an archaeological collection dating from this period, contained in a jar found in the scribal library, while one of Nabonidus' scribes, who was perhaps the 'expert' in charge of the excavations at Agade, actually took a clay 'squeeze' of an inscription of Shar-kali-sharri – now preserved in Philadelphia – which he 'found in the palace of Naram-Sin'.[52] That antiquarian interests were far from new in Neo-Babylonian times is clearly evident from such earlier examples as the library of Assurbanipal at Nineveh and Nabu-apla-iddina's 9th-century 'pious fraud' at Sippar (described on a tablet also carefully preserved by Nabopolassar). Indeed the ordinary citizens of Babylonia had long been aware of the riches contained in its ancient mounds, as can be seen in this letter from a son to his father, dated over 1000 years before:

74

> I have never before written to you for something precious I wanted. But if you want to be like a father to me, get me a fine string of beads, to be worn around the head. Seal it with your seal and give it to the carrier so that he can bring it to me. If you have none at hand, *dig it out of the ground wherever such objects are found* and send it to me. I want it very much . . .[53]

116 Dragon (*mushhushshu*) in glazed brick, one of a large number which ornamented the latest phase of the Ishtar Gate. The *mushhushshu* are hybrid creatures, scaly-coated, the head bearing the double horns of the Arabian horned viper (cf. ill. 136), seen here in profile. The front legs are feline, the hind legs end in the scaly claws of a bird of prey and the tail terminates in a scorpion sting. Ht 1·30 m. Vorderasiatisches Museum, Berlin.

6
The legacy of Babylon

Education

No other single institution contributed as much to the preservation of Mesopotamia's past as the school, known in Sumerian as the *edubba*, conventionally translated 'tablet-house'. Its primary purpose was to train scribes to fill certain administrative or 'civil-service' posts, but it achieved far more in its larger role as the centre of all learning. Not only was the rich heritage of Sumerian and Babylonian culture preserved for later generations but the *edubba* was instrumental in the dissemination of knowledge and literature throughout Western Asia. The early growth of trade – and later the march of empire – carried the Sumerian system of cuneiform writing, and with it some imitation of the Mesopotamian school, from Sumer to Iran, Syria and Asia Minor. Indeed the early prestige enjoyed by the Sumerians must to a great extent reflect their unique contribution to literacy, the invention of writing itself.

The difficult nature of the cuneiform system of writing – modern students have some 500 basic signs to learn and there are variations of these for every period – ensured the restriction of the arts of reading and writing to those few trained as scribes, and indeed as long as this cumbersome script existed, its complexity demanded years of professional training for its mastery. Despite this, an attempt in Assyria early in the 2nd millennium to reduce cuneiform to some 100 signs did not survive (the Achaemenid Persians were later to use a much-simplified alphabetic form). Although the schools appear often to be associated with the temple or palace – that this was not always so can be seen in Igmil-Sin's school at Ur – the scribes were a completely lay group. Priests as well as kings, with a very few notable exceptions, governors and even judges were illiterate. It is easy to imagine the power this gave to the educated few, a situation well illustrated in a letter from Mari:

> Because you are the one who has always read the tablets addressed to the king – and there is nobody else who reads them – I have not dispatched to you any more answers to the tablets of the king (addressed to me). Now, however, I am sending a tablet to the king and in duplicate to you. I shall repeat the previous message to you. Read this tablet and – if it is appropriate – read it to the king.[1]

A number of cuneiform texts, some of them cast as dialogues between teacher and student or between students, reveal something of the functioning of the school and indeed of contemporary humour.[2] The pupil is referred to as 'son of the tablet-house'; his teacher is the school 'father'. There are also 'elder brothers', senior students who appear to have done much of the actual teaching. Corporal punishment was freely used; there was a 'man in charge of the whip' and we read that,

> If the young son of the *edubba*
> Has not recited his tasks correctly
> The elder brother and his father will beat him.[3]

The teaching process relied on memorization, and the curriculum included what might be termed 'scientific studies', mathematics, grammar and the studying and copying of a large and diverse group of literary compositions. Already among the earliest pictographic tablets from Uruk are found word-lists apparently intended for study and practice. The Sumerians delighted in classification, to which their language was particularly suited, and these word-lists or 'glossaries', to which were later added Akkadian translations for each individual word, came to include all Sumerian and Babylonian knowledge. Among these lexical texts are lists of plants, animals (including insects and birds), countries, cities, minerals, tools, and so forth, and even Sumerian grammatical forms which were studied and copied long after Sumerian had ceased to be spoken. Such 'dictionaries' are of enormous value to modern scholars. They reveal too the extraordinary breadth and curiosity, and indeed the limitations, of Sumerian scholarship. Much of the scribe's early training consisted of copying and learning such lists, which by the Old Babylonian period had become stereotyped school exercises. Specialist subjects were also taught, including such practical skills as quantity- and land-surveying and even music.

117

The 'school-days' texts emphasize austerity, ill treatment and rebellion among the pupils and vanity not unmixed with a little cruelty on the part of the teachers. There is a decided air of satire, however, and one senses that these are burlesques of the normal school atmosphere. The student attended school from sunrise to sunset; in one text the pupil retires to bed with an injunction to his mother not to let him be late in the morning. Schooling lasted from early youth until the student became a young man:

> Come, my son, sit at my feet. I will talk to you, and you will give me information! From your childhood to your adult age you have been staying in the tablet-house. Do you know the scribal art that you have learned?[4]

This same text proceeds to enumerate a number of 'examination questions', which have proved as difficult of comprehension to the modern scholar as were the answers to the poor Babylonian student. Among the topics covered were the secret meanings of Sumerian words, all categories of songs and how to conduct a choir, the technical jargon of silversmiths and jewellers, the allotting of rations, the division of fields and the use and technique of various musical instruments. At this point in the text the candidate, unable to answer, charges the master that he has not been taught these matters, neither by the master

117 Babylonian scholars compiled numerous 'dictionaries' or word-lists, often consisting of all names in a particular category, which are of enormous value to modern students of cuneiform. This clay tablet is a syllabary, copied in the Persian period, inscribed with the names, pronunciations and meanings of a number of cuneiform signs. Dated in the 10th year of Artaxerxes I, *c.* 455 BC. Ht *c.* 14 cm. British Museum.

nor by the elder brother. The dialogue then continues with the following reprimand:

> What have you done, what good came of your sitting here? You are already a ripe man and close to being aged! Like an old ass you are not teachable any more. Like withered grain you have passed the season. How long will you play around? But, it is still not too late! If you study night and day and work all the time modestly and without arrogance, if you listen to your colleagues and teachers, you still can become a scribe! Then you can share the scribal craft which is good

fortune for its owner, a good angel leading you, a bright eye possessed by you, and it is what the palace needs.[4]

We do not know how or in what respects specialization was effected, but scribal training led to many careers, including those of royal counsellor and heads of various government ministries. We know the occupational titles of a number of types of scribe, such as 'name-writer', military scribe, scribe of the field; the ancient language was taught by a specialist 'professor of Sumerian'. Although in the Old Babylonian period there were street scribes to whom anyone could dictate a letter, most scribes seem to have been employed as administrative secretaries. There were two advanced centres of scribal learning, the 'university' of Nippur and that at Babylon which became the focus of scholarship sometime after Samsu-iluna. After the Old Babylonian period the *edubba* seems to have disappeared as an institution and, paralleling a shift in the Kassite period to a more feudal society, education seems to have fallen into the hands of a few aristocratic families.[5] In Uruk and Babylon at least, the same scribal names continued in use into Seleucid and Parthian times. Continuity of tradition was characteristic of the work of Kassite scholars themselves, who carefully transcribed and catalogued the writings of their Old Babylonian predecessors. Babylonian scribes were far more than mere copyists, however, and much of the vast treasury of literature that has come down to us from this distant age was actually composed in the scribal schools. Perhaps the greatest contribution of all was made by the scribes of the Old Babylonian period who were not only responsible for the preservation of the literary and historical heritage of the Sumerians but themselves produced some of the most vivid and lively writing of the pre-Classical world.

Literature

Our knowledge of Sumerian and Babylonian literature comes for the most part from two great sources, the royal libraries of Assur and Nineveh (12th–7th centuries) and the scribal schools of the Old Babylonian period. The earliest literary texts known come from the archives of Fara, Abu Salabikh and Ebla (sometime before 2400 BC), but relatively few Sumerian compositions have survived except in later copies. Indeed the literary 'catalogues' dutifully compiled by Old Babylonian scribes show all too clearly that only a fraction of Sumerian literature has been recovered by modern archaeologists.[6] The spiritual indebtedness of the Babylonians to the Sumerians is clearly indicated by the extent to which Sumerian language and literature continued to be studied throughout Babylonian history. We are ignorant of the real origins of this literature, however, or of the role oral tradition may have played in these early compositions. It seems likely that successive generations of storytellers and scribes must have shared in the fashioning of the final product, but some compositions clearly bear the imprint – and in later periods indeed the signature – of a single personality. That the Babylonians themselves were ignorant of the origins of their early literature would seem to be implied in Berossus' reference to the burying of all literature in Sippar 'before the Flood' and of its subsequent recovery. By the 1st millennium many literary works had acquired a standard or 'canonical' form, largely the work of Kassite scribes who were themselves the last of Babylonia's great creative writers.

From the Old Babylonian period a wide variety of written works is known. We have already mentioned legal texts, whose purpose was in some sense literary, and the variety of treatises that made up the school curriculum. Also found as school texts are a distinctive Sumerian literary genre known as 'dialogues', of which the central feature was a verbal contest between two characters, generally to assess which of the two was the more beneficial to man: Date Palm and Tamarisk, Summer and Winter, Ploughman and Shepherd, Pickaxe and Plough, and so forth. The scribes had a special name for these texts (*adaman-dug-ga*), of which the first ideogram was written Man-ᵘᵉW, i.e., 'man against man', the rest of the phrase signifying 'spoken'. Generally there was a judgment followed by a reconciliation and the two contestants departed the best of friends. Contests in prose and verse enjoyed a great vogue in later Oriental literature, and it would seem that this dramatic form was a particular legacy of the early Mesopotamian schools. It is possible that the Babylonian compositions were intended to be acted, but we cannot be certain.

During the 2nd millennium a concern with moral and ethical problems seems to have occupied the Babylonian philosopher, and a body of 'Wisdom Literature' developed, of which several major works survive.[7] The dialogues, sometimes if not too happily called 'fables', are usually classed with this traditional genre, while proverbs and maxims are also well represented. Among these there can be recognized many modern as well as biblical parallels. The Akkadian version of 'tit for tat', for example, is: 'You go and take the field of the enemy; the enemy comes and takes your field'. The loquacity of barbers would seem to be universal: 'Where servants are there is quarrel; where cosmeticians are there is slander'. And modern readers will recognize the sentiments expressed in: 'Friendship lasts but for a day, business connections forever', and, 'There is quarrelling among colleagues and backbiting among bishops'.[8]

But it is the later, 'philosophical' works that are perhaps of greatest interest. The ideal of abstract justice was slow to grow in Mesopotamia, although, as we have already noted, a royal concern for the poor and oppressed was expressed already in legal edicts dating back to the 3rd millennium. The basic Mesopotamian assumption that the universe was ruled by the gods, who punished those who neglected them and rewarded those who served them dutifully, seems hardly to have been questioned until Kassite times and even then the traditional tenet, that the individual's fate lay in his own hands, finds much support. Perhaps the best historical example of this philosophy is to be found in the Weidner Chronicle, in which a number of early rulers are said to succeed or fail depending on their devotion to Esagila (even at times when Esagila did not exist!). Beginning in Kassite times, however, texts are found in which the problem of the righteous sufferer is explored. The earliest of these, known from its opening line as *ludlul bel nemeqi*, 'I will praise the lord of wisdom', is often compared with the

Book of Job, though philosophically it is more primitive. The concept of sins of ignorance can be detected as early as the late 3rd millennium, but it was only in Kassite times that the expression of this idea gained currency:

> Mankind is deaf and knows nothing.
> What knowledge has anyone at all?
> He knows not whether he has done a good or a bad deed.[9]

The writer of *ludlul*, despairing, asserts that man can never distinguish good and bad because of the remoteness of the gods. The poem ends, however, with the sufferer's return to happiness. Another long composition of slightly later date, the so-called 'Babylonian Theodicy', considers the problem why some men oppress their fellows. Sometimes called the 'Babylonian Ecclesiastes', this work, which was apparently popular in the 1st millennium, consists of a dialogue, written as an acrostic poem, between a sceptic, who exposes the evils of current social justice, and a pious friend, who tries to reconcile these facts with his religious views.

Since the Babylonians looked for no rewards in the afterlife, the universal incidence of death was another injustice of concern to them. The desire for immortality is the theme of one of the most famous Mesopotamian stories, the Epic of Gilgamesh.[10] This epic is the longest and to the modern reader undoubtedly the finest work of Babylonian literature. However, there is no evidence that it held any special position in Babylonian literary tradition. Based on four or more separate Sumerian stories, it was woven into a unified narrative sometime early in the 2nd millennium. The poem treats a number of minor topics – man and nature, love and adventure, friendship and combat – all masterfully blended into a background for the main theme. The story concerns the adventures of Gilgamesh, a legendary king of Uruk for whom there is some historical basis, and his wild-man companion Enkidu. One of their expeditions was against Humbaba, an evil monster of the cedar forest. Enlil later decides that Enkidu must die as a punishment for the slaying of Humbaba, and it is his death that provides the turning point in the epic. The loss of his friend continues to haunt Gilgamesh who has now but one thought, to find everlasting life, despite counsel that would persuade him that his quest is in vain.

118 In the Epic of Gilgamesh the demon Humbaba was slain by Enkidu. A great variety of mask-like representations in clay depicting the face of this demon have survived, often, as in this instance, shown as the entrails of a sacrificial animal. This example probably comes from Sippar. Ht 8 cm. British Museum.

> Gilgamesh, whither are you wandering?
> Life, which you look for, you will never find.
> For when the gods created man, they let
> death be his share, and life
> withheld in their own hands.
> Gilgamesh, fill your belly –
> day and night make merry,
> let every day be full of joy,
> dance and make music day and night.
> Put on clean clothes,
> and wash your head and bathe.
> Gaze at the child that is holding your hand,
> and let your wife delight in your embrace.
> These things alone are the concern of men.[11]

Gilgamesh's search is embellished with a number of episodes, including an encounter with Utnapishtim, the Babylonian Noah. Utnapishtim tells him the famous story of the Flood (which is related in fuller detail in another Akkadian epic, Atrahasis). Ultimately Gilgamesh fails, and the tale comes to its inevitable and unhappy end.

Another great Babylonian literary work is the so-called 'Epic of Creation', known from its first line as the *enuma elish*, 'when on high'.[12] In the later periods of Babylonian civilization this composition was recited at Babylon on the fourth day of the New Year Festival. It is not the only Babylonian creation myth but is by far the longest. Its date is uncertain, but in the form in which it has been preserved is no earlier than Kassite. The *enuma elish* tells the story of the birth of generations of primeval deities to Apsu and Tiamat, the personifications of the primordial waters under the earth and of the sea 'before heaven or the firm ground below had been named'. These godly children proved so noisy and troublesome, however, that Apsu, encouraged by his vizier Mummu, was persuaded to destroy them. Ea, 'the all-wise', saw through the plot and Apsu was himself destroyed by Ea's magic. The lifeless Apsu became the motionless waters under the earth on which Ea now settled in his shrine at Eridu. Here Marduk, the real hero of the tale, was born: 8

> full-grown he came forth,
> mightiest from the first.

Tiamat was now persuaded to exact revenge, for which purpose she created an army of formidable monsters. In this crisis even Ea panicked, but Marduk stepped in and offered to do battle with Tiamat to save the other gods. Marduk's price was recognition as supreme deity, which the assembled gods solemnly affirm:

> It is you, Marduk, who are the most honoured among the great gods,
> Your destiny is unrivalled, your utterance is Anu;
> O Marduk! You are the most honoured among the great gods.
> From this day onward unchangeable shall be thy pronouncement.
> . . .
> We have granted you kingship over the universe entire.

Wishing to test the efficacy of the power they have vested in Marduk, the gods set up a constellation of stars and rather childishly demand that Marduk shall make it vanish and reappear. Delighted when he succeeds, they give him the royal insignia and send him off to defeat Tiamat. This accomplished, Marduk continues the creation of heaven and earth and the grateful gods undertake for him the construction of Babylon and Esagila. The epic ends with the enumeration of Marduk's fifty honorific names.

A number of other Babylonian myths are known, as indeed are other types of literature such as hymns and prayers to various gods, royal hymns, and such remarkable works as the Lamentation over the Destruction of Ur and the Erra Epic, to which we have earlier referred. An unsolved problem is that of the audience for whom these various

compositions were intended. Existing evidence is not informative, nor
do we know to what extent the general public was even acquainted with
the written literature. The fact that only the scribes could read and
write allows the possibility that some compositions may have been
written by them for their own edification or amusement and may have
remained unknown beyond the confines of the schools. Certainly there
was a genre of court poetry and, as we have mentioned already, a
possibility that the dialogues were actually performed; some hymns
and epics were recited at religious festivals, and textual evidence
suggests the mimed presentation of the battle between Marduk and
Tiamat. But in all these instances we have no knowledge of the extent to
which the public was allowed to participate. We assume a broad stream
of folklore which must be reflected at least to some extent in early
literary compositions, but by the Kassite period such popular traditions
may well have been lost, leaving only an intellectual literature to be
handed down through generations of scribes, one that was little known
beyond this educated circle.

Religion[13]

One of the world's most distinguished Assyriologists once wrote that 'a
systematic presentation of Mesopotamian religion cannot and should
not be written'.[14] Certainly extant evidence illuminates but a few facets
of the subject, one that in any alien society offers opportunity for
misunderstanding. Much of what has been written about Mesopotamian religion describes only that directly relevant to the priests or the
king. What part this official religion played in the lives of ordinary

119, 120 Large numbers of clay plaques survive from Mesopotamia. They were mainly votive or apotropaic in function and often depict religious subjects. Ill. 119 is a particularly fine representation of Marduk's dragon (cf. ill. 116), provenance unknown, now in the British Museum. Ht 9·2 cm. Contest scenes, common on seals, are also found among the clay plaque repertoire, as can be seen on this Old Babylonian example (ill. 120), now in the Iraq Museum. Ht c. 10 cm.

citizens we have yet to discover, but there must remain a strong presumption that its influence was relatively unimportant. Here, perhaps more than in any other aspect of Mesopotamian life, the gap in time and experience that separates us from the Babylonian world creates an almost insuperable barrier. The following brief remarks must be read in this light.

The roots of Babylonian religion lie far back in the prehistoric past. By the time sufficient textual evidence is preserved, there existed already a complicated and often seemingly contradictory amalgam of Sumerian and Semitic religious traditions.[15] In later periods it is possible to observe the fusion of one divine figure into another, often with the retention of both names; such developments produced ultimately an overwhelming confusion of minor deities. The basic structure of the pantheon, at least as recorded in the earliest preserved literature, goes back to lists of gods drawn up in the 3rd millennium. Anu, the sky, who appears as a shadowy figure throughout Mesopotamian history, originally stood at its head. Some of his attributes were later taken over, first by Enlil, and later by Marduk and Assur in Babylonia and Assyria respectively.[16] Anu's primary attribute was royalty, and it was from him that the institution of kingship and its insignia originally descended to mankind. Anu's rather colourless consort Antum was at an early period replaced by Ishtar, goddess of love and – in another guise – war, whose fertility aspects date back at least to the 4th millennium (as Sumerian Inanna, portrayed on the famous vase from Uruk). Under various names Ishtar was later to become the most important goddess throughout Western Asia. Anu was associated particularly with the city of Uruk, although he was

76

42

eventually to be overshadowed there by Ishtar, whose precinct Eanna encompassed already in the 4th millennium a most impressive array of monumental public buildings.

Enlil (Ellil), 'Lord Wind', tutelary deity of Nippur, was Anu's son. Like his father he came to be known as 'Father' or 'King' of the gods and was the first to replace Anu in the mythology. His role as national god of Sumer and bestower of kingship has already been discussed in earlier chapters. To Enlil originally belonged the Tablet of Destiny by which the fates of men and of gods were decreed, an attribute later assumed by Marduk. Another of the major gods, although perhaps not to be ranked with Anu and Enlil was Ea (Enki), lord of the underworld ocean or primeval deep, upon which, according to Babylonian mythology, the world rested (cf. above). Not only was Ea a friend of mankind and the source of all secret magical knowledge, but he was also the instructor of men in the arts and crafts. Eridu was the centre of his cult. The *enuma elish* tells us that Marduk was Ea's son, but Marduk's antecedents are obscure. Indeed he may even originally have been associated as Asalluhi with his father's city Eridu. Certainly Esagila was originally the name of a temple in Eridu and Marduk (like Asalluhi) appears with Ea in magical ritual. Surprisingly, Marduk remained subordinate to his father in matters magical; such texts contain a phrase in which he consults Ea on the proper and most efficacious procedure to be followed. As we have seen, the elevation of Marduk to the central position in the Babylonian pantheon took place no earlier than Kassite times, and perhaps even as late as Nebuchadrezzar I, as part of a deliberate move to endow Babylon, which had then become the political capital, with the aura of authority and kingship previously associated with Enlil's city, Nippur. In late Babylonian times the title *Bel*, 'Lord', became synonymous with Marduk, who like Ishtar assimilated to himself various aspects of other gods:

> Ninurta is Marduk of the hoe,
> Nergal is Marduk of the attack,
> Zababa is Marduk of the hand-to-hand fight,
> Enlil is Marduk of lordship and counsel,
> Nabu is Marduk of accounting,
> Sin is Marduk the illuminator of the night,
> Shamash is Marduk of justice,
> Adad is Marduk of rains. . . .[17]

This development, however, cannot be seen as genuinely monotheistic, since these other deities continued to be worshipped. Closely associated with Marduk was his son Nabu, god of Borsippa, patron of scribes, and, like Ea and Marduk, a god of wisdom. During the 1st millennium BC Nabu was popularized to such an extent (probably by the scribes themselves!) that at times he appears to rival Marduk and may indeed have been on the point of supplanting his father as supreme deity in the mythology.

A second group of gods consisted of the astral deities, the Sun, the Moon and the planet Venus. Of these the moon-god Sin (Nanna) was perhaps the most important. Sin's principal city was Ur, but he was also closely associated with Harran where we have already met

Nabonidus' unpopular attempts to reorganize his worship. Sin was represented by the crescent moon. The sun-god, Utu or Shamash, held a unique position as judge both of heaven and earth. As god of justice, the protection of the poor was his especial concern. Shamash, whose symbol was the sun-disk, was a son of the moon-god and was particularly associated with Sippar and Larsa. Another important god often included with this group was Adad, the weather-god. His symbol was forked lightning and his animal was the bull. Among West Semitic peoples and also in Assyria, Adad (or Hadad), was held in especially high esteem. In the early stages of Hebrew religion Yahweh (Jehovah) appears as a storm-god with attributes resembling those of Adad; like Adad Yahweh rode the clouds and his voice was thunder. Inanna-Ishtar, goddess of love and war, was, like Shamash, a child of the moon-god. She was Venus, the Morning and Evening Star, and was often represented riding on her sacred beast, the lion. Like Artemis she sometimes led a pack of hunting dogs, and as the winged goddess of war she appeared armed with bow and quiver. Her chief city was Uruk, although Kish, Agade and a number of Assyrian cities were also centres of her cult. By the 2nd millennium Ishtar had become the best-known and most widely worshipped Babylonian deity. The name Ishtar came in fact to mean simply 'goddess'.

A figure closely associated with Ishtar, but whose rank in the pantheon is obscure, is Tammuz (Dumuzi), a lesser god whose death and disappearance it was customary in certain places to mourn with solemn lamentations. Much has been written about Tammuz and the mythology associated with his name on the assumption that he underwent an annual resurrection, but the evidence for this remains controversial.[18] Originally Dumuzi seems to have been an Early Dynastic king of Uruk (or perhaps Bad-tibira) who, like Gilgamesh, became the subject of much later legend.

The ruler of the underworld, usually referred to as the 'land of no-return', was the formidable goddess Ereshkigal, joined in later times by

121 The sun-god, identified by his saw and the rays emanating from his shoulders, is often depicted on Akkadian seals being transported in his boat. The prow of the boat on this shell seal from Tell Asmar ends in the figure of a god or demon holding a forked punt-pole; a human-headed lion is tied to the prow. Ht 3·7 cm. Oriental Institute Museum, Chicago.

133

122 Old Babylonian clay plaque thought to represent Nergal, god of the nether regions, lying in a sarcophagus. He holds lion-headed maces and wears, in an upper belt, 5 daggers, and below, 2 axes and another mace. Ht 13·7 cm. Metropolitan Museum of Art, New York.

the much-feared god of pestilence, Nergal. Ereshkigal's messenger, Namtar ('fate'), appears frequently in magical texts; he was the herald of death and in his train were 60 diseases which he had power to let loose upon mankind. Another god often associated with Nergal was Erra, god of pestilence and war, against whom an amulet-shaped tablet was often placed in houses. Babylonian mythology is far from consistent in its view of death and the afterlife. There was said to be a palace with seven gates where Ereshkigal held court, but its supposed location remains unclear.[19] There seems even to have been some 'judgment' of the dead, but on the whole the Babylonian outlook on death was pessimistic and the afterlife was seen at best as but a dismal reflection of life on earth. The theme of the quest for eternal life, which reached its most inspired form in the Epic of Gilgamesh, was a popular one, and to judge from the many votive inscriptions requesting long life for the donor, life itself was held dear.

Official religion: the service of the gods

In Mesopotamia, as we have seen, both the temple and palace functioned as 'households'. Both played an important economic role, and at an early period the temple seems also to have assumed certain social responsibilities, particularly in connection with correcting the grievances of the economically underprivileged. This took such practical forms as the standardization of weights and measures and the regulation of interest rates. This role seems to have lessened after the Old Babylonian period as the economic function of the palace increased and the administration of justice became more secularized.

Central to Mesopotamian religious practice was the belief that man was created in order to serve the gods. This was interpreted literally and the deity, like the king, was cared for, fed, clothed and so forth by his courtiers, probably a more accurate word than 'priests' to describe many of the temple functionaries. A temple hierarchy in the usual sense of the word is nowhere attested. The temple staff included not only the *sanga* or 'chief priest', who was in fact as much an administrator as a priest, various types of exorcist, the *naru* or singers and the *kalû* whose duties included calming the god by music, but also such persons as scribes and the various overseers who ran the temple businesses.

Central in official Babylonian religion was the image of the god itself. The deity was considered present in its image; thus when the image was carried off in war, the deity remained absent until its return. That the role of the image was important in private worship as well is shown by the wide distribution of cheap clay replicas, and it is recorded that a son might inherit his father's 'gods'. Most temple images were made of precious wood, covered with garments plated with gold, adorned with pectorals and crowned with tiaras. They were fashioned and repaired in special workshops and had to undergo an elaborate and highly secret ritual of consecration which endowed them with 'life'.[20] The image stood on a pedestal in the cella of the temple; here the god 'lived' with his family, and was served, like the king, in courtly fashion. The god received the visits of lesser gods and the prayers of suppliants, although there is some doubt about the accessibility of the cella to the common man. The god might enjoy the company both of divine

123

courtiers and the statues of worshippers. Thus the king might install a statue of himself praying to the god. During festivals the image was carried in solemn procession through the streets.

Temple and court ritual were closely related. We read, for example, of the god Nabu going into the game park, like the king, to hunt.[21] The image was fed, in a ceremonial fashion accompanied by music, from offerings and the produce of the temple land and flocks. When the god was 'eating', he was, at least in later times, hidden from human view, even the priests, by linen curtains surrounding the image and his table. When the meal was done, the curtains were removed, but they were drawn again to enable the god to wash his fingers. Although there is no direct evidence that the Babylonian king ate behind curtains, that this practice was a feature of ritual suggests its origin in court custom. It was certainly the procedure at the Persian court. A ritual text from Uruk describes also a morning ceremonial reminiscent of the European *lever du roi*, perhaps equally a feature of the Babylonian court.[22] When the god had 'eaten', the dishes from his meal were sent to the king for consumption. What was not destined for the table of the main deity, his consort, his children or the servant gods was distributed among the temple administrators and craftsmen. The quantities of food involved could be enormous: a Seleucid text from Uruk enumerates among other offerings a daily total of over 500 kg (10 cwt) of bread, 40 sheep, 2 bulls, 1 bullock, 8 lambs, 70 birds and ducks, 4 wild boars, 3 ostrich eggs, dates, figs, raisins and 54 containers of beer and wine.[23]

There seem to have been a considerable number of regular festivals in Babylonia, including ceremonials of thanksgiving and sheep-shearing; various cities had their own calendar of seasonal feasts. The greatest festival was, of course, that of the New Year. In Neo-Babylonian times it took place during the first eleven days of Nisan, the month in which fell the spring equinox. The ritual for the first few days included various ceremonial ablutions and prayers, and on the evening of the fourth day the whole of the Epic of Creation was recited. In the view of some scholars it was actually enacted rather in the manner of a mediaeval mystery play. On the fifth day there was further ritual purification, and the god Nabu arrived from Borsippa to join in the

123 This impression of an Old Babylonian brown stone cylinder seal from Tell Asmar depicts, on the right, a worshipper bringing a sacrificial kid to the sun-god Shamash. To the left, Ishtar in the guise of goddess of war can be seen holding a 'lion mace' and a scimitar. Ht 3 cm. Oriental Institute Museum, Chicago.

124 Bronze head of a *mushhushshu*, the symbolic dragon of Marduk, found at Babylon. It shows clearly the viper's horns visible only in profile on the Ishtar Gate reliefs (ill. 116). 6th century. Ht 14·6 cm. Louvre Museum.

ceremonies. On the same day the king, whose presence was essential to the performance of the festival, made his appearance. He was permitted to enter the inner sanctuary only after the high priest had removed all his insignia. He was then humiliated by having his cheek slapped and his ears pulled, and then had to crouch down before Marduk and assure the god that during the year he had not committed any sins or neglected Esagila and Babylon. After a speech by the *urigallu* priest the king's insignia was restored, and he was again slapped on the cheek. The more painful his treatment the better, since tears in the king's eyes were deemed to signify that Marduk was well pleased. In the evening the king took part in a ceremony in which a white bull was sacrificed. The remainder of the ritual text is lost, but we know from other sources that the later ceremonies must have included not only the famous procession to the Akitu house outside the city, during which the king 'took the hand of Marduk' and led him from his shrine along the Processional Way and through the Ishtar Gate, but also the so-called Sacred Marriage. Details of how this was celebrated in Babylon in the 1st millennium are not known. Both the Sacred Marriage and the Akitu ritual appear originally to have been separate festivals which by the 1st millennium had been merged into the great New Year feast.

Personal religion

The extent to which the general public participated in these elaborate ceremonies is unclear. Certainly they were at least observers of the great processions, and one ritual text specifies that 'the people of the land shall light fires in their homes and shall offer banquets to all the gods. They shall speak the recitations . . .'[24] In Babylonia it would appear that the common man was not permitted to enter the sanctuary of the god, while ritual texts refer to other parts of the temple which were forbidden to the outsider. Such documents also mention ritual actions 'at a place which is not public'. The enormous enclosure that surrounded the ziggurat at Babylon, however, must have enabled the populace to observe, at least from a distance, whatever ceremonies were performed there.

111

Mesopotamian gods were fashioned in the image of man and were not without the shortcomings and lapses in conduct to which lesser beings are prone. Each Babylonian had his own personal god or goddess, to whom he offered prayers and sacrifices, and whose duty it was to intercede for him with the other gods and to protect him against the mass of devils and evil spirits with which the universe was believed to be inhabited and against whom even the gods were not immune. Prophylactic amulets were worn, and there existed a variety of 'priests' (*ashipu*, *mashmashu*) whose duty it was to recite incantations and to perform rituals designed to ward off such evil powers. A number of incantations have been preserved, generally addressed either to deities famed for their skill as exorcists or to the means – for example, fire – used to destroy figurines made in the image of the enemies of the sufferer. Such ritual prayers vary greatly in style, from short poetic masterpieces like the 'Prayer to the Gods of the Night' to little more than senseless, abracadabra-like sequences of words.[25] Among spirits especially feared were those of persons who had died by violence or

125 Impression of an agate seal from Babylon, showing a priest before a 5-stage ziggurrat or temple-tower. Below can be seen a fox catching a fish. Found in Merkes, 9th-8th century Assyrian in style. Ht 7·2 cm. Vorderasiatisches Museum, Berlin.

under unfavourable omens or whose burial rites had not been properly performed. Many evil spirits were believed to be the offspring of the two senior gods, Anu and Enlil, who were not always kindly disposed towards mankind. By contrast, Ea was always friendly and was thought to be the source of the beneficent arts of magic and incantation. Not all demons and spirits were ill disposed; the *shedu* and *lamassu*, represented in the form of huge human-headed winged lions and bulls, stood as guardian figures at the gates of Assyrian palaces. Private homes were protected by figures made and consecrated with elaborate ritual and buried beside the threshold. Some of these were dogs bearing such appropriate names as 'Don't stop to think, bite!' and 'Loud of bark'.[26]

Although we remain uncertain of the role played by religion in the life of the ordinary Babylonian, a number of texts, including private letters, give the impression that the various types of exorcist were frequently consulted and that prayers and sacrifices were offered at home to the individual's personal god. *Ludlul bel nemeqi* describes the devotions performed by the 'good man' (including libations to his god and prayers offered at mealtimes):

> . . . thinking only of prayer and supplication:
> Supplication was my concern, sacrifice my rule;
> The day of the worship of the gods was my delight,
> The day of my goddess' procession was my profit and wealth.
> Veneration of the king was my joy,
> And I enjoyed the music in his honour.
> I taught my land to observe the divine rites,
> To honour the name of the goddess I instructed my people.
> The king's majesty I equated to that of a god.[7]

However the texts often imply that neglect of the gods was not uncommon, while the wisdom literature suggests even a certain disillusionment.

Oh, that I only knew that these things are well-pleasing to a god! . . .
Who can understand the counsel of the gods in the midst of
heaven?[7]

Divination

Divination was undoubtedly the most important of the disciplines that
a Mesopotamian would have categorized as 'scientific', and should be
viewed not as some primitive magical or occult activity but as one of the
most basic features of Babylonian life. Indeed its senior practitioners
were men of influence, held in high esteem in their own society. They
were consulted on all important occasions both by private individuals
and officers of state. The army was always accompanied by a diviner
who in the Old Babylonian period seems to have acted also as general.
Indeed a diviner of the small state of Karana, Aqba-hammu, not only
married the king's daughter but later seized the throne from his
brother-in-law.[27]

Earlier reference has been made to the recording of 'historical'
omens, and beginning in the Old Babylonian period a variety of omens
were systematically written down and collected together in 'books' that
now constitute, in sheer numbers of texts, the largest surviving
category of Akkadian literature. Each entry in the long omen series
reads, whether deliberately or unintentionally, as did the provisions in
the contemporary law codes: if such and such happens or is observed,
then a certain consequence must follow. Babylonian divination was
considered a major intellectual achievement throughout the ancient
world, though alone among cuneiform literary forms it has no biblical
parallels, and was indeed an art derided by the Hebrew prophets.

Divination represented, basically, a technique of communication
with the gods who, according to Babylonian religious thought, shaped
the destinies of all mankind, individually and collectively. Its purpose
was to ascertain the will of the gods, to the Babylonian synonymous
with the prediction of future events. Its philosophy, of course,
presupposes supernatural cause and effect in all perceived phenomena
and assumes the cooperation of the gods in their willingness to reveal
their future intentions. Evil portended was not inevitable; there existed
a variety of purification rituals (*namburbi*) and other means of averting
unwelcome predictions. A great variety of techniques were used in
divination, including the observation of animals' entrails, oil in water,
smoke from incense, the behaviour of birds and other animals, and
celestial and other natural phenomena. A clear distinction was made
between provoked and unprovoked or natural omens. Preference for
these various techniques differed markedly from one period and area to
another. Although there exists some literature pertaining to the
interpretation of dreams, Mesopotamian philosophy was curiously
reluctant to admit that the gods made use of man himself for the
expression of divine intention – and indeed a dream was significant only
when 'interpreted' by an expert.[28] Thus shamanistic concepts, often
considered universal in primitive religion, are absent in Mesopotamia.

The behaviour of animals at the gates of a city or palace or within the
temple was considered especially meaningful; such terrestrial omens

were collected in a series numbering at least 107 tablets and known, from its *incipit*, as *shumma alu*, 'if a city'. Another series, *shumma izbu*, 'if a newborn animal', recorded the birth of malformed creatures.[29] Yet another, of some 40 tablets, is essentially 'medical' (discussed below). By the middle of the 1st millennium the emphasis lay largely on celestial portents in a development that cannot be dissociated from what would now be termed more 'scientific' advances in astronomy. Indeed the practitioners of the prophetic aspects of astronomy were viewed by the Babylonians as among their most distinguished scholars; of Babylonian methods of divination it is astrology for which that country was most celebrated. Astronomical omens of a relatively primitive type are known from the Old Babylonian period, but the real development of this essentially scientific branch of Babylonian divination came later in the 1st millennium. Evidence for this aspect of scribal activity is found particularly in large numbers of texts preserved at Nineveh in Assurbanipal's library.

Celestial omens were recorded in a series consisting of at least 70 tablets, known from its opening line as *enuma Anu Enlil*, 'when Anu and Enlil', in which observations relating to the moon alone occupy some 23 tablets. Celestial and meteorological phenomena – thunder, rain, hail, earthquakes – were thought of especial prophetic validity in matters relating to the king and state. In the Nineveh archives are preserved hundreds of reports sent by experts in the king's service, who functioned at a network of observatories throughout the country and whose responsibility it was to dispatch regular reports to the capital:

> The king has given me the order: Watch and tell whatever occurs! So I am reporting to the king whatever seems to me to be propitious and well-portending and beneficial for the king, my lord, to know.[30]

It would appear that some stations recorded celestial observations only, while at others the scribes, presumably those of more learned status, included in their reports ominous interpretations quoted from their vast compendia. By far the greatest number of these observation stations were in Babylonia – at Babylon, Borsippa, Dilbat, Nippur and Cutha – and the development of this specialized branch of ancient learning would seem to have been a particularly Babylonian contribution. A variety of astronomical texts show that at least two of these observatories, Babylon and Uruk, were still active in Seleucid times, while the Greek geographer Strabo mentions astronomical schools in Uruk and Borsippa and Pliny adds Sippar to the list. Extant copies of *enuma Anu Enlil* were actually written in Babylon, Borsippa, Dilbat, Nineveh, Assur and Kalhu (modern Nimrud – preserved on the earliest-known writing boards, chapter 4). 77

The Nineveh reports provide considerable insight into the influence at court of these astronomical experts. At times we detect even a note of jealousy among them in comments on their colleagues' competence:

> Heaven forbid that someone should write to the king my lord, 'this omen is worthless': the king my lord should not take it to heart!

Occasionally we find some royal disinclination to accept unfavourable predictions:

> The king should trust this unfavourable omen fully – how credulous
> is the king as long as they tell him favourable omens![30]

In another report the writer complains, 'The king, my lord, should not
say, "There were clouds, how could you observe?"' Even those kings,
like Esarhaddon, who were reputed to be unusually superstitious, did
not always give credence to the predictions of their diviners:

> This is what the text says about that eclipse that occurred in the
> month of Nisan: 'If the planet Jupiter is present during an eclipse, it
> is good for the king because in his stead an important person at court
> will die,' but the king closed his ears – and see, a full month has not
> yet elapsed and the chief justice is dead.[31]

Medicine[32]

The reputation of Mesopotamian medicine has suffered perhaps
unfairly owing to Herodotus' ill-informed but often-quoted remark
that physicians were quite unknown in Babylonia. In fact those who
were ill could call upon the services of two types of medical
practitioner whose cures were on the one hand magical, and no doubt
psychologically highly efficacious, and on the other, wholly medicinal,
based on the prescription of a wide variety of remedies. The expert in
magic was called *ashipu*, the practical physician and pharmacist, *asu*.

Already in the 3rd millennium there is evidence for the practice of
medicine. The oldest medical text known, an Ur III pharmacopoeia,
written in Sumerian, contains a list of more than a dozen medical
prescriptions, utilizing such raw materials as milk, snake skin, turtle
shell; plants such as cassia, myrtle, asafoetida and thyme; and products
of the willow, pear, fir, fig and date.[33] The remedies prescribed were
both salves and filtrates to be applied externally and liquids to be taken
internally, often dissolved in beer. The text reveals, indirectly, a
considerable acquaintance with a number of relatively elaborate
chemical operations and procedures; potassium nitrate (saltpetre) is
mentioned, a product which could only have been obtained with some
chemical knowledge, and there are instructions to 'purify' several of the
substances employed. Both the Sumerians and the Babylonians
attributed numerous diseases to the presence of harmful demons in the
patient's body, but there is no reference in this particular text to spells
or incantations, and it is clear that even at this early period practical
medicine could be quite independent of magic. Unfortunately there is
no mention of the diseases for which the remedies were intended.

A lengthy tablet of the Neo-Assyrian period, signed by the physician
Nabu-le'u, provides further, though regrettably rare, evidence for
medical treatment.[34] This text is divided into three columns, giving
respectively the names of the plants, the diseases for which they were
prescribed and the method of administration. The first column
enumerates a *materia medica* of more than 150 items, specifying what
part of the plant to use and indicating any necessary precautions. The
third column gives the temperature, frequency of dose, time of day, and
so forth, for its application and, notably, whether the patient must fast
beforehand.

The largest body of 'medical' texts from Mesopotamia, however, is a series we have already mentioned in the general discussion of omens, relating to the activities of the *ashipu*.[35] This handbook, 'If the exorcist is going to the house of a patient', is a late compilation consisting of some 40 tablets, grouped into 5 sections. The form used is similar to that of other omen collections. The *protases* or 'if-clauses' refer exclusively to the appearance of the patient's body or his behaviour, and each entry informs the *ashipu* of the nature of the disease and often the prognosis, 'He will get well', 'He will die'. With the exception of the badly damaged fourth section, no form of treatment is mentioned. The first 2 tablets, as the *incipit* suggests, are concerned solely with ominous happenings the *ashipu* may encounter on his way to the patient's house. In the second section (12 tablets) the symptoms are grouped according to the various parts of the body, beginning with the skull and ending with the toes. The names of the diseases mentioned are not medical, but designate the deity or demon that has caused them:

> If the patient keeps crying out 'My skull! My skull', it is the hand of a god.
> If he grinds his teeth, and his hands and feet shake, it is the hand of the god Sin; he will die.

In the third section (10 tablets) the prognoses are grouped chronologically, according to the progress of the disease from day to day. At the end of this section groups of symptoms are listed indicating specific diseases:

> If a man's body is yellow, his face is yellow, and his eyes are yellow, and the flesh is flabby, it is the yellow disease [jaundice].

The fourth section is badly damaged but contains fragments referring to treatment in specific cases and a description of various syndromes:

> If a man is stricken with a stroke of the face and his whole torso feels paralysed, it is the work of the stroke; he will die.

The fifth and last part of the work (6 tablets) was apparently devoted to the diseases of women, particularly those arising out of pregnancy and malnutrition.

The medical texts relating to the practice of the *asu* are also arranged in the manner of omen texts, but here specific symptoms are enumerated, followed by detailed instructions regarding the appropriate medication. The level of medical practice reflected in these texts can be traced back at least to the Old Babylonian period, but it would appear that the *asu*, a practitioner of some status at this time, was to some extent superseded in later periods by the *ashipu*. Unfortunately many of the relevant texts remain ill understood, and indeed unstudied, and we do not know to what extent this impression – or indeed any of our reconstruction of Babylonian medical practice – reflects the specific interests of scholarly circles, especially at Nineveh and Assur where the majority of the surviving handbooks were copied and studied. As with so many other aspects of Mesopotamian life, we know something of the activities of court circles and next to nothing of those pertaining to the common man.

Equally, the distinction between the *ashipu* and the *asu* was not always as marked as this brief summary may seem to suggest. Certainly the *ashipu* treated his patient largely by incantations and other magical means, but he did sometimes resort to the use of drugs, if only in a magical sense:

> These are 25 drugs for an ointment against the hand of a ghost . . . the secret of *ashiputu* [magical practice].

At the same time the *asu* is known to have had occasion to employ magical practice, although sometimes acknowledging that the 'incantation is not mine, it is an incantation of Ea . . .', i.e. the true province of the *ashipu*. The two forms of treatment were certainly not mutually exclusive and there is even evidence to suggest that under certain circumstances the *ashipu* and the *asu* were accustomed to work together:

> If the work of the hand of a ghost [often thought to be the cause of conditions of the ears and eyes] is so tormenting that the *ashipu* is unable to eradicate it, you [the *asu*] mix together eight drugs . . .,

and an Assyrian letter reads, 'let him appoint one *ashipu* and one *asu*, and let them together perform their treatment on my behalf'.[36]

Two passages from *ludlul bel nemeqi* illustrate in striking fashion the complexity, indeed the essential unity, of the various aspects of Babylonian thought that we have isolated under such conventional headings as divination, religion and medicine:

> My affliction increases, right I cannot find,
> I implored my god, but he did not turn his countenance;
> I prayed to my goddess, but she did not raise her head,
> The diviner (*baru*) through divination did not discern the situation.
> Through incense-offering the dream interpreter (*sa'ilu*) did not explain my right.
> I prayed to the *zaqiqu*-spirit but it gave me no instructions.
> The conjurer (*mashmashu*) through magic did not dispel the wrath against me.
> Whence come the evil things everywhere? . . . . .
> My symptoms troubled the *mashmashu*,
> And my omens have confounded the *baru*.
> The *ashipu* has not diagnosed the nature of my complaint,
> Nor has the *baru* put a time limit on my illness.[37]

Although we in the 20th century AD must confess a serious lack of understanding of the dichotomy of Babylonian medicine, there seems to have been no confusion in the Babylonian mind between the specific spheres of medicine (*asutu*) and magic (*ashiputu*). Insofar as the texts are in any way revealing of the nature and extent of Babylonian medical practice, they show a level of typical herbal medicine dependent on an extensive pharmacopoeia and including a number of drugs of known medicinal value. They reveal too the recognition and treatment of a wide variety of diseases. A number of tablets mention conditions of the eye, respiratory ailments, hepatic disease, and gastric conditions, though here the fact that Akkadian *libbu* can refer to the heart, abdomen, entrails or womb makes translation more than usually difficult. Conditions such as enteritis, colic, diarrhoea, intestinal obstructions and probably dysentery are mentioned; other tablets treat ailments of the genital organs and diseases of the legs, including gout. Mention is made of clinical examination: the temperature of the sick man was tested in several parts of his body, the rhythm of the pulse was apparently recognized, discolorations of the skin, inflammations, and in some instances the colour of the urine noted. The recognition of contagious disease is also attested.

There is little evidence for surgery and it is perhaps revealing that the lancet was referred to as the 'barber's knife'. The Code of Hammurapi tells us, however, that surgical operations were performed and that surgeons were skilled in setting broken bones. Indeed it seems more than likely that much medical skill was learned by observation and practical training, and that such practical knowledge is not reflected in the handbooks. There is, for example, no mention of the practice of trepanation in the texts, yet trepanned skulls have been found, one recent discovery dating from as early as 5000 BC.[38] An Old Babylonian text mentions a Caesarean section, but one apparently performed after the patient's death. Some evidence, unfortunately ambiguous, may suggest the treatment of cataracts by surgical means; a Neo-Babylonian text provides a unique reference to a medical specialist, an eye doctor. Midwifery was in the hands of women and there is a single mention of a woman physician in an Old Babylonian text from Larsa.[39]

The Code of Hammurapi also tells us something of physicians, including the fees they were paid (graded according to the social status of the patient and not the doctor!). Mutilation and even death were the penalties for surgical errors. Private physicians seem to have been rare, though they are mentioned in the Ur III and Old Babylonian periods; most seem to have been attached to the palace. At the time of the 14th-century BC Amarna letters we hear of court physicians being sent abroad, presumably with the object of increasing the Babylonian king's prestige by impressing foreign rulers with the skill of his doctors. Similar references can be found in the Mari letters. One of the most humorous Babylonian texts, 'The tale of the poor man of Nippur',[40] a story reminiscent of the Arabian Nights recounting three pranks played by the poor man on an avaricious mayor, tells in its second episode of the activities of the prankster disguised as a physician (*asu*). It is one of the few texts that reveal something of ordinary medicine, providing even a description of the doctor's appearance: clean-shaven and carrying the two insignia of his calling, a libation jar and a censer. Other texts indicate that the physician carried also a bag of herbs. The rogue doctor of the story announces himself as a native of the learned city of Isin where the temple of the goddess Gula, goddess of healing, has 61 recently been excavated (chapter 4). Most of our knowledge of Babylonian medicine comes from the learned handbooks of the scribal schools and libraries. The simple story of the poor man of Nippur reveals all too clearly how limited is our view of ordinary everyday medical practice at this time.

126 Old Babylonian mathematical tablet now in the British Museum. The problem illustrated by the concentric circles, which represent a village with surrounding ditch and dike (outer circle), involves certain geometric calculations given the circumference of the village, a constant distance between village and ditch, and ditch and dike, the depth and volume of the ditch and the inclination of the dike. '. . . beyond the ditch I made a dike, one cubit per cubit is the inclination of this dike. What is the base, the top and the height of it? And what is its circumference?' Ht of tablet 22·9 cm. For solution, see *RA* 29, 1932, 60-61!

Mathematics[41]

The complex mathematical system developed by the Babylonians represents a truly remarkable achievement. Unfortunately, owing to the relatively very small number of specifically mathematical texts recovered, we know nothing of its origins, although number symbols occur on the earliest tablets. The majority of mathematical documents so far known are school texts, such as those from Tell Harmal. These date from the Old Babylonian period, by which time the system appears fully developed. Already there are tables for multiplying and dividing and for calculating squares and square roots, cubes and cube roots, reciprocals, exponential functions, the sums of squares and cubes needed for the numerical solution of certain types of cubic equations, and so forth. On one tablet approximations of reciprocals of irregular

5

56

numbers are evaluated; approximations for $\sqrt{2}$ and $\sqrt{3}$ are also known. The system of tables alone, as it existed in 1800 BC, puts the Babylonians well ahead of all other arithmeticians in antiquity.

Along with the table texts there existed also problem texts, comprising a great variety of documents concerned with the formulation or solution of algebraic or geometric problems, including such practical matters as excavating or enlarging canals, military engineering, earth-moving, quantity-surveying, and so forth. Many of the arithmetical tables are combined with tables of weights and measures, a clear indication of the essentially practical purpose of Babylonian mathematics. Tables of exponential functions were used in the computing of compound interest, and there existed special lists of 'coefficients' required for specific calculations in handling such everyday materials as bricks, asphalt, copper and barley.

126

Babylonian mathematics seems to have been largely algebraic in operation, although the step to a consciously algebraic solution was never made. Numerous types of problem were solved by reduction to the normal form of quadratic equation, in itself a remarkable development. There exist also examples which are equivalent to solving special types of equations of the 4th and 6th order; one tablet from Susa implies a special problem of the 8th degree.[42] Geometrical concepts seem to have played little part in Babylonian mathematics, although the scribes commonly employed the Pythagorean theorem more than a thousand years before Pythagoras as well as such geometrical principles as similarity. In general, however, geometry seems to have been considered only one of many subjects in practical life to which arithmetical procedures could be applied. Geometric interpretation in the Euclidean fashion was unknown. This is evident from solutions where areas and lengths are added or areas multiplied. However, one tablet, enumerating problems relating the area of a circle to that of polygonal forms, seems indisputably of a theoretical nature (ill. 127).[43] With more evidence our present conception of Babylonian geometry may well have to be revised.

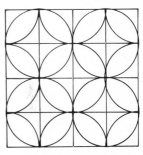

127 A number of complex geometrical relationships were known to Old Babylonian mathematicians. This diagram is copied from one of the few Old Babylonian maths texts that appear theoretical in content. The tablet was inscribed with geometrical exercises in which the student had to calculate the areas of various shapes. 'A square, the side is 1. Inside it are 4 quadrants and 16 boat-shapes. I have drawn 5 regular concave-sided tetragons. This area, what is it?' After Saggs.

Babylonian mathematics was based on the Sumerian sexagesimal system of notation, that is, one in which 60 units of one kind are written as one of the next higher order. A decimal substage is recognizable in this number system, but was rarely employed in mathematical calculations. Sixty as a base has many advantages including a large number of divisors which makes, inter alia, for simpler calculations involving fractions. Originally a bigger number was indicated simply by a bigger sign, but already by the 19th century BC a system of place-value or positional notation had developed. In our own system 526, for example, represents $(5 \times 10^2) + (2 \times 10) + 6$; in the sexagesimal system 526 would indicate $(5 \times 60^2) + (2 \times 60) + 6$, or 18,126 in decimal notation. Among ancient mathematicians only the Babylonians developed place-value notation; like our own Hindu-Arabic system, it allowed a flexibility of number writing which would have encouraged the growth of higher mathematics.

The Babylonian system had two inherent disadvantages: the symbolism was clumsy and no special sign for zero had yet been developed. The lack of such a concept was obviously felt by some Old

Babylonian mathematicians, for they occasionally left blanks where a zero should have been. A sign for zero, however, was invented sometime in the 1st millennium, probably in the Persian period, but possibly as early as 700 BC.[44] It was regularly employed in Seleucid astronomical texts, though never at the end of a number. It was left to Hindu mathematicians over 1000 years later to contribute the final step, namely the use of such notation for the smaller decimal units, the system we use today. Oddly, despite its obvious advantages, the Greeks and Romans failed to adopt place-value notation, although for astronomical computations the sexagesimal system was taken over by Hellenistic astronomers, their followers in India, and later by Islamic and European scholars. Indeed we use it still for the measurement of arcs and angles and for divisions of time. The Babylonian day was divided into 12 'double hours', each divided into 60 'double minutes', in turn containing 60 'double seconds', a system adopted by the Jews after the Babylonian captivity and subsequently by the Greeks and Romans. The 24-hour day is a Hellenistic device ultimately of Egyptian origin.

Weights, measures and exchange

The Babylonians developed a systematic series of weights and measures remarkable for their consistent and simple convertibility. This system was essentially sexagesimal. The true value of these measures, however, varied from town to town and from one historical period to another, a situation not unknown even in modern Iraq where the Baghdad and Mosul *huga* still differ in weight. Thus it is not possible to give any consistent value for the various measures expressed. Weights were based on the arbitrary concept of the 'load' which could be carried by a man or animal, the smaller units being assigned conventional values. Thus the load or talent (*biltu*) was divided into 60 minas (Akkadian *manû*) and a mina into 60 shekels (*shiqlu*). The mina weighed about 0.5 kg (18 oz), the talent thus approximating some 30 kg (67 lb). Occasionally the *she*, literally a 'grain', was used, a reflection of the early function of corn as a measure of both weight and value. In the Neo-Babylonian period, however, small weights were expressed as fractions of the shekel. Measures of length were based on the cubit or 'elbow' (very approximately 0.5 m). The Babylonian 'mile' (*beru*) was something over 10 km in length. This land distance was the equivalent in walking time to the Babylonian double-hour, also *beru*. The basic unit of capacity was the *qa*, which varied considerably from one period to another (from *c*. 0.4 to 0.85 litres). In Assyria the *imeru* ('donkey-load' or homer) was also used as a measure of capacity. The basic land measure was the *ikû* or 'field', *c*. 0.35 ha. The largest unit of land was a *buru* (18 *ikû*, *c*. 6.3 ha.). From the Kassite period onwards areas of land were often expressed in terms of the quantity of grain required to sow them.

128

Corn was the original measure of both weight and value but as early as the 3rd millennium silver had become the basic standard. As a means of payment silver was used in ingots and other forms which were weighed; ordinary transactions based on silver were generally carried

128 Babylonian weights were commonly made of haematite in the form of a duck. This is one of the largest ever discovered, weighing 29·68 kg. It was found at Babylon in one of the store-rooms on the eastern side of the ziggurrat precinct. According to the inscription it was a 'correct talent'. Length 40 cm. Archaeological Museum, Istanbul.

out without the silver changing hands. Silver 'currency' was stamped to indicate a certain minimum percentage of the metal, but at least in the Neo-Babylonian period this was often inferior to industrial silver and there are references to refusals to accept the inferior bullion: 'Stamped silver is not to be paid. Take pure silver.'

The invention of coinage is generally ascribed to the Lydians in the 7th century BC, but a casual reference in the annals of Sennacherib shows that small copper 'coins' were in use already in Mesopotamia by this time (704–681): 'I built clay moulds, poured bronze into each and made their figures perfect as in the casting of half-shekel pieces.'[45] In 493 BC an edict of Darius I introduced silver coinage into the Persian Empire, including Babylonia. In the Seleucid period the value of silver coins depended not only on their weight but also on the ruler under whom they were struck. With the freer manipulation of money that the circulation of coinage made possible, private banking flourished on a scale previously unknown in Babylonia, and from the late 6th century onwards we know of a number of dynastic banking houses, such as the Egibi family in Babylon and the Murashu in Nippur, who made colossal fortunes, inter alia, by lending money at exorbitant rates of interest. In regions to the west the Babylonian practice of charging interest on certain types of loan was regarded as ungentlemanly if not positively wicked. This is clearly reflected in the Old Testament attitude towards usury and the Hebrew contempt for the merchants of Babylon. Thus a letter from Ugarit (on the Syrian coast): 'Give the 140 shekels which are still outstanding from your own money but do not charge interest between us – we are both gentlemen!'[46]

Astronomy

The earliest extant records of astronomical observations in Mesopotamia are those preserved in astrological omens of the reign of the Old Babylonian king Ammi-saduqa, noting the appearance and disappearance behind the sun of the planet Venus. These documents, although they have some importance for chronology, are not astronomically remarkable. Thereafter a growing body of celestial observations is attested, primarily associated with the interpretation of omens but perhaps also important to the regulation of the calendar. We have already mentioned *enuma Anu Enlil*, the long astronomical omen series which seems to have acquired its final form during Kassite times, and the systematic reporting of astronomical omens, probably beginning at the time of Nabu-nasir and well documented from 7th-century Nineveh. Another three-tablet series known as *mul-apin*, 'plough star', after its first entry, also preserved in the library of Assurbanipal, summarizes the astronomical knowledge of the time, classifying the fixed stars according to three parallel 'paths', describing the movements of the moon and planets, and so forth. At the same time astronomical 'diaries' were kept, also predominantly observational in character but containing a number of 'predicted' data, particularly relating to solstices and equinoxes, eclipses and planetary phenomena.[47] These early aspects of Babylonian astronomy were relatively crude and largely qualitative; it is not until the Seleucid period that a genuinely mathematical astronomy is known, though this development almost certainly begins at least as early as Achaemenid times.[48] The astronomical theories of the Seleucid period were highly sophisticated, comparable in all respects to contemporary Greek systems. Indeed the Greeks themselves attributed to the Babylonians an ancient astronomical tradition, though the story later related by Simplicius (6th century AD) that a nephew of Aristotle, Callisthenes, while campaigning with Alexander, sent his uncle a complete list of eclipses ostensibly observed by the Babylonians over 1900 years (i.e. from the end of the 3rd millennium) is probably apocryphal.

A major incentive for the development of accurate astronomical observation would have been the attempt to achieve regularity in the calendar; associated with this was the necessity for accurate prediction of certain celestial events. As in most ancient societies, the Mesopotamian calendar was lunar. The lunar year is marginally more than 11 days short of the solar year. Thus an extra month is required roughly every three years to keep the two calendars synchronized. Down to about 450 BC the regulation of the calendar was somewhat haphazard, as is illustrated by Hammurapi's decree: 'This year has a gap. Let the following month be called a second Elulu.' The king hastened to add that taxes must be paid by the 25th of the additional or intercalary month, not by the 25th of the following normal month! Sometime after the middle of the 5th century (certainly from 380 BC onwards) a cyclic scheme of 7 intercalations in 19 years was introduced,[49] the so-called Metonic cycle, named after a 5th-century BC Greek astronomer despite the fact that his proposals failed to be adopted in Athens. This cyclical computation, first used in Babylonia, formed the basis of both the Seleucid calendar and the later Jewish and Christian religious calendars.

The adoption of the lunar calendar created another problem which proved more difficult to solve. The Babylonian month, like the Jewish and Islamic, began with the first sighting of the new crescent moon. A popular misconception about Babylonian astronomers is that their observations were extremely accurate owing to the exceptional

brilliance of the night sky in Mesopotamia. In practice they were concerned for the most part with the appearance and disappearance of celestial bodies, that is, observations made just above the horizon which in Mesopotamia is seldom sharply defined and frequently obscured by dust. Indeed the Greek astronomer Ptolemy, who lived in Alexandria in the 2nd century AD, noted that although almost complete lists of eclipses going back to the reign of Nabu-nasir (747 BC) were available to him, Babylonian planetary observations were on the whole unreliable.

The problem not only of seeing but of predicting accurately the date of the new moon led Seleucid astronomers to compose texts known as 'ephemerides', which are similar to modern nautical almanacs. The positions of the sun, the moon and the visible planets were carefully computed for regular time intervals and compiled in lists whose final purpose was the prediction of planetary and lunar phenomena. Specific functions such as the velocity of the sun, of the moon, certain complex corrections and so on were frequently computed for many years ahead. Closely related to these documents are the so-called 'procedure texts', giving the rules and methods for such computations. Unfortunately these texts are few in number and poorly preserved and their terminology is far from clear. The Babylonians' surprisingly skilful methods for calculating lunar and planetary ephemerides were probably developed during the 5th–4th centuries BC; certainly they were in common use by 250. Seleucid astronomical texts of known attribution come from two schools, at Babylon and Uruk. The Uruk archive seems to end with the occupation of Babylonia by the Parthians, but the Babylon school continued for some time thereafter, the latest cuneiform document known being an 'almanac' for AD 75.[50]

129 Seleucid astronomical text of the time of Antiochus I, found at Uruk. On the left is the planet Jupiter; a winged snake with the forepaws of a lion represents the constellation Hydra and standing on this fabulous beast is a lion, defined by its inscription as the zodiac sign lion. Extant ht of tablet 9·5 cm. Vorderasiatisches Museum, Berlin.

129

Horoscopic astrology

Closely connected with the development of mathematical astronomy late in the 1st millennium BC was the invention of the zodiac and the beginning of horoscopic astrology. We have already remarked on the rather primitive astrological omens preserved from the Old Babylonian period and later in *enuma Anu Enlil*. Such predictions were concerned, however, not with individuals but with national events; indeed celestial phenomena were interpreted solely with regard to the future of the country and/or the king:

> If the sun stands above or below the moon, the foundation of the throne will be secure.
> When the moon and sun are seen together on the sixth day of the month, war will be declared on the king.[51]

The modern signs of the zodiac appear on cuneiform texts of the mid-1st millennium BC, but the tradition of the zodiacal constellations is much earlier. The first evidence for personal horoscopes comes also from Babylonia; the earliest known example is dated to 410 BC and there are several 3rd-century texts of this type.[52] The tradition of horoscopic astrology is often thought to be Hellenistic, but much of our general knowledge of Hellenistic astronomy comes only from Roman times and no known Greek horoscope antedates 4 BC, with the single exception of the famous monument of Antiochus I of Commagene (62 BC). The early horoscopes from Babylon and Uruk record the date of birth and in one instance the date of conception, followed by an astronomical report concluding with predictions concerning the future of the child. Two were actually cast by Babylonian astrologers for individuals with Greek names. Despite this evidence for its early development, there is little reason to believe that Babylonian astronomers were particularly concerned with this branch of astrology, and during the Seleucid period their energies were devoted largely to the genuinely scientific observation of celestial phenomena. Astrology as well as mathematics and astronomy was much developed and expanded in the Classical world, and Hellenistic science – later transmitted through Arab sources – was to dominate the ancient world and western Europe until the time of Newton. But its roots lay undoubtedly in Babylonia, and the Babylonian astronomy of Seleucid times, with over a millennium of remarkable mathematical development behind it, was without question a major force in the development of true science in the ancient world.

Babylonian technology[53]

Several aspects of ancient technology have already been mentioned – the manufacture of glass, the brewing of beer, the early use of copper, the late spread of iron, vaulting and other building techniques, the pharmaceutical competence of the *asu* and so forth. With the exception of the relatively few tools and manufactured products that are non-perishable and may thus survive in the archaeological record, our evidence for Babylonian science and technology comes almost entirely from cuneiform texts in which the wealth of technical terms has proved, among ancient vocabulary, the most difficult of translation. Our knowledge of this area of Babylonian life is limited too by the same constraints that serve to conceal the everyday aspects of medicine. Whereas a variety of lexical texts listing minerals, chemical substances and other technical vocabulary reveal something of Babylonian methods of classification (largely by association) and of the range of scribal interests in what we might term 'scientific' knowledge, ordinary technological practice is seldom described. Recipes for the manufacture of glass, perfumes, and bronze are exceptions, but even these often fail to reveal the precise technology employed. As we have already observed, the scribes' approach was in general empirical rather than theoretical, and what was common practice or knowledge was often not recorded. Nonetheless, evidence from economic archives, particularly those relating to manufacturing industries, from letters and other types of text, together with that from archaeological investigation, indicates both a wide knowledge and understanding of the properties of many of the substances listed in the lexical texts and a considerable technological skill in such fields as practical chemistry and engineering.

The medicinal use of herbs and minerals has already been mentioned, and it is clear that the Babylonian *asu*, who was his own pharmacist, knew something of the true therapeutic properties of many of these substances. An Assyrian compendium on plants and drugs, preserved in the Nineveh and Assur libraries, contains more than 400 Sumerian names for plants, fruits, etc., and nearly twice as many Semitic synonyms; of the 100 or so commonly used in medical prescriptions and another 150 found less frequently, a substantial number have definite medicinal properties. The preparation of aromatic substances used in medicine, for magic and ritual and for cosmetics, was a major Babylonian industry. The texts reveal that women played an important part in perfume chemistry, even appearing in the role of 'author' or authority for the recipes.[54] Before 3000 BC chemists were experimenting with lime, soda and silicates in combination with coloured mineral substances to produce glazes, frits and eventually true glass. Soap, prepared from a vegetable oil and vegetable alkali, was also known as early as the 3rd millennium, though its use was largely medicinal. Archaeological evidence also shows a remarkable technical development. Among the chemical apparatus found have been crucibles, vessels for filtering, equipment for distillation and extraction, drip bottles and so forth.

Many aspects of Babylonian technology have their roots so far back in prehistory that it is impossible to trace their origins and development. We know from written sources, for example, that the wool industry was of great importance in ancient Sumer, and that the arts of bleaching, spinning, fulling, dyeing and weaving were fully developed by the 4th millennium. Archaeology reveals spindle-whorls for spinning at all early village farming settlements in Mesopotamia and, though rarely, the impressions of textiles preserved on clay containers or their stoppers. The chance find of actual textile fragments in unusual conditions of preservation at Çatal Hüyük in Turkey demonstrates a complex variety of woven stuffs already by the 6th millennium. Tanning too was an important Babylonian industry and

130 Rafts floated on inflated skins were used for heavy transport in Babylonia, while lighter local traffic was carried in coracles, such as this one, similar to the modern Arab *gufa* still to be found along the Euphrates. The modern *gufa* is made of wickerwork covered with bitumen, but this ancient Assyrian example, a detail from a relief of Sennacherib now in the British Museum, appears to have been covered with skins. The detail also shows a man fishing, supported by an inflated goatskin. After Layard.

one of certain ancient pedigree. Leather and skins were employed for a great variety of purposes, from shields and harnesses to small boats or 130 coracles of a type still in use today, inflated skins as 'floats' for swimming rivers, goatskin bags for drinking water, pouches for milk and butter, sandals, and so on. By the 1st millennium BC there is evidence for parchment, used mainly for cursive Aramaic writing.[55]

Two of the oldest industries are those of the potter and metal-worker. The earliest pottery yet discovered comes from the prehistoric site of Mureybet in northern Syria (*c.* 8000) and by the 6th millennium a wide variety of types is found throughout Mesopotamia. Although ordinary kitchen pots probably continued to be made 'at home', by this time there were already professional potters. At Yarim Tepe, in northern Mesopotamia, an 'industrial' area containing a number of elaborate two-chambered kilns is found not long after 6000, and tests using the scanning electron microscope show kiln temperatures already 131 well above 1000°C at this time.[56] The potters' wheel was in widespread use not long after 4000 BC.

131 Seal impressions from a late-4th-millennium clay bulla found at Susa show potters at work and 'commercial' pottery kilns. Simple two-chambered kilns are found as early as the 6th millennium. After Amiet.

Of early metal we know far less since metal can be melted down for re-use and it was too valuable a commodity to be lost in any quantity. Before 7000 native copper was already being made into simple tools and ornaments by cold-hammering, and by 6000 both lead and copper were being smelted (Çatal Hüyük and Yarim Tepe). Evidence for casting, probably in open moulds, appears by the latter part of the 5th millennium.[57] Although the source of ancient Middle Eastern tin has yet to be established, tin bronzes are found by *c.* 3000 and constitute some 12% of 3rd-millennium 'copper' objects so far analyzed from Mesopotamia.[58] The skill of Akkadian smiths can be seen particularly in the casting of such remarkable pieces as the head from Nineveh and the almost life-size naked figure of the time of Naram-Sin. The fact that the alloying of copper with tin, lead or arsenic greatly facilitates casting – copper is particularly difficult to cast because of the large quantities of gas given off during solidification – was certainly known to the smiths of this period, who were well acquainted with bronze; yet a recent analysis of the Naram-Sin statue, the surviving portion of which weighs 160 kg, shows it to have been cast of almost pure copper, a remarkable testament to ancient technological skills.[59] Unfortunately rare is the type of discovery made at Tell al Dhiba'i in 1965 of a fully equipped coppersmith's shop dated to the early 2nd millennium.[60]

15
17

The use of gold is attested by *c.* 4000, while the earliest pictographic sign for silver suggests that it was already cast in ingot form by the late 4th millennium. The sign for copper occurs frequently on the earliest (Uruk IV) texts, also in the form of an ingot. Among craftsmen mentioned on these texts are the chief smith and the carpenter. Other pictographs in use at this time represent chariots (both two- and four-wheeled), a wheeled carriage, a sledge, a seeder-plough and some form of musical instrument, possibly a harp or lyre; weapons include the socketed axe, throwing-spear, dagger and bow and arrow, all attested archaeologically long before in prehistoric times. The skill of jewellers, stone-carvers, smiths, glass-workers and a variety of other Mesopotamian craftsmen is readily apparent in any museum collection representative of their products. One must imagine also an even greater variety of perishable commodities – textiles, carpets, furniture – of which no trace survives.

Food and farming

We have earlier referred to the fact that the world's oldest known farming communities are to be found in the Upper Euphrates valley and in the foothill areas adjacent to Mesopotamia. By *c.* 6000 virtually

132 This Kassite seal impression provides an excellent picture of a Babylonian seeder-plough, drawn by two humped oxen. The central figure has a bag of seed-corn slung over his shoulder and is feeding seed into a funnel through which it passes down a seed-drill into the ploughed furrow. Several examples of this impression were found at Nippur on a clay tablet dated to the reign of Nazi-Maruttash (*c.* 1300). After Clay.

all the staple crops known from later textual sources were being grown, and the basic herd animals – sheep, goat, cattle and pig – had been domesticated.[61] By this time too the practice of irrigation was well established, at least in northern Babylonia, and the use of some form of primitive plough seems highly probable, though this cannot yet be proved. The development of irrigation and plough agriculture – and the easy availability of such profitable cereals as wheat and barley – paved the way for the growth of the large-scale farming that was to make Babylonia, despite its arid climate, the richest agricultural area of the ancient world. The lack of drainage, owing to the very flat land surface, was ultimately to create problems of soil salinization, for which there is already textual evidence before 2000.[62] This irreversible process was to cause the abandonment of large areas of previously highly fertile arable land and was undoubtedly one factor in the northward shift of settlement, and indeed political power, which we have earlier observed in the first part of the 2nd millennium.

Although both wheat and barley were grown in Babylonia, barley, which tolerates greater salinity and aridity than wheat, soon became the basic staple. This cereal provided not only flour for the unleavened bread which still remains the basis of Iraqi diet (*khubz*), but also the raw material for the brewing of beer, the liquid which 'makes the liver happy and fills the heart with joy'.[63] Millet, which has not so far been identified at prehistoric sites, was less commonly grown; rice was not introduced until the 1st millennium, probably in Persian times. Pulses and legumes were of considerable importance in the prehistoric diet, but are mentioned infrequently in later texts. It should be borne in mind, however, that these texts deal largely with essential staples produced for temple and palace, or on large estates, and not with common garden cultivation. The most frequently mentioned vegetables are onions, then as now a staple item in the diet, garlic and leeks; turnips, lettuce and cucumber are also found. A number of spicy and aromatic seeds were employed, such as cress, mustard, cumin and coriander. The Akkadian form of the word 'sesame' appears in the texts, but up to now no oil seeds other than linseed, a crop cultivated already before 6000, have been found among palaeobotanical specimens. Sesame closely resembles linseed, except that it is lighter in colour, and it is possible that the word may originally have referred to linseed which was replaced, perhaps as late as early Islamic times, by what we now know as sesame, introduced from the east.[64] Pistachios and almonds would have provided further sources of plant fat in the diet, but these trees grew only in the foothills. Olive oil, though known, was not locally produced. It would appear that Sennacherib attempted to cultivate 'the oil tree' in the gardens of Nineveh, but the olive was never grown successfully in lowland Mesopotamia.[65] The same Assyrian king was also responsible for the first introduction of cotton ('the wool-bearing tree').

The date palm occupied a unique position, comparable to the olive in the Mediterranean. It was probably first brought into cultivation somewhere in the Lower Mesopotamian basin.[66] As well as a crop of great nutritional value, which could be preserved and stored, it was the source of numerous useful products such as wood for light

6, 132

133 Limestone stele of Shamash-resha-usur, an 8th-century governor of Suhi and Mari. The inscription commemorates his achievements, the one of which he was most proud being the introduction of honey-bees into the land of Suhi. The governor is shown standing before Adad with his bolts of lightning and Ishtar with her bow. The stele was found in the 6th-century museum at Babylon (northern palace). Ht of relief panel 60 cm. Archaeological Museum, Istanbul.

construction, fibres for ropes, leaves for roofing, and so forth. The young palm sprout provided a celery-like vegetable, and in the 1st millennium an alcoholic beverage was made from the fruit. From the early 2nd millennium there are lexical texts listing some 150 words for the various kinds of palms and their different parts. Dates also provided the basic sweetener. Honey was known, collected apparently from wild bees, but was rare in ancient times and expensive even in the 1st millennium; the wax was used for a number of purposes, including medicines and to provide the surface on writing boards. The introduction of bee-keeping is described on a stele of a governor of Suhi and Mari (8th century), found in the museum at Babylon:

133

> I introduced the flies which collect honey, which in the time of my predecessors nobody knew nor introduced, and located them in the garden of the town Gabbarini that they might collect honey and wax; I even understood how to separate the honey from the wax by boiling; my gardeners also knew this.[67]

The date and the pomegranate were the most common fruits; apples, figs, pears, and some kind of plum were also known.

Animal products such as meat, yoghurt and cheese were eaten. Meat was not an important item in the diet, the poor probably eating it only at festivals. Milk, which spoils rapidly in hot climates, was not popular as a drink but was commonly employed in medicines. It was often stored in the stomachs of animals, the resulting contact with rennen producing a particularly useful product which, like cheese and ghee, was slow to spoil. Animals were kept not only for their meat and milk, but for their hides and wool. Sheep provided a curly and industrially useful wool, which had appeared as the result of a mutation after their domestication; a clay figure of a sheep from Tepe Sarab (near Kermanshah), on which the curly fibres are clearly depicted, shows

134, 135 Camels were not widely known in Mesopotamia until the 1st millennium BC and even then were used largely by nomadic Arab tribes. This detail (ill. 134) is from a stone relief from Nineveh, now in the British Museum, illustrating Assurbanipal's expedition against the Arabs. The whole relief shows the Assyrian army with chariots, horse and foot soldiers falling upon the Arabs who escape on their camels, depicted here shooting backwards as they flee. (After King.) The seal impression, of Achaemenid date, shows soldiers mounted on a horse and a camel. It is inscribed with the name of the owner. Dark blue chalcedony seal, ht 2·9 cm. British Museum.

that this development had taken place at least by the 6th millennium. Some 200 Sumerian words are known designating the various types and varieties of sheep; among the most economically important were the 'fattened', 'fat-tailed' and the 'mountain' sheep. Goat hair was also used for weaving carpets and containers. Pigs were kept for their fat and skin as well as their meat. In early periods the ox was the only draught animal, but by the late 4th millennium the onager was used to pull wheeled vehicles. The donkey was the major beast of burden and remained so even after the introduction of the horse which was used in the 2nd millennium largely for drawing fighting chariots and only later in the 1st millennium for mounted troops.[68] The camel was not native to Mesopotamia. Although known from early times it was not widely used until the 1st millennium, and even then largely by the nomadic Arab tribes. In the 7th and 6th centuries the punitive expeditions against the Arabs by the Sargonid and Neo-Babylonian monarchs resulted in the capture of large numbers of camels, the price of which consequently fell very low in Babylonian markets.

Fishing provided an important addition to the diet in early times, and economic texts up to the Old Babylonian period enumerate large quantities of various fish (over 50 different types are mentioned in Sumerian texts). After this time, however, fish and fishing are rarely referred to; in Neo-Babylonian Uruk the word fisherman even came to have the connotation of a lawless person.[69] Ducks and geese and various other, perhaps wild, birds are mentioned in the texts, as is the fowler or bird-keeper. The chicken was a relative late-comer, arriving only in the 1st millennium and moving westwards to reach Greece c. 600 BC.[70] In Syria it was known as the 'Akkadian bird' in the same fashion as the New World turkey, brought in from the east in recent times, is called in Baghdad the 'Basra chicken'. Locusts, which were considered a delicacy, provided another item in the diet; a stone relief from Khorsabad shows attendants at a royal banquet serving them on long skewers.

Two meals a day were apparently the normal custom, morning and night. For the wealthy the usual repast included not only bread, beer and meat, but also various fatty dishes and honeyed pastries. In

provisioning the army flour and wine were the staple items. Rations of wine were also issued to administrative officials, the quantity varying according to their status. Wine was made from a variety of fruits including, at least in the 1st millennium, both red and white grapes.

In retrospect

The perceptive reader will have observed how difficult it is to classify the textual material discussed in this last chapter, a fact which emphasizes the cultural as well as chronological gap that separates us from the Babylonian world. He will have realized that we are forced by the limits of language as well as the habits of thought into an ethnocentric terminology that, as in the case of the economic, religious and political institutions discussed in earlier chapters, tends to isolate concepts and institutions which in the Babylonian mind were inseparable. Such semantic problems obscure the real structure of Babylonian society, while our attempts to reconstruct its institutions and ideology, as indeed its history, are biassed by the disjointed nature of our sources and the wholly random circumstances of their preservation and discovery. Often we are forced to base what synthesis is possible on data of only limited temporal and spatial relevance, yet not to attempt an overall view would be to reduce the history and archaeology of Mesopotamia to no more than dull catalogues. The picture we have sketched is based on evidence that might be differently interpreted. Any study of Babylonian civilization is, and will remain, an amalgam of near-truths, misunderstandings and ignorance, but this can be said of more periods of history than most historians would admit. In our case the single stroke of an archaeologist's pick can revise whole chapters of ancient history, a point well illustrated by recent excavations at such sites as Tell Mardikh and Habuba Kabira South.

The history of Babylon may appear well known, at least in broad outline, and in parts is seemingly well documented by textual and archaeological evidence. Certainly we have, in some periods, substantial archives of a sort unknown to historians of Greece and Rome: the records and correspondence of a ruler, a temple or a merchant, preserved because they were written on clay tablets. In the Classical world such documents are hardly known, except by the fortuitous preservation of papyrus under very dry conditions in Egypt and – even more rarely – in Palestine and Syria. Yet it remains difficult to explain why Babylon attained its cultural supremacy in Western Asia. Its moments of political and military hegemony outside southern Mesopotamia were brief, perhaps because the Babylonians were always more interested in making money than war. Until the period of the Kassite kings – for whom the sources are more than usually laconic – Babylonia as a nation did not in fact exist, and it is one of the paradoxes of Babylonian history that the first monarchs to be successful in restraining the divisive individualism of the ancient city-states – earlier 'empires' were but temporary exceptions to the normal fragmented pattern – were foreigners. Certainly Mesopotamian civilization in its later days owed much of its vitality and persistence to this non-Babylonian dynasty, whose rulers were so zealous in their maintenance of traditions they clearly considered superior to their own. It is surely apparent – and this is where the purely political view of history forced on us by the nature of the official records may conceal the issue – that the real prosperity of the Babylonians, as distinct from the occasional imperial aspirations of their rulers, depended on their very fertile land and their focal position in Western Asiatic trade. Babylonian imperialism succeeded only briefly at any period, and it may well be that the farmers and merchants were better served by rulers who had no expensive military ambitions. Certainly one of the greatest fascinations of Babylonian archaeology is that many of its most interesting questions remain still to be answered.

136 The god Marduk and his dragon as portrayed on a massive lapis-lazuli cylinder (*kunukku*), dedicated to Marduk by Marduk-zakir-shumi I (9th century). Together with a number of other valuable objects plundered from the treasury of Esagila, it was found at Babylon in a house on the mound of Amran belonging to a Parthian manufacturer of beads. The elaborate decoration on Marduk's garments probably represents gold ornament. Ht of *kunukku* 19 cm. After Andrae.

Mesopotamian chronology

Presargonic Kings of Kish
   (2630–2316)

(En)-mebaragesi	2630–2600
Mesalim	*c.* 2550

Lagash
   (2570–2342)

En-hegal	*c.* 2570
Lugal-sha-engur	*c.* 2550
Ur-Nanshe	2494–2465
Akurgal	2464–2455
E-ana-tuma	2454–2425
En-ana-tuma I	2424–2405
En-temena	2404–2375
En-ana-tuma II	2374–2365
En-entar-zi	2364–2359
Lugal-anda	2358–2352
Uru-ka-gina	2351–2342

Kings of Sumer

	En-shakush-ana	2432–2403
Ku-Baba		
Puzur-Sin		
Ur-Zababa	Lugal-zagesi	2340–2316

Dynasty of Akkad
   (2334–2154)

Sargon	2334–2279
Rimush	2278–2270
Manishtushu	2269–2255
Naram-Suen (Naram-Sin)	2254–2218
Shar-kali-sharri	2217–2193
Igigi Nanium Imi Elul-dan	2192–2190
Dudu	2189–2169
Shu-Turul	2168–2154

Ensis of Lagash
   (2230–2111)

Gudea	2141–2122

Third Dynasty of Ur
   (2112–2004)

Ur-Nammu	2112–2095
Shulgi	2094–2047
Amar-Suena (Amar-Sin)	2046–2038
Shu-Suen (Shu-Sin)	2037–2029
Ibbi-Sin	2028–2004

Larsa Dynasty
   (2025–1763)

First Dynasty of Isin
   (2017–1794)

Ishbi-Erra	2017–1985	Naplanum	(2025–2005)
Shu-ilishu	1984–1975	Emisum	(2004–1977)
Iddin-Dagan	1974–1954	Samium	(1976–1942)
Ishme-Dagan	1953–1935	Zabaya	(1941–1933)
Lipit-Eshtar	1934–1924	Gungunum	1932–1906
Ur-Ninurta	1923–1896	Abisare	1905–1895
Bur-Sin	1895–1874		
Lipit-Enlil	1873–1869	Sumu-El	1894–1866
Erra-imitti	1868–1861	Nur-Adad	1865–1850
Enlil-bani	1860–1837	Sin-iddinam	1849–1843
Zambiya	1836–1834	Sin-eribam	1842–1841
Iter-pisha	1833–1831	Sin-iqisham	1840–1836
Urdukuga	1830–1828	Silli-Adad	1835
Sin-magir	1827–1817	Warad-Sin	1834–1823
Damiq-ilishu	1816–1794	Rim-Sin	1822–1763

First Dynasty of Babylon
(1894–1595)

		Kings of Assyria	
Sumu-abum	1894–1881		
Sumulael	1880–1845		
Sabium	1844–1831		
Apil-Sin	1830–1813		
Sin-muballit	1812–1793	Shamshi-Adad I	1813–1781
Hammurapi	1792–1750	Ishme-Dagan I	1780–1741
Samsu-iluna	1749–1712		
Abi-eshuh	1711–1684		
Ammi-ditana	1683–1647		
Ammi-saduqa	1646–1626		
Samsu-ditana	1626–1595		

Kassite Dynasty

Gandash			
Agum II (kakrime)	c. 1570		
Burna-Buriash I	c. 1510	Puzur-Assur III	c. 1521–1498
Kashtiliashu III	c. 1490		
(Ulamburiash)			
Agum III	c. 1465		
Kara-indash	c. 1415	Assur-bel-nisheshu	1419–1411
Kadashman-Harbe I			
Kurigalzu I	c. 1390		
Kadashman-Enlil I	c. 1370	(Amenophis III in Egypt)	
Burna-Buriash II	c. 1350		
Kara-hardash		Assur-uballit I	1365–1330
Nazi-Bugash			
Kurigalzu II	1345–1324	Enlil-nirari	1329–1320
Nazi-Maruttash	1323–1298	Arik-den-ili	1319–1308
Kadashman-Turgu	1297–1280	Adad-nirari I	1307–1275
Kadashman-Enlil II	1279–1265	Shalmaneser I	1274–1245
Kudur-Enlil	1264–1256		
Shagarakti-Shuriash	1255–1243	Tukulti-Ninurta I	1244–1208
Kashtiliashu IV	1242–1235		
(interregnum)	1234–1228		
Enlil-nadin-shumi } Kadashman-Harbe II }	1227–1225		
Adad-shuma-iddina	1224–1219		
Adad-shuma-usur	1218–1189	Assur-nirari III	1203–1198
Meli-Shipak	1188–1174		
Marduk-apla-iddina I	1173–1161	Assur-dan I	1179–1134
Zababa-shuma-iddina	1160	(Shutruk-Nahhunte in Elam)	
Enlil-nadin-ahi (Enlil- shuma-usur)	1159–1157		

Second Dynasty of Isin
(1158–1027)

Marduk-kabit-ahheshu	1158–1141		
Itti-Marduk-balatu	1140–1133	Assur-resha-ishi I	1133–1116
Ninurta-nadin-shumi	1132–1127		
Nebuchadrezzar I	1126–1105	Tiglath-Pileser I	1115–1077
Enlil-nadin-apli	1104–1101		
Marduk-nadin-ahhe	1100–1083		
Marduk-shapik-zeri	1082–1070	Assur-bel-kala	1074–1057
Adad-apla-iddina	1069–1048	Shamshi-Adad IV	1054–1051
Marduk-ahhe-eriba	1047		
Marduk-zer-x	1046–1035		
Nabu-shumu-libur	1034–1027		

Second Dynasty of the Sealand
(1026–1006)

Simbar-Shipak	1026–1009
Ea-mukin-zeri	1009
Kashshu-nadin-ahi	1008–1006

Dynasty of Bazi
(1005–986)

Eulmash-shakin-shumi	1005–989
Ninurta-kudurri-usur I	988–986
Shirikti-Shuqamuna	986

Elamite Dynasty

Mar-biti-apla-usur	985–980

Dynasty of E
(979–732)

Nabu-mukin-apli	979–944		
Ninurta-kudurri-usur II	944		
Mar-biti-ahhe-iddina	943–		
Shamash-mudammiq	c. 905	Adad-nirari II	911–891
Nabu-shuma-ukin I	c. 895	Tukulti-Ninurta II	890–884
Nabu-apla-iddina	c. 870	Assurnasirpal II	883–859
Marduk-zakir-shumi I	c. 854–819	Shalmaneser III	858–824
Marduk-balassu-iqbi	c. 818–813	Shamshi-Adad V	823–811
Baba-aha-iddina	812		
(5 unknown kings)		Adad-nirari III	810–783
Ninurta-apla-x			
Marduk-bel-zeri		Shalmaneser IV	782–773
Marduk-apla-usur			
Eriba-Marduk	c. 770	Assur-dan III	772–755
Nabu-shuma-ishkun	c. 760–748	Assur-nirari V	754–745
Nabonassar	747–734	Tiglath-Pileser III	744–727
Nabu-nadin-zeri	733–732		
Nabu-shuma-ukin II	732		

'Ninth Dynasty of Babylon'

Nabu-mukin-zeri	731–729		
Tiglath-Pileser III (Pulu)	728–727		
Shalmaneser V (Ululaiu)	726–722	Shalmaneser V	726–722
Merodach-Baladan II	721–710	Sargon II	721–705
Sargon II	709–705		
Sennacherib	704–703	Sennacherib	704–681
Marduk-zakir-shumi II	703		
Merodach-Baladan II	703	(Hezekiah in Judah)	
Bel-ibni	702–700		
Assur-nadin-shumi	699–694		
Nergal-ushezib	693		
Mushezib-Marduk	692–689		
Sennacherib	688–681		
Esarhaddon	680–669	Esarhaddon	680–669
Shamash-shuma-ukin	667–648	Assurbanipal	668–627
Kandalanu	647–627		
(Assyrian interregnum)	626	Assur-etel-ilani	626–623

Chaldaean Dynasty
(625–539)

Nabopolassar	625–605
Nebuchadrezzar II	604–562
Evil-Merodach	561–560
Neriglissar	559–556
Labashi-Marduk	556
Nabonidus	555–539

Achaemenid Rulers

Cyrus II	538–530
Cambyses II	529–522
Bardiya	522
Nebuchadrezzar III	522
Nebuchadrezzar IV	521
Darius I	521–486
Xerxes I	485–465
Bel-shimanni	482
Shamash-eriba	482
Artaxerxes I	464–424
Darius II	423–405
Artaxerxes II Memnon	404–359
Artaxerxes III Ochus	358–338
Arses	337–336
Darius III	335–331

Macedonian Rulers

Alexander (III) the Great	330–323
Philip Arrhidaeus	323–316
Alexander IV	316–307(?)

Seleucid Dynasty
(Seleucid Era year 1 = 311 BC)

Seleucus I Nicator	311–281
Antiochus I Soter	281–261
Antiochus II Theos	261–246
Seleucus II Callinicus	246–225
Seleucus III Soter	225–223
Antiochus III (the Great)	223–187
Seleucus IV Philopator	187–175
Antiochus IV Epiphanes	175–164
Antiochus V Eupator	164–162
Demetrius I Soter	162–150
Alexander Balas	150–145
Demetrius II Nicator	145–139
Antiochus VI Epiphanes	145–142
Antiochus VII Sidetes	139–129
Demetrius II Nicator	129–125
Alexander II Zabinas	128–123
Antiochus VIII Gryphus	125–96
Seleucus V	125

Sin-shumu-lishir	623
Sin-shar-ishkun	623–612
Assur-uballit II	611–609

Parthian or Arsacid Dynasty

Arsaces	c. 250–248
Mithradates II	c. 122

NOTE: None of these dates is certain, but from Ur III onwards the error is unlikely to exceed 2–3 decades and after 900 BC, only 1–2 years. All rulers of Babylon are included with the exception of the early Kassites for whom the evidence is virtually non-existent. The Assyrian and Seleucid lists are incomplete and contain only those rulers relevant to Babylon. The chronology followed is based on Sollberger and Kupper 1971; Brinkman, J. A. 1972, *AJA* 76, 272–73; *PKB* and Parker, R. A. and Dubberstein, W. H. 1956, *Babylonian Chronology 626 BC–AD 75* (Providence). The latest Kassite data can be found in Brinkman, J. A. 1976, *Materials and Studies for Kassite History*, Chicago.

Notes on the text

Abbreviations

AAA   *Annals of Archaeology and Anthropology*, Liverpool

AASOR   *Annual of the American Schools of Oriental Research*

ABL   Harper, R. F. *Assyrian and Babylonian Letters*, London

AfO   Archiv für Orientforschung

AJSL   *American Journal of Semitic Languages and Literatures*

ANET   Pritchard, J. B. 1955 *Ancient Near Eastern Texts Relating to the Old Testament*, Princeton, 2nd edn

An. St.   *Anatolian Studies*

AOAT   Alter Orient und Altes Testament

AOS   *American Oriental Series*

ARMT   *Archives royales de Mari*, texts in transliteration and translation

AS   *Assyriological Studies*

Bi. Or.   *Bibliotheca Orientalis*

CAD   *The Assyrian Dictionary* of the Oriental Institute, Chicago

CAH   *Cambridge Ancient History*, 3rd edn

HUCA   *Hebrew Union College Annual*

JAOS   *Journal of the American Oriental Society*

JCS   *Journal of Cuneiform Studies*

JESHO   *Journal of the Economic and Social History of the Orient*

JNES   *Journal of Near Eastern Studies*

JSS   *Journal of Semitic Studies*

LAR   Luckenbill 1926, 1927

MDOG   *Mitteilungen der Deutschen Orient-Gesellschaft*

MIO   *Mitteilungen des Instituts für Orientforschung*

Or.   *Orientalia*

PKB   Brinkman 1968

RA   *Revue d'assyriologie et d'archéologie orientale*

RCAE   Waterman, L. 1930 *Royal Correspondence of the Assyrian Empire*, Ann Arbor

RLA   *Reallexikon der Assyriologie*

St. Or.   *Studia Orientalia*

UE   *Ur Excavations*

UVB   *Vorläufiger Bericht uber die . . . Ausgrabungen in Uruk-Warka*, Berlin, 1930–

WVDOG   *Wissenschaftliche Veröffenlichung der Deutschen Orient-Gesellschaft*

YOS   *Yale Oriental Series*

ZANF   *Zeitschrift für Assyriologie*, neue folge

Chapter 1

1 Oates 1968, 8.

2 Masry, A. H. 1974, *Prehistory in Northeastern Arabia*, Miami; Kapel, H. 1967, *Atlas of the Stone Age Cultures of Qatar*, Aarhus; Oates, J. 1976, *Antiquity* 50, 20–31; 1977, *Antiquity* 51, 221–34.

3 Lees, G. M. and Falcon, N. L. 1952, The Geographical History of the Mesopotamian Plains, *Geog. Jl* 118, 24–39; Larsen, C. E. 1975, The Mesopotamian Delta Region: a reconsideration of Lees and Falcon, *JAOS* 95, 43–57.

4 The most recent survey is that of Gibson, McG. 1972, *The City and Area of Kish*, Miami; see also Weiss, H. 1975, Kish, Akkad and Agade, *JAOS* 95, 434–53.

5 Gibson 1972; Adams, R. McC. and Nissen, H. J. 1972, *The Uruk Countryside*, Chicago, 42 ff.

6 Kraeling, C. H. and Adams, R. M. 1960, *City Invincible*, Chicago, 26, 36–37; Adams, R. McC. 1969, The Study of Ancient Mesopotamian Settlement Patterns and the Problem of Urban Origins, *Sumer* 25, 111–24. See also ch. 6, n. 62.

7 Finkelstein, J. J. 1963, Mesopotamian Historiography, *Proc. Am. Phil. Soc.* 107, 463.

8 Jacobsen, T. 1939, The Sumerian King List, *AS* 11; Gelb, I. J. 1954, Two Assyrian King Lists, *JNES* 13, 209–230; Landsberger, B. 1954, Assyrische Königsliste und 'Dunkles Zeitalter', *JCS* 8, 31–73, 106–33; Grayson 1975.

9 Landsberger, B. (1943–45), Three essays on the Sumerians, trans. M. D. Ellis, Los Angeles, 1974; Jones, T. B. (ed.) 1969, *The Sumerian Problem*, New York, London; Kramer 1963, 41.

10 Albright, W. F., The Evidence of Language, *CAH* I, 1, 145–52.

11 Oates, J. 1960, Ur and Eridu: the prehistory, *Iraq* 20, 32–50.

12 Cooper, J. S. 1973, Sumerian and Akkadian in Sumer and Akkad, *Or.* 42, 239–46; Biggs, R. D. 1967, Semitic Names in the Fara Period, *Or.* 36, 55–66; see also Gelb, I. J. 1961, *Old Akkadian Writing and Grammar*, Chicago, 2–6, and *Genava* 8, 1960, 241–71.

13 Oates 1968, 15.

14 Adams 1969, 119 (see n. 6).

15 Smith, S. 1940, *Alalakh and Chronology*, London. For further discussion of the problems of Mesopotamian chronology, see also Rowton, M. B. *CAH* I, 1, 193–237; Parrot, A. 1963, Archéologie mésopotamienne II, 332 ff.; Landsberger, B. 1954, *JCS* 8; Oates, D. 1968, ch. 2; Brinkman, J. A. 1973, *Or.* 42, 306–18.

16 Diakonoff, I. M. (ed.) 1969, *Ancient Mesopotamia*, Moscow, 173–203; 1972, Socio-economic Classes in Babylonia and the Babylonian Concept of Social Stratification, *München Ak.-Abh. phil.-hist.*, 41–52.

17 Jacobsen, T. 1943, Primitive Democracy in Ancient Mesopotamia, *JNES* 2, 159–72; 1957, Early Political Development in Mesopotamia, *ZANF* 52, 91–140.

18 Hallo, W. W. 1957, *Early Mesopotamian Royal Titles*, New Haven.
19 Jacobsen 1957, 104–09.
20 Sollberger and Kupper, 59–60 and esp. n. 2.

Chapter 2

1 Heinrich, E., Strommenger, E., *et al.*, excavation reports in *MDOG* 101, 1969 onwards; a plan of the walled town, which includes Habuba Kabira South and Tell Qannas, can be found in Strommenger, E. Habuba Kabira Sud 1974, in *Annales archéologiques arabes syriennes* 24, 1974; see also Finet, A. Les Temples Sumériens du Tell Kannas, *Syria* 52, 157–74.
2 Weiss, H. and Young, T. C. Jr, 1975, The Merchants of Susa, *Iran* 9, 87–96; Kohl, P. L. in press, The Balance of Trade in Southwest Asia in the Mid-third Millennium BC, *Current Anthropology*.
3 For example, Kramer, S. N., 1952, *Enmerkar and the Lord of Aratta*, Philadelphia. See now Kramer 1977, Commerce and Trade: Gleanings from Sumerian Literature, *Iraq* 39, 59–66.
4 Sollberger and Kupper, 1971, 59 and esp. 57, n. 10. This book is the basic source for most of the inscriptions referred to or quoted in this chapter; some can also be found in *ANET* and Kramer 1963; for chronicle references, see Grayson 1975, and for Assyrian inscriptions, Grayson 1972.
5 Guterbock, H. G. 1964, Sargon of Agade mentioned by Hattusili of Hatti, *JCS* 18, 1–6.
6 Pettinato, G. 1976, The Royal Archives of Tell Mardikh-Ebla, *Biblical Archaeologist* 39, 44–52; Matthiae, P. 1977, *Ebla: un impero ritrovato*, Turin; on the language of Ebla, see now Gelb, I. J. 1977, Thoughts about Ebla, *Syro-Mesopotamian Studies* 1, 1.
7 Cf. Moortgat 1969, pls. 125–7 and Eannatum's Stele of the Vultures.
8 Sollberger and Kupper 1971, 128
9 Sollberger and Kupper 1971, 122, 129; Hallo, W. W. Gutium, *RLA* 1971, 712.
10 Delougaz, P., Hill, H. D. and Lloyd, S. 1967, Private Houses and Graves in the Diyala Region, *OIP* 88; Lamberg-Karlovsky, C. C. 1972, Trade Mechanisms in Indus-Mesopotamian Interrelations, *JAOS* 92, 222–29.
11 Hallo, W. W. and van Dijk, J. J. A. 1968. *The Exaltation of Inanna*, New Haven.
12 Westenholz, A. 1974, Early Nippur Year Dates and the Sumerian King List, *JCS* 26, 154.
13 Speiser, E. A. 1954, Authority and Law in the Ancient Orient, *JAOS* supplement 17, 8–9.
14 Kramer 1963, 62–6; also Falkenstein, A. 1965, *ZANF* 57, 43–124.
15 Sollberger, E. 1959–60, Byblos sous les rois d'Ur, *AfO* 19, 120–22.
16 Goetze, A. 1963, Šakkanakkus of the Ur III Empire, *JCS* 17, 1–31.
17 Kang, S. T. 1973, *Sumerian Economic Texts from the Umma Archive*, Urbana; some of the thousands of known Drehem texts are published in Jones, T. B. and Snyder, J. W. 1961, *Sumerian Economic Texts from the Third Ur Dynasty*, Minneapolis; see also Jones, T. B.

Sumerian Administrative Documents: an Essay, *AS* 20, 41–61.
18 Curtis, J. B. and Hallo, W. W. 1959, Money and Merchants in Ur III, *HUCA* 30, 103–39; for the use of silver as a unit of value in the Agade period, see now Foster, B. R. Commercial Activity in Sargonic Mesopotamia, *Iraq* 39, 31–43.
19 Falkenstein, A. 1956, 1957, *Die neusumerischen Gerichtsurkunden*, I–III, Munich; see also Kramer 1963, 85 ff.
20 Finkelstein, J. J. 1968–9, The Laws of Ur-Nammu, *JCS* 22, 66–82; for Urukagina's reforms, see Kramer 1963, 320–21.
21 Mallowan, M. E. L. 1947, Excavations at Brak and Chagar Bazar, *Iraq* 9; Oates, D. 1977, The Excavations at Tell Brak, 1976, *Iraq* 39, 233–44; for Tell Taya, see Reade, J. 1973, *Iraq* 35, 155–87, 1968, *Iraq* 30, 234–64.
22 Oates, D. 1972, Form and Function in Mesopotamian Temple Architecture, paper given at the XXème rencontre assyriologique, Leiden, cf. *Archaeology* 26, 1973, 142.
23 Oates, D. 1973, Early Vaulting in Mesopotamia, in Strong, D. E. (ed.) *Archaeological Theory and Practice*, London, 184–91.
24 Hallo, W. W. 1966, The Coronation of Ur-Nammu, *JCS* 20, 133–41; see also Hallo 1970, The Cultic Setting of Sumerian Poetry, XVIIème rencontre assyriologique, Bruxelles (ed. A. Finet), 116–34.
25 Gadd, C. J., Babylonia *c.* 2120–1800 BC, *CAH* I, 2, 909–10.
26 Oates, D. 1972, The excavations at Tell al Rimah, 1971, *Iraq* 32, esp. 80–82.
27 Groenewegen Frankfort, H. A. in Frankfort, Frankfort, Wilson and Jacobsen 1949, 155; for a more recent translation of the complete text, see *ANET* 455–63.
28 Weadock, P. N. 1975, The *Giparu* at Ur, *Iraq* 37, 104.
29 Civil, M. 1967, Šu-Sin's Historical Inscriptions, *JCS* 21, 31; Kramer 1963, 164.
30 Some scholars have made a distinction between Ur III 'Amorite' and Old Babylonian 'West Semitic', *inter alia*, Gadd, C. J. *CAH* I, 2, 627; the more commonly held view now emphasizes the strong similarities between the names of the two periods, cf. Buccellati, G. 1966, *The Amorites of the Ur III Period*, Naples; Gelb, I. J. 1968, An Old Babylonian List of Amorites, *JAOS* 88, 39–46. In the present book both groups are referred to as Amorite or Amurru as they were known in Akkadian.
31 *ARMT* VI, 76.
32 Kupper 1957; Oates 1968, 8–15, 38.
33 Oppenheim 1968, 96–8; *ARMT* I, 6; II, 48.
34 Oppenheim, A. L. 1954, The Seafaring Merchants of Ur, *JAOS* 74, 6–17; ancient Dilmun almost certainly included Bahrain and parts of the adjacent mainland as well. See also Hallo, W. W. and Buchanan, B. 1965, A 'Persian Gulf' Seal on an Old Babylonian Mercantile Agreement, *AS* 16, 199–209.
35 van Dijk, J. 1965, Une insurrection générale au

pays de Larsa avant l'avenement de Nuradad, *JCS* 19, 1–25; Jacobsen, T. and R. M. Adams 1958, Salt and Silt in Ancient Mesopotamian Agriculture, *Science* 128, 1252. See also S. D. Walters 1970, *Water for Larsa*, New Haven.

Chapter 3

1 Gibson, M. 1972, *The City and Area of Kish*, Miami, 37, n. 49.

2 Gelb, I. J. 1955, The Name of Babylon, *Journal of the Institute of Asian Studies* 1, 1–4.

3 Finkelstein, J. J. 1966, The Genealogy of the Hammurapi Dynasty, *JCS* 20, 95–118.

4 Dossin, G. 1938, Les archives épistolaires du Palais de Mari, *Syria* 19, 117.

5 The chronology for this period is far from certain. A contract written in Babylon and dated to the 10th year of Hammurapi's reign associates the names of Hammurapi and Shamshi-Adad in the oath. If Hammurapi's accession is placed in 1792, Shamshi-Adad must then still have been alive in 1782, yet the Assyrian King-List makes this impossible, cf. Oates 1968, 27–8. On present evidence these discrepancies cannot be resolved.

6 Published in *Archives royales de Mari*, texts in transliteration and translation (*ARMT*) I–XIX, Paris, 1950– . Letters cited include I, 61; I, 108; IV, 70; II, 23; II, 31; II, 34; II, 49; II, 72. Cf. also Laessøe, J. 1963, *People of Ancient Assyria*, London, 44–53; Kupper, J.-R. 1967, *La Civilisation de Mari*, XVème rencontre assyriologique, Liège.

7 *ARMT* II, 33; Munn-Rankin, J. M. 1956, Diplomacy in Western Asia in the Early Second Millennium BC, *Iraq* 18, 68–110.

8 *ARMT* VI, 76; Drower, M. S. 1969, The domestication of the horse, in Ucko, P. J. and Dimbleby, G. W. (eds.) *The domestication and exploitation of plants and animals*, London; also S. Bökönyi 1972, An early representation of domesticated horse in North Mesopotamia, *Sumer* 28, 35–38, (but note that the Selenkahiye bones are no longer thought to be horse).

9 Thureau-Dangin, F. 1939, Sur les Étiquettes de Paniers à tablettes provenant de Mari, *Studia et Documenta ad Iura Orientis Antiqui Pertinentia, P. Koschaker Dedicatae*, Leiden, 119–20.

10 Diakonoff, I. M. 1972, Socio-economic Classes in Babylonia and the Babylonian Concept of Social Stratification, *München Ak.-Abh. phil.-hist.*; the best general discussion of Mesopotamian social structure is to be found in Oppenheim 1964; for the Old Babylonian period see also Harris, R. 1975, *Ancient Sippar*; also Oppenheim, A. L. 1967, A New Look at the Structure of Mesopotamian Society, *JESHO* X, 1–16.

11 Jacobsen, T. 1943, Primitive Democracy in Ancient Mesopotamia, *JNES* 2, 163–4.

12 The most recent discussion is to be found in Kraus, F. R. 1972, *Vom mesopotamischen Menschen der altbabylonischen Zeit und seiner Welt*, Amsterdam; see also Speiser, E. A. 1958, The Muškênum, *Or.* 27, 19–28; von Soden, W. 1964, *ZANF* 56, 133–41.

13 Goetze, A. 1956, The Laws of Eshnunna, *AASOR* 31, 51–2; Sollberger, E. 1969, Old-Babylonian Worshipper Figurines, *Iraq* 31, 90–93.

14 Oppenheim 1964, 356, n. 1; Goetze 1956, 128–9; see also Gelb, I. J. 1976, Quantitative Evaluation of Slavery and Serfdom, *AOAT* 25, 195–207.

15 Laessøe, J. 1965, IM 62100: A Letter from Tell Shemshara, *AS* 16, 189–96; Oates 1968, 39.

16 Landsberger, B. 1955, Remarks on the Archive of the Soldier Ubarrum, *JCS* 9, 121–31.

17 Harris, R. 1963, The Organization and Administration of the Cloister in Ancient Babylonia, *JESHO* 6, 121–57; 1975, *Ancient Sippar*, Leiden.

18 Driver, G. R. 1931, A Problem of River-traffic, *ZA* 40, 228. For the *tamkarum*, see Leemans, W. F. 1950, *The Old Babylonian Merchant*, Leiden; 1960, *Foreign Trade in the Old Babylonian Period*, Leiden.

19 Finkelstein, J. J. 1961, Ammisaduqa's Edict and the Babylonian 'Law Codes', *JCS* 15, 99 n. 11; also Goetze 1956, *op. cit.*, 56 ff.

20 The precise meaning of *mar-awilim* is not clear but it appears generally to refer to free men (perhaps *awilum* but not heads of households(?)).

21 Driver, G. R. and Miles, J. C. 1952, 1955, *The Babylonian Laws*, Oxford; see also *ANET* and, for a more recent edition, Finet, A. 1973, *Le Code de Hammurapi*, Paris.

22 Edzard, D. O. 1967, The Old Babylonian Period, in Bottéro, Cassin and Vercoutter, 221. See also Kraus, F. R. 1960, Ein Zentrales Problem des altmesopotamischen Rechtes, *Genava* 8, 283–96.

23 Kraus, F. R. 1958, *Ein Edict des Königs Ammi-ṣaduqa von Babylon*, Leiden; also Finkelstein 1961, *JCS* 15, 91–104.

24 Finkelstein, J. J. 1965, Some New *Misharum* Material and its Implications, *AS* 16, 236.

25 Woolley, Sir Leonard and Sir Max Mallowan 1976, The Old Babylonian Period, *UE* VII, London; Woolley, Sir Leonard 1954, *Excavations at Ur*, 175 ff.

26 Baqir, T. 1959, *Tell Harmal*, Baghdad.

27 Lenzen, H. J. *et al.* 1964, Der Sinkašid-Palast, *UVB* 20, 28–32, and pl. 35.

28 Oates, D. 1967, The Excavations at Tell al Rimah, 1966, *Iraq* 29, 90, 94–5.

29 Oates, D. 1966, The Excavations at Tell al Rimah, 1965, *Iraq* 28, pl. XXXIV, b.

Chapter 4

1 Landsberger, B. 1954, *JCS* 8, 70, n. 181; Hallo, W. W. 1963, Royal Hymns and Mesopotamian Unity, *JCS* 17, 116–17.

2 Neugebauer 1952; for the most recent publication see Reiner, E. and Pingree, D. Babylonian Planetary Omens, 1: the Venus Tablet of Ammisaduqa, *Bibliotheca Mesopotamica* 2.

3 Oppenheim, A. L. 1970, *Glass and Glass Making in Ancient Mesopotamia*, 59 ff.

4 Brinkman, J. A. 1974, The Monarchy in the Time of the Kassite Dynasty, in *Le Palais et la Royauté*, XIXème rencontre assyriologique, Paris, 396, n. 7; Unger 1931, 276–9.

5 The conventional interpretation of this ceremony

has been questioned by Grayson, A. K. 1970, in *Chronicles and the Akitu Festival*, XVIIème rencontre assyriologique, Bruxelles, 164–70.

6 Brinkman op. cit., 395; in the 19th century some 18,000 tablets of the Kassite period were recovered from Nippur alone (Hilprecht, H. V. 1903, *Explorations in Bible Lands*, Edinburgh, 414). Major sources for Kassite studies are Balkan, K. 1954, Kassitenstudien: Die Sprache der Kassiten, *AOS* 37, and Jaritz, K. 1958, Quellen zur Geschichte der Kaššu-Dynastie, *MIO* 6, 187–265. A major new work, unfortunately not available when this book was written, is Brinkman, J. A. 1976, *Materials and Studies for Kassite History* I, Chicago.

7 Recent neutron activation analyses of the letters of Tushratta, a king of the Mitanni who presumably wrote from Washshukanni, and clays from the Khabur triangle in northern Syria have now eliminated this area as a possible location for the Mitanni capital, including Tell Fakhariyah, the site most frequently identified as Washshukanni (A. Dobel, pers. comm.).

8 Drower, M.S. 1973, Syria *c.* 1550–1400 BC, *CAH* II, 1, 493 ff. See also ch. 3, n. 8, above.

9 Knudtzon, J. A. 1915, *Die el-Amarna Tafeln*; Leipzig. A number of the letters relating to Babylon can be found in Oppenheim 1968.

10 Brinkman, J. A. 1972, *AJA* 76, 274.

11 Edzard, D.O. 1960, Die Beziehungen Babyloniens und Ägyptens in der mittel-babylonischen Zeit und das Gold, *JESHO* 3, 38–55.

12 Brinkman, J. A. 1969, review of The Kassite Period and the Period of the Assyrian Kings (*UE* VIII), *Or.* 38, 315.

13 Boissier, A. 1932, Document Cassite, *RA* 29, 93–104; W. G. Lambert 1964, The Reign of Nebuchadnezzar I, in McCullough, W. S. (ed.), *The Seed of Wisdom*, Toronto, 3 ff.

14 EA = 'el-Amarna', the numbers refer to the conventional order of publication, cf. n. 9 above.

15 Oppenheim 1968, 139–46.

16 Brinkman, J. A. 1970, Notes on Mesopotamian History in the Thirteenth Century BC, *Bi. Or.* 27, 312, n. 136; Porada, E. 1965, Cylinder Seals from Thebes, *AJA* 69, 173.

17 Brinkman, J. A. 1972, *AJA* 76, 275.

18 Brinkman, J. A. 1970, *Bi. Or.* 27, 308, n. 82.

19 Grayson 1975, cf. Synchronistic History and Chronicle P; see also Grayson 1965, Problematical Battles in Mesopotamian History, *AS* 16, 337–42. For another view on the accuracy of Chronicle P see Röllig, W. 1967, *Heidelberger Studien zum Alten Orient*, 173–84, but cf. Brinkman, J. A. 1970, *Bi. Or.* 17, 302.

20 Sollberger and Kupper 1971, 144 (IIIA2s).

21 Assyrian royal inscriptions down to the end of the reign of Assurnasirpal II (859) are quoted from Grayson 1972, 1976; for later inscriptions, see Luckenbill 1926–7 (*LAR*).

22 Lambert, W. G. 1957–58, Three Unpublished Fragments of the Tukulti-Ninurta Epic, *AfO* 18, 38–51.

23 For a fuller account of this period see Munn-Rankin, J. M. 1975, Assyrian Military Power 1300–1200 BC, *CAH* II, 2, 274–306, and review by Brinkman 1970, *Bi.Or.* 27, 301–14; also Wiseman, D. J. Assyria and Babylonia *c.* 1200–1000 BC, *CAH* II, 2, 443 ff.

24 Brinkman, J. A. 1970, *Bi.Or.* 27, 311.

25 Labat, R. 1975, Elam and Western Persia *c.* 1200–1000 BC, *CAH*, II, 2, 487; see also Tadmor, H. 1958, Historical Implications of the Correct Reading of Akkadian *dâku*, *JNES* 17, 138.

26 Tadmor, *op. cit.*, 138, l. 10; also Lambert, W. G. 1957–8, *AfO* 18, 399; although Chronicle P leaves Marduk in Assur throughout this period (ll. 12–13), cf. n. 19 above.

27 Baqir, T. Iraq Government Excavations at Aqar Quf, *Iraq* supplement 1944, 1945; *Iraq* 8, 1946, 73–93.

28 A document purported to come from the 'foundation level' of room 15, Palace Area, is dated to the reigns of Nazi-Maruttash (1323–1298) and Kadashman-Turgu (1297–1280); if this attribution is correct then phase III of the palace must also be later than Kurigalzu II. Gurney, O. R. 1949, Texts from Dur-Kurigalzu, *Iraq* 11, 133–5.

29 Baqir, T. 1945, *Iraq* supplement, 12. The number of Kurigalzus is far from certain, cf. Brinkman 1969, *Or.* 38, 320 ff.; Goetze, A. 1964, The Kassites and Near Eastern Chronology, *JNES* 18, 97–101; Jaritz, K. 1958, *MIO* 6, 210; etc. Note also that there is another (?earlier) name for Dur-Kurigalzu, which is Parsâ.

30 Reuther, O. 1926, Merkes, Die Innenstadt von Babylon, *WVDOG* 47, 16.

31 Huot, J.-L. *et al.* 1976, Larsa, rapport préliminaire sur la sixième campagne, *Syria* 53, 1–45.

32 Strommenger and Hirmer 1964, pl. 180.

33 Lambert, W. G. 1957, Ancestors, Authors and Canonicity, *JCS* 11, 1–9.

34 Gurney, O. R. 1952, *The Hittites*, Harmondsworth, 83.

35 Snodgrass, A. M. n.d., Early Iron Working, British Academy – Russian Academy of Sciences Symposium, Cambridge 1974; on iron generally, cf. Maddin, R., Muhly, J. D. and Wheeler, T. S. 1977, How the Iron Age Began, *Sci. Am.* 237, 4.

36 Brinkman, J. A. 1972, *AJA* 76, 278; the basic source for post-Kassite Babylon is an important and extensive work by the same author, A Political History of Post-Kassite Babylonia 1158–722 BC, *An.Or.* 43, 1968, hereafter abbreviated *PKB*.

37 Wiseman, D. J. 1975, *CAH* II, 2, 455; King, L. W. 1912, *Babylonian Boundary Stones*, London, no. 6.

38 Lambert 1964, see n. 13 above.

39 *PKB* 101 ff.

40 Grayson 1976, 3ff.

41 Oates and Oates 1976, 134.

42 Grayson 1975, 189; *PKB* 130.

43 The interpretation given here is far from certain but would seem to be implied in Grayson, Chronicle 24, ll. 7–8; see also 165 and *PKB* 130 ff.

44 Jacobsen 1976, 227; cf. also Lambert, W. G. 1957–8, *AfO* 18, 395–401.

45 *PKB* 166 ff.
46 Lambert 1957–8, *AfO* 18, 398–9; King, L. W. 1912, no. 36.
47 Oates, D. 1963, The Excavations at Nimrud (Kalhu), 1962, *Iraq* 25, 20 ff.
48 *PKB* 22, 227; Grayson 1975, 13–14; Sachs, A. 1948, A Classification of the Babylonian Astronomical Tablets of the Seleucid Period, *JCS* 2, 285–6; the earliest preserved 'diary' is dated to Nebuchadrezzar year 37, Sachs, A. 1952, A Late Babylonian Star Catalog, *JCS* 6, 149.
49 Chronicle 15, l. 23; see also Drews, R. 1975, The Babylonian Chronicles and Berossus, *Iraq* 37, 44–5; Wiseman, D. J. 1955, Assyrian Writing-Boards, *Iraq* 17, 3–20.
50 *PKB* 227.
51 Saggs, H. W. F. 1955, The Nimrud Letters, *Iraq* 17, 24.

Chapter 5

1 II Kings 20:12 ff.; Isaiah 39. For a history of Merodach-Baladan, see Brinkman, J. A. 1964, Merodach-Baladan II, in *Studies Presented to A. Leo Oppenheim*, Chicago; also 1965, *JNES* 24, 161–6.
2 See ch. 4, n. 21.
3 For the possibility that Sargon was in fact a son of Tiglath-Pileser III, see *AfO* 9, 1933–4, 79; also *ABL* 99, rev. 3–4, a letter to the king 'before, when your father was ruling'.
4 Clay, A. T. 1915, Miscellaneous Inscriptions, *YOS* Bab. Texts I, 60–61; Grayson 1975.
5 Brinkman, J. A. 1973, Sennacherib's Babylonian Problem, *JCS* 25, 93.
6 II Kings 19, 36–7; Brinkman 1973, 95, n. 34; *ANET* 288, quoted here on p. 123, lines 25–31.
7 Wiseman, D. J. 1958, The Vassal-Treaties of Esarhaddon, *Iraq* 20.
8 *LAR* II, 381 (988).
9 The royal brick was moulded in more esoteric materials, see Ellis, R. S. 1968, *Foundation Deposits in Ancient Mesopotamia*, New Haven, 178–9.
10 Oates, J. 1965, Assyrian Chronology, 631–612 BC, *Iraq* 27, 135–59; Reade, J. 1970, The Accession of Sinsharishkun, *JCS* 23, 1–9.
11 *LAR* II, 379; Postgate 1977, 133.
12 Woolley, Sir Leonard 1962, The Neo-Babylonian and Persian Periods, *UE* IX, pl. 29.
13 Cf. Warka King-List, van Dijk, J. 1962, Die Inschriftenfunde, *UVB* 18, 53; also Oates, J. 1965, *Iraq* 27, 135–59.
14 Oppenheim, A. L. 1955, 'Siege-Documents' from Nippur, *Iraq* 17, 69–89; van Dijk, J. 1962, *UVB* 18, 39–62.
15 Oates, D. 1960, 1961, The Excavations at Nimrud (Kalhu), *Iraq* 23, 9; *Iraq* 24, 12–13.
16 The account of Josephus differs substantially from that of the Babylonian Chronicles; cf. Wiseman, D. J. 1956, *Chronicles of the Chaldaean Kings*, London, 33–5.
17 II Kings 24, 14–16.
18 *ANET* 308.
19 The most recent information about the wall north of Baghdad, which has long been identified as the Median Wall, can be found in Barnett, R. D. 1963, Xenophon and the Wall of Media, *Journal of Hellenic Studies*, 1–26; Reade, J. E. 1964, El Mutabbaq and Umm Rus, *Sumer* 20, 83–9.
20 II Kings 25, 22–6; Wiseman 1956, 94–5.
21 Grayson 1975.
22 Gadd, C. J. 1958, The Harran Inscriptions of Nabonidus, *An.St.* 8, 35–92; other texts of Nabonidus can be found in Grayson 1975 and *ANET*; see also Tadmor, H. 1965, The Inscriptions of Nabunaid: Historical Arrangement, *AS* 16, 351–63, and Dougherty, R. P. 1929, Nabonidus and Belshazzar, *YOS* 15.
23 Oppenheim, A. L. 1956, The Interpretation of Dreams in the Ancient Near East, *Trans. Am. Phil. Soc.* 46, 250.
24 Saggs 1962, 147–8, 261 ff.
25 Harran Inscription H2, cf. n. 22.
26 Milik, J. T. 1956, Prière de Nabonide et autres écrits d'un Cycle de Daniel, *Revue Biblique* 62, 408. On Taima, see Röllig, W. 1964, Nabonid und Tema, XIème rencontre assyriologique, Leiden, 21–32.
27 *ANET* 314.
28 Grayson 1975, 109–10.
29 *ANET* 315.
30 Cardascia, G. 1951, *Les archives des Murašu, une famille d'hommes d'affaires babyloniens à l'Époque perse (455–403)*, Paris; Ungnad, A. 1941–4, Das Haus Egibi, *AfO* 14, 57–64.
31 Jacobsen, T. 1957, Early Political Development in Mesopotamia, *ZANF* 18, 139–40, n. 115.
32 *ANET* 317; see also n. 9 above.
33 Unger 1931, 168; Pallis 1956, 31, n. 2.
34 Tarn, W. W. 1951, *The Greeks in Bactria and India*, Cambridge, 187–8.
35 Unger 1931, 319 ff.
36 Strassmaier, J. N. 1888, Arsaciden-Inschriften, *ZA* 3, 146.
37 Sachs, A. 1976, The Latest Datable Cuneiform Tablets, *AOAT* 25; for late Babylonian texts actually written in the Greek alphabet, see Sollberger, E. 1962, Graeco-Babyloniaca, *Iraq* 24, 63–72.
38 Classical and biblical references to Babylon can be found in the appendices of an excellent but now little-consulted book, Lane, W. H. 1923, *Babylonian Problems*, London.
39 The official publications of Koldewey's excavations can be found in *WVDOG* 15, 32, 47, 48, 55, 59, 62 (1911–1957); for a summary of the earlier of these reports see Unger 1931. See also brief reports in *Sumer* since 1958.
40 Koldewey, R. 1914, *The Excavations at Babylon* (transl. A. S. Johns), London, v.
41 Langdon, S. 1905, *Building Inscriptions of the Neo-Babylonian Empire* I, Paris, 85.
42 Cf. n. 18 above.
43 Unger 1931, 229 ff.
44 For the possibility that the earlier ziggurrat may have been part of Esagila, see the Creation Epic VI, 63 (*ANET* 69).
45 Unger 1931, 191, 246; see also Busink, T. A.

1949, *Die Babylonische tempeltoren*, Leiden; von Soden, W. 1971, Etemenanki vor Esarhaddon, *Ugarit-Forschungen* 3, 253–63; Wiseman, D. J. 1975, The Temple Tower Again, *Le Temple et le Culte*, XXème rencontre assyriologique, Leiden, 150.

46 Koldewey 1914, 212; recent German excavations have recovered Islamic remains in the area of the alleged Neo-Babylonian precinct walls of Etemenanki, H. Lenzen, pers. comm.; *Sumer* 23, 1967, i.

47 Woolley, Sir Leonard 1962, *UE* IX, pls. 15, 70.

48 Koldewey 1914, 131.

49 Clay, A. T. 1915, Miscellaneous Inscriptions, *YOS* Babylonian Texts I, 69 ff., 62 ff.

50 Langdon, S. 1915/16, New Inscriptions of Nabunaid, *AJSL* 32, 105.

51 *PKB* 145, n. 874; 301, n. 1975; Weiss, H. 1975, Kish, Akkad and Agade, *JAOS* 95, 446–7.

52 Hilprecht, H. V. 1903, *Explorations in Bible Lands*, Edinburgh, 516 ff., squeeze ill. p. 517; Sollberger and Kupper 1971, 112–13.

53 Oppenheim 1968, 87.

Chapter 6

1 Oppenheim, A. L. 1965, A Note on the Scribes in Mesopotamia, *AS* 16, 254; *ARMT* II, 132.

2 For Mesopotamian education generally, see Gadd, C. J. 1956, *Teachers and Students in the Oldest Schools*, London; Kramer 1963, ch. 6; Å. Sjöberg 1976, The Old Babylonian Eduba, *AS* 20, 159–79.

3 Gadd 1956, 20.

4 Landsberger, B. 1960, Scribal Concepts of Education, in Kraeling, C. H. and Adams, R. M. (eds.), *City Invincible*, Chicago, 100–01.

5 Cf. ch. 4, n. 33.

6 Kramer, S. N. 1975, Two British Museum iršemma 'Catalogues', *St. Or.* 46, 141–66. See also Hallo, W. W. 1976, Toward a History of Sumerian Literature, *AS* 20, 181–203.

7 Lambert 1960; see also *ANET*.

8 Lambert 1960, 259; see also *CAD, kinattūtu*.

9 Lambert 1960, 16.

10 Inter alia, *ANET*; Jacobsen 1976.

11 Frankfort *et al.*, 1949, 226.

12 Inter alia, *ANET*; Jacobsen 1976.

13 See, inter alia, Dhorme, E. 1949, Les religions de Babylonie et d'Assyrie, Paris; Bottéro, J. 1952, La religion babylonienne, Paris, Frankfort *et al.* 1946; Oppenheim 1964, ch. 4; Jacobsen 1976.

14 Oppenheim 1964, 172.

15 Jacobsen, T. 1970, Mesopotamian Gods and Pantheons, in *Toward the Image of Tammuz* (ed. W. L. Moran), Cambridge, Mass., 16–38; Kramer, S. N. 1960, Sumero-Akkadian Interconnections: Religious Ideas, *Genava* 8, 272–83.

16 According to documents from Lagash Enlil had become the leading deity already in the 24th century BC, Kramer 1960, 277, n. 25.

17 Jacobsen 1976, 235.

18 Jacobsen 1976, 25 ff.; Kramer 1969, 107–33; Gurney, O. R. 1962, Tammuz Reconsidered, *JSS* 7, 147–60; also von Soden, W. 1955, *ZANF* 17, 130–66.

19 Kramer, S. N. 1960, Death and Nether World

According to the Sumerian Literary Texts, *Iraq* 22, 59–68.

20 Smith, S. 1925, The Babylonian Ritual for the Consecration and Induction of a Divine Statue, *JRAS*; see also ch. 4, n. 46.

21 *ABL* 366 (trans. *RCAE*).

22 Oppenheim 1964, 183–98; Thureau-Dangin, F. 1921, *Rituels accadiens*, Paris, 89 ff.

23 *ANET* 343–45; Thureau-Dangin 1921, 62 ff.

24 *ANET* 339.

25 *ANET* 390–91; Reiner, E. 1958, *Šurpu, a Collection of Sumerian and Akkadian Incantations*, Graz.

26 Gurney, O. R. 1935, Babylonian Prophylactic Figures and their Ritual, *AAA* 22, 31–96.

27 Dalley, S., Walker, C. B. F. and Hawkins, J. D. 1976, *The Old Babylonian Tablets from Tell al Rimah*, London, 33.

28 Oppenheim, A. L. 1956, The interpretation of Dreams in the Ancient Near East, *Trans. Am. Phil. Soc.* 46. For divination generally, see *La Divination en Mésopotamie ancienne*, Paris 1966.

29 Leichty, E. 1970. *Šumma izbu*, New York.

30 Oppenheim, A. L. 1969, Divination and Celestial Observation in the Last Assyrian Empire, *Centaurus* 14, 97–135, quotations from pp. 115, 118, 120.

31 Oppenheim 1964, 227.

32 Labat, R. 1963, Mesopotamia, in Taton, R. (ed.), *Ancient and Medieval Science*, London, 78–89; Oppenheim, A. L. 1962, Mesopotamian Medicine, *Bull. of the Hist. of Medicine* 36, 97–108.

33 Kramer, S. N. 1956, *From the Tablets of Sumer*, Indian Hills, Colorado, 100–04; Civil, M. 1960, Prescriptions médicales sumériennes, *RA* 54, 57–72.

34 Labat 1963, 79–80.

35 Labat, R. 1951, *Traité akkadien de diagnostics et prognostics médicaux*, Leiden.

36 Ritter, E. K. 1965, Magical-Expert (=Ašipu) and Physician (=Asû), *AS* 16, 308, 315, 320.

37 Lambert 1960, 39, 45.

38 I. Hijara, 1976 excavations at Arpachiyah.

39 Oppenheim 1964, 376, n. 14.

40 Gurney, O. R. 1956, The Tale of the Poor Man of Nippur, *An.St.* 6, 145–64.

41 Neugebauer 1952; see also R. Labat 1963 (n. 32, above); Powell, M. A. 1973, Sumerian Area Measures and the Alleged Decimal Substratum, *ZA* 62, 165–221.

42 Neugebauer 1952, 48.

43 Saggs, H. W. F. 1960, A Babylonian Geometrical Text, *RA* 54, 141.

44 Neugebauer 1952, 27, n. 14.

45 Cf. *ze'pu, CAD; LAR* II, 176.

46 Oppenheim 1964, 88.

47 Cf. ch. 4, n. 48.

48 Sachs, A. 1948, *JCS* 2, 271–90.

49 Sachs, A. 1952, Sirius Dates in Babylonian Astronomical Texts, *JCS* 6, 114.

50 Cf. ch. 5, n. 37.

51 Saggs 1962, 455.

52 Sachs, A. 1952, Babylonian Horoscopes, *JCS* 6,

49–75; van der Waerden, B. L. 1952–53, History of the Zodiac, *AfO* 16, 216–30; van der Waerden 1949, Babylonian Astronomy II, the 36 Stars, *JNES* 8, 6–26.

53 Very little has been published on Babylonian technology. The most extensive book is Levey, M. 1959; see also Oppenheim, A. L. 1970, *Glass and Glass Making in Ancient Mesopotamia*, Corning, N. Y.

54 Levey 1959, 142–3.

55 Levey 1959, 67; on the tanning industry, see Crawford, V. E. 1954, *Sumerian Economic Texts from the First Dynasty of Isin*, New Haven.

56 Oates and Oates 1976, 42; Tite, M. S. and Maniatis, Y. 1975, Examination of ancient pottery using the scanning electron microscope, *Nature* 257, 122–3.

57 See general discussion in Oates and Oates 1976; the earliest known worked metal comes from Çayönü in Turkey, Braidwood, R. J. *et al.* Feb. 1974, Beginnings of Village-Farming Communities in Southeastern Turkey, *Proc. Nat. Acad. Sci. USA*, 71, 568–72; early evidence for casting comes from Arpachiyah (Mallowan, M. E. L. and Rose, J. C. 1935, *Iraq* II, pl. X) and from clay models of metal shaft-hole axes found at T. 'Uqair (Lloyd, S. and Safar, F. 1943, *JNES* II, pl. XVIII).

58 Eaton, E. R. and McKerrell, H. 1976, Near Eastern alloying and some textual evidence for the early use of arsenical copper, *World Archaeology* 8, 169–91; see also Muhly, J. D. 1977, The Copper Ox-Hide Ingots and the Bronze Age Metals Trade, *Iraq* 39, 74 ff.

59 Al-Fouadi, A. H. 1976, Bassetki Statue, *Sumer* 32, 65–6.

60 Al-Gailani, L. 1965, Tell edh-Dhiba'i, *Sumer* 21, 37–8.

61 See, most recently, van Zeist, W. 1976, On macroscopic traces of food plants in southwestern Asia, *Early History of Agriculture, Phil. Trans. R. Soc. London*, 27–41; Bökönyi, S. 1976, Development of early stock rearing in the Near East, *Nature* 264, 19–23; general discussion in Oates and Oates 1976.

62 Jacobsen, T. and Adams, R. M. 1958, Salt and Silt in Ancient Mesopotamian Agriculture, *Science* 128, 1251–8; see also Oates, D. and J. 1976, Early irrigation agriculture in Mesopotamia, in Sieveking, G. de G., Longworth, I. H. and Wilson, K. E. (eds.), *Problems in Economic and Social Archaeology*, London, 109–35.

63 Civil, M. 1964, A Hymn to the Beer Goddess and a Drinking Song, in *Studies Oppenheim*, Chicago, 74; for brewing, see Hartman, L. F. and Oppenheim A. L. 1950, On Beer and Brewing Techniques in Ancient Mesopotamia, *JAOS* supplement 10.

64 Helbaek, H. 1966, The Plant Remains from Nimrud, in Sir Max Mallowan, *Nimrud and its Remains* II, London, 616; sesame pollen has, however, been reported in Khuzistan, F. Hole, pers. comm.

65 *LAR* II, 173 (403).

66 Zohary, D. and P. Spiegel-Roy 1975, Beginnings of Fruit Growing in the Old World, *Science* 187, 323.

67 Levey 1959, 94–5 (n. 53 above); *PKB* 219.

68 See ch. 3, n. 8.

69 Oppenheim 1964, 46.

70 Oppenheim 1964, 317.

Sources of the illustrations

The photographs used for the undermentioned illustrations are reproduced by courtesy of:

Archives Photographiques, Louvre, 14, 24, 25, 34, 40, 44, 47, 50; Trustees of the British Museum, 16, 18, 19, 72–4, 81, 82, 89, 92, 93, 117–19, 126, 135; M. Chuzeville, 114; Deutsche Orient-Gesellschaft, 71, 90, 91, 95, 96; Directorate-General of Antiquities, Baghdad, 7, 8, 12, 15, 17, 36–8, 48, 52, 55, 56, 60, 63, 64, 86, 97, 99, 105, 111, 112, 120; Giraudon, 41, 45, 70; Hirmer Verlag, München, 115; H. Lenzen, 30; L. Majewski, 113, 128, 133; Metropolitan Museum of Art, New York, Rogers Fund, 31, 84, 104, 122; M. Munn-Rankin, 94; D. Oates, 13, 28, 59, 68, 75, 76, 85,

103, 106, 107; J. Oates, 65, 109, 110; Oriental Institute, University of Chicago, 20, 21, 22, 35, 39, 46, 49, 121, 123; A. Parrot, 33, 53, 124; E. Porada, 87; Staatliche Museen, Berlin, 62, 78, 83, 102, 108, 116, 125, 129; University Museum, University of Pennsylvania, Philadelphia, 23.

Ills. 2 and 100 were drawn by P. Bridgewater, ills. 42, 54 and 69 by S. Ebrahim, ills. 79, 80, 130 and 136 by T. Holland; other maps and drawings are by the author, unless otherwise acknowledged in the captions.

Select bibliography

General

Cambridge Ancient History, 3rd edn, 1970– , ed.
I. E. S. Edwards, C. J. Gadd, N. G. L. Hammond,
E. Sollberger.
Hallo, W. W. and Simpson, W. K. 1971. *The Ancient
Near East*, New York.
Kramer, S. N. K. 1963. *The Sumerians*, Chicago.
Laessøe, J. 1963. *People of Ancient Assyria*, London.
Lloyd, S. 1947. *Foundations in the Dust*, Oxford.
Moortgat, A. 1969. *The Art of Ancient Mesopotamia*,
London.
Oates, D. 1968. *Studies in the Ancient History of
Northern Iraq*, Oxford.
Oates, D. and J. 1976. *The Rise of Civilization*,
Oxford.
Oppenheim, A. L. 1964. *Ancient Mesopotamia*,
Chicago.
Oppenheim, A. L. 1968. *Letters from Mesopotamia*,
Chicago.
Saggs, H. W. F. 1962. *The Greatness that was Babylon*,
London.
Strommenger, E. and Hirmer, M. 1964. *The Art of
Mesopotamia*, London

Texts

Grayson, A. K. 1972, 1976. *Assyrian Royal In-
scriptions*, vols. 1, 2, Wiesbaden.
Grayson, A. K. 1975. *Assyrian and Babylonian
Chronicles*, New York.
Luckenbill, D. D. 1926, 1927. *Ancient Records of
Assyria and Babylonia*, vols. I, II, Chicago.
Pritchard, J. B. 1969. *Ancient Near Eastern Texts
relating to the Old Testament*, 3rd edn, Princeton.
Sollberger, E. and Kupper, J.-R. 1971. *Inscriptions
Royales Sumériennes et Akkadiennes*, Paris.

Chapters 2–3

Bottéro, J., Cassin, E. and Vercoutter, J. 1967. *The
Near East : the Early Civilizations*, London.

Edzard, D. O. 1957. *Die 'Zweite Zwischenzeit'
Babyloniens*, Wiesbaden.
Kupper, J.-R. 1957. *Les nomades en Mésopotamie au
temps des rois de Mari*, Paris.

Chapters 4–5

Brinkman, J. A. 1968. *A Political History of Post-
Kassite Babylonia, An. Or.* 43, Rome.
Koldewey, R. 1914. *The Excavations at Babylon*,
London.
Olmstead, A. T. 1948. *History of the Persian Empire*,
Chicago.
Pallis, S. A. 1956. *The Antiquity of Iraq*, Copenhagen
(excellent source for history of Babylon, post-539
BC).
Postgate, N. 1977. *The First Empires*, Oxford.
Tarn, W. W. 1948. *Alexander the Great*, Cambridge.
Unger, E. 1931. *Babylon : die heilige Stadt nach der
Beschreibung der Babylonier*, Berlin.

Chapter 6

Contenau, G. 1954. *Everyday Life in Babylon and
Assyria*, London.
Dhorme, E. 1949. *Les religions de Babylonie et
d'Assyrie*, Paris.
Frankfort, H. *et al.* 1946. *The Intellectual Adventure of
Ancient Man*, Chicago (also published as *Before
Philosophy*, Harmondsworth, 1949).
Jacobsen, T. 1976. *The Treasures of Darkness*, New
Haven.
Kramer, S. N. K. 1969. *The Sacred Marriage Rite*,
Bloomington.
Lambert, W. G. 1960. *Babylonian Wisdom Literature*,
Oxford.
Levey, M. 1959. *Chemistry and Chemical Technology
in Ancient Mesopotamia*, London.
Neugebauer, O. 1952. *The Exact Sciences in Antiquity*,
Princeton.

Index